SOUTH OF SOMEWHERE

AT TABLE

South of Somewhere

WINE, FOOD, *and* *the* SOUL *of* ITALY

ROBERT V. CAMUTO

UNIVERSITY OF NEBRASKA PRESS
LINCOLN

All photographs courtesy of the author.

Library of Congress Cataloging-in-Publication Data
Names: Camuto, Robert V., author.
Title: South of somewhere: wine, food, and
the soul of Italy / by Robert V. Camuto.
Description: Lincoln: University
of Nebraska Press, 2021.
Identifiers: LCCN 2021007917
ISBN 9781496225962 (paperback)
ISBN 9781496229168 (epub)
ISBN 9781496229175 (pdf)
Subjects: LCSH: Wine and wine making—
Italy. | Wineries—Italy, Southern. | Italy,
Southern—Description and travel. |
Camuto, Robert V.—Travel—Italy.
Classification: LCC TP559.I8 C2753
2021 | DDC 641.2/20945—dc23
LC record available at https://lccn.loc.gov/2021007917

Set in Questa by Laura Buis.
Designed by N. Putens.

To the memory of my grandparents
Raffaele Cioffi (b. Vico Equense, 1895) and
Concetta Guidone (b. Vico Equense, 1909)

CONTENTS

PHOTOGRAPHS

ACKNOWLEDGMENTS

The two greatest rewards of my career have been to explore this world as a journalist and to travel in the world of wine.

In recent years I've had the privilege to take a deep dive into European terroirs and meet some original and sometimes heroic characters. I am extremely grateful to *Wine Spectator* for helping support the journey, to countless Italian winemakers and their staffs for their openness and hospitality, and to Italians who have welcomed us in our new home.

Writing is in itself a solitary and often lonely activity, and I thank my wife and son for supporting and participating in my peripatetic life over the years as well as the many readers whose letters and emails have encouraged me to write more.

Thanks also to the University of Nebraska Press team of editors and artists who have helped to realize this project, my agent, Barbara Rosenberg, and to independent editor Gretchen Stelter.

SOUTH OF SOMEWHERE

Introduction

Italy began for me south of Naples, in a modest-sized town perched on a tuff stone cliff above the Mediterranean. Since Roman antiquity Vico Equense has been a slice of paradise, of seaside villas with stunning views over the Gulf of Naples to Mount Vesuvius. It was also the birthplace of my maternal grandparents, who immigrated to New York between the great wars and presided over an Italian-style deli on First Avenue called Ralph's.

As a very young boy, I'd seen photographs and heard of Vico's unrivaled beauty and the sweet produce from its volcanic soils. I'd gotten a taste of this world in my grandmother's tiny Manhattan kitchen—in her earthy baked artichokes, her deeply aromatic wine-stewed *Genovese Napoletana* pasta sauce, and the melting layers of her eggplant parmigiana. This was where I first learned that food could alchemize into emotion and that a meal could be an intoxicating adventure. Accompanying it all was the wine.

By the time I came around, my grandfather Raffaele (Ralph) had stopped fermenting California grapes in the deli's basement and instead brought home straw basket bottles (*fiaschi*) of Chianti, which he taught me to uncork.

More than anything I sensed that my grandparents' old country had taught them a different way of being in the world. Ralph was a joyful, big-nosed, singlet-wearing, cigar-smoking southerner who had traveled to New York as a young man. Apparently, after having too much of a good time there as a bachelor in the roaring twenties, his family arranged for him to return to Vico to marry a young woman—my grandmother—from a Vico family. After they wed the couple returned to New York.

What I remember most about Ralph was his untroubled outlook and generosity. Family legend had it that after he'd lost his savings at the start of the Great Depression, he'd spent the last two dollars in his pocket on a show. His reasoning was that he'd started in the United States with nothing and would do it again. If people from the neighborhood didn't have enough money to pay their grocery bills, Ralph offered credit, making notes in the store ledger. If a homeless person came in, Ralph made him a meatball sandwich.

My grandmother, who carried herself with deliberate formality, her silver hair tightly pinned up, was generous, but her generosity was limited to family. In addition to producing miracles in her kitchen, serving as defender of her grandchildren against parental scorn or spankings, and listening to the tear-inducing operas of Giuseppe Verdi, she served as the more practical and serious half of the couple. It was her job to balance the books, close the cash register, and fret that her husband's largesse would bankrupt them.

Ralph's big heart, which had been pumping since the end of the nineteenth century, gave out at the relatively young age of sixty-eight, leaving my grandmother a widow in her fifties. Ralph died with the store ledger full of IOUs. My aunt and uncle gradually took over the store. And in the summer of 1968, my widowed grandmother took a pair of cousins and me to Vico. I was ten years old, and it turned out to be the magical summer of my childhood.

We stayed with relatives in town and spent our days and evenings in Vico's marina area, known as "Seiano," with its panoramic views of Naples and Vesuvius—the same view I'd seen depicted in Italian restaurant murals painted in New York or Boston's North End. In Seiano the extended family—cousins, uncles, aunts, and in-laws— gathered at O'Saracino, the seafront restaurant owned and run by my grandfather Ralph's nephew Ciro Aiello. My cousins and I spent our days diving off the docks of O'Saracino into the sea with our Italian cousins. At lunchtime we ate spaghetti on the shaded terrace. We followed our cousins around Vico's streets, and at night we gathered again on O'Saracino's terrace to eat long rectangular pizzas that stretched down the center of the table.

The two sides of the family mingled, but they were very different. My grandmother's side, the Guidones, were like my grandmother: fair-skinned, fine-featured, and reserved. They were teachers and professors, the kind of upright people others called "Dottore." My grandfather's family—the Cioffis—were louder, fleshier, and more fun. Their swarthy Mediterranean skin tanned more deeply, their faces were rounder, laughter came easily to them, and their vocabulary included a rich assortment of theatrical expressions and gestures.

It was as carefree as summer gets, and I learned a few Italian phrases: "Andiamo a giocare Ping-Pong" (Let's go play Ping-Pong) and the ten-year-old-pleasing "Dov'e il gabinetto?" (Where is the toilet?). Whenever we kids had a question—"Can we go to . . . ?"; "Can we have an ice cream?"; "Can we play with pizza dough?"; "Can we take a raft out in the bay?"—the answer always seemed to be an easy shrug accompanied by "Why not?"

The grown-ups seemed like ideal adults to me. They were so elegant in the way they combed their hair, moved with ease, and wore sunglasses driving their tiny Fiats, which glimmered in the sun. I also loved the way they lingered at the table, discussing what appeared to be important matters in hushed Italian. At mealtime wine was always present—not in fancy bottles but ubiquitous carafes, always there on the table as an accessory of adulthood, white and red, mingling on the adults' breath with the smells of garlic, spices, and tobacco, just as it had with my grandfather.

It was my summer of love. A far cry from the San Francisco version, with sex, drugs, and music, mine was spent surrounded by family and infused with the flavors of the Mediterranean. I remember the intimate smells of the apartment buildings and of the wild fields between sea and town. I can still see my grandmother's sister's breakfast table next to the garden window that opened near a fig tree. On top of the lace tablecloth rested a small bowl of fresh figs, whose strange, sweet pulp I tasted for the first time. There also sat the dish of lemon-scented breakfast cake, the intoxicating aromas from a stovetop espresso moka hovering over all.

That summer I fell in love with a way of living. It saddened me to leave, even if that life was very different from my much more varied urban life as an American kid. Vico was my Proustian madeleine—in fact, an assortment of them, that marked me for life, and that I have been in search of ever since.

The longer I have lived, the more time I have spent in Italy. And the more time I have spent in Italy, the more I have traveled south. A few years ago, I approached my wife with an idea: Why not move to Italy?

At that point, we had lived in the South of France near Nice about fifteen years. I was an established wine storyteller with a regular gig writing for *Wine Spectator*. We both loved traveling to Italy. Our son had gone off to study and work in London, liberating us from the academic calendar and his school. She agreed to think about it.

For me, the jump across the Franco-Italian border, just an hour from our home in France, would be easy. I prefer simple Italian foods, the melody of the language, and the complex vernacular of hand gestures and expressions used by extroverted Italians. But I knew that for my wife, Gilda, it would not be easy. She was reared in California but is French, from Nice. Her name is pronounced the Italian way with a soft G, thanks to her opera-loving grandmother, who enjoyed *Rigoletto*, but she is essentially a Gaul when it comes to suspicion of Rome.

Despite the fact that Nice was the birthplace of the nineteenth-century Italian unification hero Giuseppe Garibaldi, as well as part of the Piedmont-Sardinian kingdom prior to the 1860 Treaty of Turin, it is still French. And the Italian side of the border is often viewed as a poorer cousin and rival. Jean Cocteau once famously said that the French are Italians in a bad mood. But, in fact, the two countries are worlds apart.

France is, of course, a beautiful country that has inspired poets and painters. Modern France is a world where most everything seems to have been engineered or at least considered by experts—from the well-kept highways to country roundabouts and a codified selection of cheeses and baguettes.

Italy, in contrast, feels like it was designed by mad sculptors and anarchists. The art gracing Italy's grand piazzas—from Michelangelo to Bernini, the Trevi Fountain to Sicilian Baroque—conjures gods and demons, flesh and muscle, at the limit of overwhelming. Yet few things in Italy are well organized. Not far from heart-stopping beauty, you can often find blight and confusion in the form of garish modern construction, abandoned cement skeletons of buildings, crumbling infrastructure, or a spontaneous dump. In just a few minutes' drive, you can feel as though you've gone from the apogee of civilization to the depths of the third world.

It would take an entire book to describe all the differences between the two countries. One word that sums up the cultural divide is the Latin verb *sentire* (to feel). In Italian *sentire* not only means "to feel" but also "to hear." In French *sentir* not only alludes to feeling but also means "to smell." In other words, Italians associate emotions with verbal communication, and the French associate their feelings with a sense of smell. Italians want to hear each other, which explains why they can regularly be found in those dramatic public squares taking their evening *passeggiata*, often *ciao ciao*-ing loudly into their *telefonini* while the more sophisticated French generally remain standoffish, sussing things out.

After a few days of sniffing around my question, my wife returned with her answer.

"Okay," she said. "But Rome and south is not possible."

"Rome and south" meant she didn't want to leave the norms of Western Europe to live in what she feared would be a primitive cradle of corruption. As a woman she was not willing to live in some sort of dark age, where the men went out to the bar in the evening and the women stayed home and ironed shirts.

These are, of course, clichés. But I didn't argue and eagerly took the deal to move to the North. And, honestly, I was glad to move to a place where we knew public services would work, the trash would get picked up, and there was little risk that an earthquake could, at any moment, turn our lives upside down.

We considered towns in the northern half of the country: Florence was too touristy, Milan was too big, the entire Piedmont lacked olive trees, and Venice was sinking. We settled on Verona: a beautiful and historic human-scale city on the Adige River that also happens to be a capital of the Italian wine trade.

Italy is not just world's largest wine producer, but it is also an endless source of stories. It also has a long and checkered wine history, from the spread of the vine through Europe during the Roman Empire to the modern postwar industrialization of vineyards and mass-scale cooperative wineries.

Italy's movement to modern fine wine, which we recognize today on wine shop shelves and high-end restaurant wine lists, began in earnest only after a horrifying, deadly scandal shook the world's faith in Italian wine. In 1986 twenty people died, and dozens were blinded, after drinking inexpensive table wines fortified with poisonous quantities of methanol—a cheap wood alcohol commonly used to produce formaldehyde and automobile fuel additives. Ironically, the scandal was not centered in some poor southern province controlled by Mafia bosses, but in Northern Italy's esteemed and somewhat snobby Piedmont, close to France. It was also here, in a kind of grand-scale atonement, that the reset of Italian wines began.

Making better wines meant not only enologists, modern testing labs, good and clean equipment, and dedicated winemaking spaces, but also years of research in selecting varietals and studying soils. Perhaps the greatest challenge was a change of attitude: choosing to favor quality over quantity. Transforming wine from a source of calories in the countryside to a source of exquisite pleasure in the cities, where people now live, has taken time—as has convincing old-school *contadini* (peasant farmers). Naturally, it took longer for some parts of the South to get the memo.

Rural southerners—long under the yoke of feudalism or the church—often lacked the entrepreneurial instincts that benefit small-scale commercial winemaking. Up until a couple of generations ago, agriculture was a life of misery. Who had money to spend on wine?

Thankfully, mentalities and opportunities have changed. Wine, like communication, was once controlled by a few who had access to investment technology and markets. In recent decades, as technology, access, and education have been democratized, so has winemaking. With even a small investment and a bit of time, good wine can be made anywhere you can grow good grapes.

Italy's greatest strength is its culture of renaissance—not the Renaissance period, but the idea of inspired renewal in what may seem a very dark hour. So it was in wine. Today you find that spirit of renaissance when a daughter of contadini uses her grandfather's grapes in some forgotten patch of countryside to launch her own wine label.

Of course, it is one thing to make great wine and another to sell it. Thanks to new generations of adventurous wine drinkers from the United States, northern Europe, and elsewhere across the globe, there is a growing thirst for "new" discoveries among old vineyards. While it's become popular to bash globalization, in fact the wine world would dry up without it. One of the beautiful things about a connected world is that, for the first time, the aforementioned daughter of contadini in the deep South of Italy can develop an ardent following for her wines in Tokyo, London, Brooklyn, or Los Angeles.

Italians need the world outside its borders to thrive. It's been that way for thousands of years. The world also needs Italians, for their sense of beauty and design and their hands that make products including finished marble, Ferraris, and ferrazzuoli pasta. Italians,

7

with their high tolerance for chaos, also serve as an antidote to a very stressed-out modern world. In one way or another, Italy's lifestyle has spread through the world—you can find Italian restaurants in the Himalayas—but Italians have yet to conquer their own land.

Italy is not a country in the classic sense. Except for the World Cup or European soccer championships every two years, or under the roof of the worldwide Eataly food emporiums, the various tribes of Neapolitans, Sicilians, Milanese, Romans, Lucani, Abbruzzese, Pugliesi, and Calabrese have little or nothing in common. All roads may have once led to Rome, but ever since, Italy has been about the detours—and the detours in the detours. Officially, the history books say unification was completed in 1871, but Italy never really united. It has remained a collection of culturally distinct regions, provinces, towns, and even neighborhoods with their own dialects, saints, and fears; their own ways of eating, drinking, and viewing the world. Loyalty is to the local bell tower.

I've asked Italians many times where to find the best olive oil, and the answer is usually as parochial as it gets: "My sister-in-law" or "From those trees over there." Everywhere in Italy defines itself in contrast to its neighbors. Everywhere is south of somewhere else. In the absence of national cohesion, local geography is primal, right down the slender Mediterranean boot with coasts that face in all directions. Naturally, business-minded northerners look down on what they consider lazy, ignorant southern *terroni*—a term making an insult out of *terra* (land). Southerners often resent affluent, polenta-eating northerners whose cuisine is bland compared to their own. Still, they travel north or leave the country altogether in search of work. Meanwhile, Sicilians—long the rival of the Piemontese, who carried out unification under their king—cleverly manage to find their way into high political posts.

I love the South because it is less sophisticated, more agricultural, more familial. It remains truer to the heart of the Italy I remember from my childhood. Northern Italy may be far wealthier, but the messier and poorer South wins hands down with its embarrassment of natural riches: its sunshine and volcanic soils, its fragrant, varied lemons and oranges and peppers, its fresh mozzarella and ricotta cheeses, its myriad heirloom crops and grapevines.

The Italian South is vital to the wine world because of the parts of it that were never industrialized by tractors and homogenized with cloned vines from elsewhere. In the late nineteenth century, most of Europe's vineyards were destroyed by the American root-ravaging vine louse *phylloxera*. In the early twentieth century, vineyards were replaced with standardized varieties grafted onto American (*phylloxera*-resistant) rootstock. It's an odd thing to realize that now nearly all the world's vineyards, from large to miniscule, use a system deployed throughout the fruit industry with one plant variety serving as the roots and another as the fruit bearer.

Southern Italy's volcanic soils, however—particularly around active volcano Mount Etna in Sicily, now-dormant Vesuvius, and Basilicata's extinct Vulture—were hostile to *phylloxera*, which find it difficult to tunnel through volcanic sands. That meant that some old vineyards stocked with an array of local nineteenth-century cultivars survived. Hundreds of old varieties and subvarieties still live on in the South, making it one of the world's genetically richest vineyard areas. That's interesting not just for drinkers seeking something new to pour, but also for agronomists looking for plants with a natural resistance to modern vineyard epidemics and climate change.

Will the South achieve its wine potential? In some places it will, thanks largely to a new generation of educated, environmental, and open-minded winemakers who are combining the best of their schooling with the traditions of their ancestors.

Your average wine-drinking Italophile is probably able to name a handful of Italian wine appellations. But Italy has about four hundred of them, classified as either DOC (Denominazione di Origine Controllata) or the higher "guaranteed" standard DOCG (Denominazione di Origine Controllata e Garantita) under an often byzantine system that originated in the early 1960s and has been periodically updated for better or for worse. Nearly as many grape varieties are used to make wine. In Italy, and concerning Italian wine, the farther south you go, the more you travel into the unknown. Scratch the surface, and it's a jungle out there. That's a good thing.

After some years living here, I am still learning about twenty-first-century Italy and reconciling it with the ideal given to me by my grandparents and Vico Equense. I grew up an American during the happy dawn of modern postwar Italy. I was born the same week that the song known as "Volare" (officially "Nel Blu Dipinto di Blu") was released by Italian singer-songwriter Domenico Modugno, a Puglia native who, decades later, became a politician in Italy's fringe Radical Party.

I know it is common for people of a certain age to get nostalgic for the "good old days." This seems to be a particular affliction of Italians. I remember the words of an elderly Roman cab driver in the 1980s who lamented the state of his country to me and my wife while we were on our honeymoon.

"Even the Mafia has become corrupt," he sighed.

There is a basis for Italian malaise—in the last three decades, the "Italian miracle" of postwar economic boom has waned, and the future, as in most places these days, is uncertain. The Naples I visited in the 1960s fell for a time into a pit of crime and drugs and only in recent years has managed to partially climb out of it. Corruption persists at the highest levels. Public debts are the steepest in Europe, and the birth rate is the lowest. The young are seeking jobs elsewhere. And, with all the challenges facing it, Italy's political leaders are still fuming about wanting to take Leonardo da Vinci's *La Gioconda* (Mona Lisa) back from the Louvre in Paris! Yet somehow Italians manage.

From time to time I have returned to Vico Equense, which also happens to be the hometown of the maternal grandparents of Bruce Springsteen (who is celebrated at his family's historic café). My first time back in Vico was just months before the world banking crisis of 2008 came to Italy and left lasting economic wounds. I dropped in with my wife and son and my mother, who'd flown in from New York.

We arrived with no telephone numbers or addresses of relatives, just memories—my mother's and mine—and some names. The town has more than twenty thousand people, but it only took one trip to Vico's cathedral-like and now-famous pizzeria with its mouthful of a name (Pizza a Metro da "Gigino" L'Università della Pizza) to get on the relatives' circuit again. We simply described parts of the family tree to a waiter, and he pulled out his phone.

Forty years and a few months after my summer in Vico, we dropped into O'Saracino for dinner, accompanied by a pair of my mother's Cioffi cousins, Vittorio and Franco. Both men were lifelong bachelors whose strong features and good looks were now long faded, but whose broad grins hinted at lives well lived. The restaurant, with its simple wood walls and windows that looked out to the sea, seemed smaller than in my memories. In fact, it was larger, having been rebuilt after a fire in in 1985. Ciro Aiello, shrunken by age, was well into his eighties. He greeted us affectionately, recalled the summer of my youth, and refused to let me pay for dinner.

"When I come to America, you pay," he said. I don't think Ciro has made it to the United States yet.

When I returned to Vico another decade on, he was ill and in his nineties. Cousin Franco had passed away. And O'Saracino had been demolished in a messy only-in-Italy zoning dispute. Just across the street, however, in a medieval lookout tower Ciro bought in the 1980s, his daughter, Vittoria, ran one of Southern Italy's most famous restaurants with one of the country's most celebrated chefs. The extensive wine list was filled with fine wines from across Campania and an Italy that didn't even exist when I'd come as a boy. Renaissance still happens.

I now live in an Italy that seems to move from one crisis to the next. Yet, in between imminent disasters, life is woven with feast days for parochial saints; celebrations of local artichokes, beets, onions; and the wine of the local soils. On a daily basis the true center of life can be found at modern Italy's secular temples—its bars and cafés, where communion is dispensed in the form of espresso, the mind-expanding flavors of gelato, or an afternoon *aperitivo* or glass of wine.

I remember about a decade ago walking with my wife through the gridlocked traffic and piled-up garbage at the edge of old Naples. We took refuge in a local café, where, standing at the counter we were served by a barista in a white jacket and bow tie. The place was busy but serene, with opera playing faintly in the background, and the air sweetly scented with the orange-flower aromas of Naples's sublime Easter tart *pastiera*. The barista put before us a pair of fine white espresso cups on top of saucers with fancy paper coasters. Inside the cups were thimble-sized portions of perfection I will never forget. The price was nothing—the same one euro you would pay at a roadside service stop. For an extra coin, you could pay for an espresso for a local who couldn't afford that small luxury.

To me this is the essence of Italy: chaos that gives birth to inspiration. It is the force of Italian life and of Italian wine. I live in the more settled, predictable North, but some inner compass constantly pulls me to other parts in search of some seed of brilliance—south of wherever I am.

1   *Thus Spoke Giuseppe*

I don't remember when I picked up the idea that Calabrese were hard-headed *testa dura* people—somehow more set in their ways than other Italians. Was I born with it? Could I have learned it from my grandmother while in my mother's womb?

Many years later, I decided Calabria might be the most "Southern" place in Southern Italy. Sure, Calabria is the meridional extremity of the continent, isolated on the toe of the Italian boot, about to punt the island of Sicily into the gap between Tunisia and Sardinia. But Calabria's southern-ness is really more about psychographics than geography.

This was confirmed for me at the 2017 Vinitaly: the annual spring gathering of the Italian wine trade in Verona that is part fair, part business, and a lot of party. I'd received an invitation for a soirée of the Regione Calabria, featuring wines and regional foods at Verona's stately neoclassical Teatro Nuovo. But before heading over to the check-in with the Calabrese, my wife and I stopped in for a more exclusive private *aperitivo*, at the home of Veneto fashion and wine magnate Gaetano Marzotto.

The Marzotto family famously rose from running a wool mill in the Veneto in the early nineteenth century to a modern fashion powerhouse that's bought and sold brands like Valentino and Hugo Boss. Marzotto modern-day counts and countesses have included industrialists, politicians, flamboyant socialites, and sportsmen. Over more than eighty years, four generations built its Santa Margherita estate into a formidable wine company that expanded across Italy while making Pinot Grigio a ubiquitous white wine by the glass in the United States.

Gaetano Marzotto, the sexagenarian businessman and president of the Santa Margherita group, greeted his guests graciously at his palazzo apartment in Medieval Verona, bowing as he air-kissed the hands of female guests. The worn-by-time marble floors and restored frescoes on the walls created an old-world picture of eternal elegance. The white-gloved staff poured sparkling wines into crystal glasses and served guests from elaborate food stations laid with mountains of *salumi*, pasta, and cooked meats. For company you couldn't have asked for a more distinguished parade of great Italian producers who dropped by. But I was disoriented by the courtly whispers, the eerie hush of perfectly restrained high society.

Is this really Italy? I wondered. It seemed more *northern* than any place I'd ever been. More like the southern frontier of the old Austrian empire, which Verona was for the half century before its annexation to the newly united Italy in 1866. So I figured the Regione Calabria gathering we were going to next was sure to be its antidote. It did not disappoint.

Staffing one of the great entry doors of the Teatro Nuovo were a pair of young, dark-suited women acting as gatekeepers.

"We are on the guest list," I explained to them.

"What is your name?" asked one of the sentries with a detached look. I spelled it out for her.

"Okay," she said. "Wait."

There was a minute or so of awkward confusion. She stood there, aloof. What were we waiting for? As far as I could tell, she had no list.

"Is there a list somewhere?" I inquired.

She shrugged, gave me a heavy-lidded *I just work here* roll of the eyes, and said, "We had the list, but now nobody can find it." Then she asked, "You are on the list?"

"Yes," I reaffirmed.

"Okay," she said, taking my word for it and swinging the door open for us into the lobby, which was filling up with a crowd.

Long tables lined the central lobby, with wine being poured next to plates of Calabrian salumi and cheeses. In a second room to the side, a group of cooks was chopping, sautéing, and boiling in a cloud of steam on top of a makeshift stage. Within minutes, enough people showed up to pack the place like canned *alici* (anchovies). In contrast to the evening's earlier event, they tended to be fleshy, flashy, demonstrative, and visibly tattooed.

When the cooks started handing down small plates of pungent, bright-red pasta, the crowd lurched toward them, and the energy in the place surged. I don't recall what music was playing; it was drowned out by the crowd, who passed the plates, hand to hand, to all corners of the room, mingling the sharp aromas of onion, garlic, and hot peppers with the floral, spice, and citrus of competing perfumes. It was a food rave with an open bar—delicious chaos.

To the event's organizers, it was also, I later learned, a complete disaster. Bills didn't get paid. Nothing had gone as planned, resulting in a lot of shaking heads. I doubt they ever found the guest list.

One thing that happened that night that seemed like fate was I met Giuseppe. It took all of five minutes for me to determine that Giuseppe Ippolito would be my *cicerone* (guide), my Virgil, in the first rings of Calabria. Giuseppe is a small wine producer from Cirò, which hangs above deep Calabria's Ionian coast and is its most promising appellation. He is also a fervent believer, student, and teacher of all things Calabria.

At fifty-one he seemed lit up by an energy that emanated from his core. He could talk above the din of hundreds of others, as he did that evening in Verona. He had a theatrically elastic, round face topped by a high forehead and receding whitish curls. He was a free-spirited guy who'd never learned to speak in polite shades of gray. A few weeks later, I headed south to meet up with him.

My first hours in Cirò were not the stuff of which travel brochure dreams are made. The airport in nearby Crotone—on the eastern Greece-facing shores of the Ionian—had been shut down after a series of scandals that confirmed the region's reputation as the South's lawless sinkhole. So instead I flew into Lamezia Terme on the western shores of the Tyrrhenian coast and drove across the ball of the foot of the Italian boot.

The Calabrian interior in spring is an idyllic Southern Italian landscape. In every direction stretched green hillsides of wheat and olives and Mediterranean scrub splashed with the colors of wildflowers. The Ionian came into view, deep blue and rimmed by endless miles of wild sandy beaches. Then I arrived in Cirò Marina—the modern seaside town that sprawled just a few miles from the mountaintop medieval village of Cirò—and my heart sank. The room I had booked in a local bed-and-breakfast sat above a supermarket. The entrance and terrace looked onto the parking lot and a set of tired-looking dumpsters.

An afternoon walk by the sea only made things worse. Cirò Marina's beach strip was lined with shuttered cafés, pizzerias, and gelaterias, the sidewalks sprouting weeds and blown trash. One small effort of green—a strip that vaguely recalled a lawn—held a stand of windswept olive trees that looked as anemic and withered as abandoned scarecrows. In the fine, dimpled sand of the beach itself lay piles of debris and human neglect: flattened plastic containers, shards of Peroni bottles, and last season's cigarette butts. How did this happen? It's a question I've asked myself often in Italy's blighted undersides so close to so much beauty. By the last light of the day, Giuseppe had arrived to answer this question and others.

He pulled up in front of the dumpsters in the parking lot in his small minivan and sprang from the front seat to greet me with a dramatic cry that made me feel like a long-lost friend. He was clad in black: a T-shirt and down vest that covered his firm torso, large black wraparound sunglasses over his soft, deep-set eyes, a strip of leather holding a large shark tooth around his neck, and black tattoo ink seeming to crawl out from under his short sleeves.

Giuseppe grabbed my right hand as though readying to arm wrestle and embraced me with his left. After making sure I was well settled into the supermarket accommodations, he flipped open the passenger door. Mosquito corpses caked the van's gray exterior, long ago baked into the paint by the Calabrian sun. The cloth seats were covered with road dust and dog hair, and the seat belts for both driver and passenger were fastened in front of the seatback, rendering their use impractical. I got in and Giuseppe sped through the streets of Cirò Marina.

"In the 1970s and the 1980s, with the economic boom, all the old houses up in the village were abandoned, and people built here," he said, driving down a street lined with unfinished cinderblock and brick houses, their top floors partially framed with roofs and columns but never filled in with walls and windows. "The people who had property in Cirò sent their sons to university in the North and sold their land to build homes down here. But the sons never came back." His hands flew off the wheel, fingers pinched together to form the shape of dangling overripe figs. "Look how terrible these houses are. Brutto . . . bruttissimo . . . bruuuuuuuuuutttttttissssssssssssiiiiimmmmmmo."

He accelerated around a corner, drove halfway down a side street of anonymous cinderblock construction, and abruptly stomped on the brakes, stopping in front of an abandoned building built from river stones and brick with tall, arched windows. A rotted door barely hung on to a noble-looking doorway—a reminder of an earlier time when craft mattered.

"All the houses were like this." He shook his head and seemed ready to spit. "This whole area was orange trees, olives, and vines. I remember when I was a boy, all the houses had had their own cellars for making wine. Now look at it."

Giuseppe contemplated this for about the time it would take to say *Che puttana di merda*. He removed his sunglasses—the sun was setting—and hung them on the neckline of his vest before leaping to another thought.

"But the interior of Cirò has remained intact." He held up an index finger and put his foot to the gas. "That's the secret!"

Over the course of a couple of days, I observed Giuseppe as a man in constant motion, who seemed to spend his every moment sensing, feeling, and expressing himself with his entire being, from his hand gestures to his facial tics and constant commentary. Within minutes his thoughts would jump from the despoiling of the Calabrian coastline and its history to the region's geography and its Sila mountains, then on to more far-flung topics like South America, women, Calabrian food, and Cirò wine.

"Tonight," his voice boomed, and his right hand chopped the warm evening air, "we will eat Cirotana . . . and drink Cirotana."

Calabria produces a miniscule amount of wine by Italian standards. Yet, within the region, Cirò is its largest-producing area. Cirò is all about Gaglioppo—a little-understood red-wine grape that researchers have genetically linked to Sangiovese. At their worst, when the vines are young and the grapes less than fully ripe and when produced without much care, Gaglioppo wines are so astringent and bitter they can make you gasp for air. But, in recent years, things have improved as a new generation has taken more care, giving more time for grapes to ripen and to age for longer periods in the cellar before release. Giuseppe is part of Cirò's renaissance. Ippolitos have been making wine here for generations, and Cirò's famous Ippolito 1845 is now owned by cousins who produce nearly a million bottles per year. His father, Giovanni, was one of Southern Italy's first agronomists who wrote the rules for the Cirò appellation in 1969. In 2007 Giuseppe—after flirting with becoming a lawyer and traveling the world—came home to work with his father, who was selling grapes to Ippolito 1845. Giuseppe decided to try something different. He rented cellar space from his cousins and began to make his own wines under the Du Cropio label, artfully sealed and dribbled with Ferrari-red wax.

Giuseppe stopped his car in front of a blackened stone wall with an iron gate, and we walked into a courtyard full of olive trees and all kinds of citrus and tropical plants. On the other side of a pair of heavy wooden doors was his family's old wine cellar—a room with thick stone walls and cracked terra-cotta floors and crammed with antique winery equipment, sculptural corpses of vines, and vintage Cirò wines. I sat at a wood table that was set for dinner as Giuseppe stuck his head outside the room and called, "Elena!" He was answered by a female voice as loud and insistent as his own.

Giuseppe's young and round-figured housekeeper arrived with food, starting with an olive wood board heaped with salumi and another dish with a round, pizza-like bread. In great detail Elena explained the latter to be a classic Calabrian Pitta di Sambuco, a pizza topped with elder-flowers now in bloom across great swaths of Europe. We tore off pieces. The aroma of the hot bread mingled with the flowers' sweet scent.

Giuseppe grinned broadly. "To go to a restaurant in Calabria is nothing! Yes, we have restaurants with stars now—one or two stars. But our Calabrian home cooks have twenty stars. Like Elena, they learned from Mamma and Nonna."

Elena beamed confidently and disappeared.

Giuseppe took a knife, held it over the salumi, and cut a bright, nearly orange-colored round of coarsely pressed whole-pig *soppressata*. He stabbed it and held it in my direction. One bite painted the inside of my mouth with the carnivorous intensity of spice and fat.

For the first time that evening Giuseppe said, "Now take some wine." I did.

The process was repeated with a slice of fat-streaked *capocollo*, aged pecorino (sheep) cheese that vaguely smelled of the wooly source of its milk, and *sauza*, a heady Calabrian dish made from baked fava bean pods, bread, sausage, and hot pepper.

"Take a forkful . . . then some wine!" Giuseppe instructed.

His point was to demonstrate how well Cirò wines paired with rustic, spicy food. And they did. They were not the kind of wines you would want to drink by themselves. Like Calabrians themselves, they need company to discuss, argue, and express themselves. With each bite and sip, Giuseppe's wines, with their piercing acidity and bitter tannins, cut right through the flavors and textures of the food.

Elena returned and set down a platter of more of her typical home preparations: artichoke hearts and sweet peppers in oil, pickled fennel and Tropea onions—Italy's most famously sweet onion, brought to the toe of the Italian peninsula by ancient Greeks. At the center of the platter was a small bowl of fiery red paste that, even now, as I read this, much later in the cold of winter at the other end of Italy, revs my gastric juices. Calabrian *sardella*, also known as "poor man's caviar," is made from the millions of anchovy and sardine spawn that swarm off the coast in spring. These *bianchetti* are fished in fine nets and, while fresh, kneaded with oil, hot red pepper, and wild fennel into a loose spread.

Giuseppe dipped a slice of raw Tropea onion into the bowl of sardella and held it out to me.

"This," he said, "is number one."

I took it and put it in my mouth. It screamed with flavors—saltiness, spiciness, pungency. I could feel and smell the sea, imagine the garlands of vulgar red peppers drying in the shade, and see the warm, sandy coastal soils that grew the onions, which were piled up and sold off the back of a three-wheeled Ape truck.

"Now the wine," Giuseppe ordered. "My father said the purpose of wine is to cleanse the mouth."

He watched my reaction as his Cirò red scrubbed the oils and flavors of the sardella from my cheeks, tongue, and gums. "You see?"

I did. It was an exercise we would repeat many times over a pair of days: bite of food, Cirò. Bite of food, Cirò. Wine as a kind of rinse cycle or mouthwash was not the most inspiring or appetizing thought in the world, but it worked.

In Cirò and eating Cirotana, these bold wines were the perfect pairing. Southern Italians don't drink wine to drink, but to eat and share at the table. Cirò does produce small amounts of easy, fruity white wine from Calabria's Greco Bianco grape (which can also be used in small percentages in Cirò reds). But for Giuseppe and others dedicated to Cirò red, white Cirò was an aberration.

"For me, white wine is not even wine," he said, and passed an earthy, sweet-smelling platter of roasted eggplant and peppers.

In that moment, I could agree.

"Bruttissima!" Giuseppe bellowed the following morning in his car, drawing the word out. As we drove out of Cirò Marina under the crystalline blue sky, he couldn't help but heap insults on the architectural crimes by the side of the road.

We headed north along the coast. The buildings yielded to open landscapes, white beach, and an expanse of Ionian Sea that somewhere out there on the horizon splashed up on the Greek island Corfu. Giuseppe sang the praises of Cirò's Ionian light. He spoke of how the bianchetti were completely different—firmer—in the cooler, deeper waters just north of Cirò Marina and the Punta Alice headland at the opening of the Gulf of Taranto, in the arch of the Italian boot. He turned to go up into the hills and to a countryside of narrow, winding roads, vineyards, and green wheat. Flocks of sheep grazed in olive groves, and uncultivated fields were dabbed with a stunning palette of spring color: yellow from flowering broom and ferula, blue from thistle, and bold red carpets of wild *sulla* (a.k.a. cock's head or French honeysuckle).

"By August, this will all be brown," Giuseppe said. He veered onto a dirt road through a wooded area of oak, acacia, and eucalyptus trees and drove onto a ridge-top clearing.

Giuseppe cut the engine and pushed his door open. I followed him to the ridge's edge, which was cooled by a morning breeze. We looked out over a collection of gently sloping hillsides with neatly partitioned agricultural plots separated by forest, all of it ending miles away with the backdrop of the sea.

"This," Giuseppe said in a near-whisper, "is a point of meditation."

It seemed an odd statement coming from Giuseppe. His life, as he recounted it, had been led by instinct and impulse rather than reflection.

Growing up here, he'd always helped with work on the family farm. As a young man, at the urging of his father, he went to Rome to study law, a popular vocation in Italy for those seeking *la dolce vita*. It was a time when Cirò's main markets—Calabrian home winemakers along with northern producers who needed ripe southern grapes to give their wines a boost—were waning. Giuseppe was in no hurry to finish his studies at the University of Rome, which proceeded "molto slow," over seven years instead of the standard five. Those two extra years were spent knocking around Cuba and Central and South America, following Che Guevara's trail.

"I would call my father and he would say, 'Come back and study,'" Giuseppe said with a laugh.

Finally, when he did finish his degree work, Giuseppe began a requisite internship prior to Italy's equivalent of a bar exam. He worked for a lawyer cousin in Rome but, after some weeks, decided the profession wasn't for him. "I couldn't stand being enclosed by four walls," he said. He returned to Calabria and the farm, selling the entire crop of grapes with his father for more than a decade before taking a portion of the harvest to make his own boutique wines.

We stepped over the freshly plowed clods of red clay in this high vineyard that had been planted by Giuseppe's father in 2007, three years before his death. The vines were arranged in *abinate* style: paired off side by side with single spurs that shot in opposite directions along a training wire. They were low to the ground, no more than knee height. The whole system was carefully designed to yield lower quantities of smaller, more concentrated Gaglioppo.

"My father said that if you weren't going to higher quality, you were going nowhere," Giuseppe said.

With about seventy-five acres, Giuseppe had enough workers to do the hard labor in his vineyards, allowing him to still indulge his wanderlust.

Back in the car, along the blacktop to Cirò village, Giuseppe mentioned his current girlfriend, who lived in Rome. I asked if he'd ever considered settling down to start a family.

"Matrimonio?" he said with a look of horror. "Never!"

The family line, like that of many men in Italy I have come to know, will likely end with him. The conversation then turned back to more comfortable turf.

"Like all beautiful things, Gaglioppo is difficult to cultivate," he said. "If you pick Gaglioppo a week too soon, it is too astringent. If you don't harvest well, you destroy all your work for the year."

We spent the next hours visiting his vineyards, stopping for an espresso in Cirò's largely abandoned medieval old town, and touring a handsome, well-executed municipal exhibit on the town's most famous son: the sixteenth-century mathematician and astronomer Aloysius Lilius, considered the first author of the Gregorian calendar. Then we visited what Giuseppe called his "open Louvre."

"It is a museum with no lines and no tickets," he promised.

He drove through a hilltop grove of centuries-old olive trees with some of the most twisted, tortured-looking trunks I'd ever seen.

"You see, every one is a sculpture," Giuseppe said. He stopped the car in front of a tree that was like a Rorschach in three dimensions. It could have been an early twentieth-century Italian futurist sculpture by the likes of the fiery but short-lived Calabrian artist Umberto Boccioni. Or a detail of Rodin's *Gates of Hell*.

On the way back to his house, Giuseppe took a winding back road that had washed out in a flood four years earlier. In some spots half the road had simply cratered; in others it had spilled down the hillside. To add insult to injury, some piles of broken asphalt had been turned into spontaneous dumps by opportunists looking for a place to leave their trash. Each sight was, of course, more *bruttissimo* and *cattivo* than the last.

"In Calabria and Sicily, we have a much longer history in wine than Tuscany or the Piedmont, but they are much more bravi for investing in their culture," Giuseppe said somberly. "The big problem of the South is we don't valorize what we have."

In the afternoon light, Giuseppe's yard exploded into full view, the ground a mix of gravel and sprouting weeds. It was an exotic Eden blending the Mediterranean with the Americas and Asia—citrus, mulberry, and pecan trees along with palms, two-story-tall succulents, and a giant avocado tree.

A pair of dirt bikes stood in the shade. A small, primitive stone wine *palmento* once used for stomping and pressing grapes lay hidden behind overgrown shrubs. At the back of the property, in full sun, was a large, unfinished gray block of construction with a roof but no walls. Giuseppe said this was to be his new winery when finished, perhaps the following year. For now he still worked out of his cousins' winery and sold off about two-thirds of his grape harvest.

We walked under a loquat tree, heavy with clusters of orange and red fruit, and picked some, peeling the skin, sucking on the sweet and tart flesh, and spitting out the thick seeds, our hands sticky with juice. Elena called out from the kitchen above that it was time for lunch, and we moved to Giuseppe's cellar table. She brought us a plate of flat, handmade gnocchi tossed in a clear sauce of fresh, lightly sautéed anchovies, along with other plates of cooked greens, fried *baccala* (salted cod) croquettes, and anchovy *frittelle* (fritters).

"I eat frittelle," Giuseppe explained, "when the wine is good." If you eat the anchovies without wine, the taste covers everything else. "Here, eat this." Giuseppe pointed to the plate of frittelle. "Now the wine," he instructed. "You see?"

Yes, once again, I saw. His Cirò red easily cut through the oils and flavors and left the palate clean for the next bite. This was about as far as you can get from the innumerable technical and sometimes church-like swirling, sniffing, and sipping sessions I've attended in which wine is dissected down to its various components—aromas, fruit flavors, mouthfeel, tannins, attack, and finish.

"Now this one," he said pointing to the baccala croquettes. "Now the wine."

And so the lunch continued, ending with some potent pecorino cheeses paired with Giuseppe's Cirò Riserva (a designation requiring two years of aging).

Afterward, we sat outside in the shade. My eyes felt heavy. Giuseppe asked if I wanted to take a nap. Instead we jumped into his car and drove to a nearby café for an espresso. On the way back to his home, he cursed his Calabrese brethren for their lack of interest in the region's patrimony—the history, the nature, the light. "People from here are interested in none of it. The problem is the Calabrese don't know their own land. It's like the Romans who don't know Rome!"

Back in his garden, we met his cousin and enologist Vincenzo Ippolito, still one of the owners of the family's Ippolito 1845, along with his two brothers, three cousins, and an uncle. But, he said, he left the family business in 2012 because he couldn't take disputes with his father.

"At forty-three years old, I said, 'Basta,'" said Vincenzo. "My father arrived at eight in the morning and stayed until midnight, and we fought the whole time." He still looked young, with a dark beard, a full head of hair, and blue eyes that were not yet resigned.

Though his father died less than a year before our meeting, Vincenzo had decided to stay out of the family winery's operations. He was Giuseppe's enologist and had built up his own consulting practice across Calabria. We drank some of Giuseppe's Cirò Riserva, and Vincenzo spoke about the complexities of Cirò winemaking. "Gaglioppo is like Nebbiolo," he said. "It is very tannic, and it needs to be mature. It needs to be worked the same way. It quickly makes sugar and can produce alcohol, and so many became convinced that it has tannins, but they are rougher tannins." Yet beyond the actual work in the vineyards and winery, Vincenzo believed the fate of Cirò lay in the aesthetics of the place itself.

"The problem with Calabria," he said wearily, as if he'd said this a thousand times before, "is too much trash, too many ruins of houses, too many unfinished houses. When you sell a wine, you sell the *territorio*. Here, people don't understand that. Yes, the interior of Calabria is beautiful, but the coast is destroyed. The problem is the roads are on the coast, and nobody wants to go inside. When people come from the outside and they drive along the coast to Cirò and they see trash and disorder, they don't want to drink the wine." He sighed. "When they choose a wine, they want to see little birds."

Giuseppe echoed his words and shook his head. I thought Vincenzo was finished, but he continued.

"Reggio Calabria is even more southern—more backward," he said of the region's largest city on the straits of Messina facing Sicily.

"In Reggio they are bravo for the vineyards, but for wine they are backward. It's a Sicilian province, not Calabrian."

"In what way?" I asked.

He sipped the wine. Looked up at the blue sky and down again. "Reggio is like Sicily fifty years ago. They are in the Middle Ages." After another pause he said, "In the way they think, they are a little north of Libya."

Cataldo Calabretta is known locally in Cirotano dialect as "the nose." The label doesn't come from his sense of smell but from the hooked beak in the center of his round, welcoming face. At forty he had a quick smile, green eyes, and salt-and-pepper stubble that formed both his beard and his receding hairline.

He drove south of Cirò in a Fiat Panda 4x4, up into the hills, where the road gave way to a pair of tracks through the wild sulla and a vineyard at the top of a ridge. The land was completely different from Giuseppe's red clay vineyards to the north. Here, in the southern part of Cirò, we were surrounded by carpets of broken white rock with no apparent soil at all.

"There is not just one Cirò," Cataldo said. "With all the different vineyards we have, there are many Ciròs. Look at how hard and wild the landscape is—the wines must reflect that. I don't want to make a Cirò that is *morbido* [soft]," he said. "The drinkability doesn't come from sweetness; it comes from the saltiness!"

We drove down and across the valley to another white stone vineyard, this one close to the busy two-lane road. I followed Cataldo as he marched across the vineyard, parallel to the road. He squatted in a concrete drainage ditch, pointing at a white crystalline powder. He licked the finger, swabbed some of the white substance, and put it in his mouth.

"Salt," he said.

I was a little doubtful on this one. Salt? Nevertheless I followed his lead. My taste buds detected chalkiness but nothing I would call salt.

"It's the salt of the earth," Cataldo said.

Cataldo was emblematic of Cirò's wine renaissance. He was a fourth-generation grower with an expanded worldview—the first to produce commercial amounts of wine (about thirty thousand bottles) from his family vineyards. He studied enology in Milan, worked in Emilia Romagna and Abruzzo, and returned home in 2008 to prepare the vineyards organically for his own wine label. In 2011 he installed a simple cellar below his parents' house in Cirò Marina, and the following vintage produced his first Cirò red under his name. He was one of the young producers in Cirò hoping to create a new identity on the model of Sicily's Mount Etna, an ancient wine area that had been rediscovered, then became fashionable on tables in Milan, Paris, and New York.

"Cirò is a paradox," he lamented. "It's a small appellation with only four and a half million bottles total. But you can find it on supermarket shelves with Gaglioppo blended with Cabernet and Merlot." Anyway, Cataldo said matter-of-factly, without a miracle, the vineyards would continue to shrink. "Because one hectare of this kind of hillside vineyard takes three hundred to four hundred hours of work per year. It takes farmers to work a vineyard!"

But what about the young vintners like himself? I asked.

"There is a lot of talk about young people returning to the land," he said. "But in my opinion, it is propaganda."

We drove up to Cirò village and descended the same broken road I'd gone down days earlier with Giuseppe. He used his right hand to gesture toward a concrete wall that had dissolved into a heaping obstruction on the asphalt.

"If you want to promote the area and the agriculture, then fix the roads," he spat. "For fifty years, the South of Italy has been governed by contractors—and it's all badly built. They thought reinforced concrete would be the solution for everything. And so they built without respect for nature, and with the force of the water, it all comes down. Then," he said, calming himself as he pointed to a thick ancient fortress of a stone wall, "you have dry stone walls that last a thousand years."

That afternoon, at his parents' house above his winery, we ate lunch prepared by his mother, who was descended from the Albanian diaspora, which began in the fifteenth century with the Ottoman defeat of the country. She hails from the perched village of San Nicola dell'Alto which speaks Arbëreshë, the language of Italo-Albanians. We were joined by his father and his Mexico City–born girlfriend, Mavi Pena, whom he met at a friend's wedding in Amsterdam.

His mom, wielding a large bowl of linguini tossed with calamari and tomato sauce, shuffled slowly in her slippers to the end of the table near the kitchen as her husband, a thin, small man who appeared exhausted from decades of work, sat at the other. She returned to the kitchen and came back with plates of stuffed calamari and fried anchovies. I took what I thought to be good-sized helpings, considering that it seemed I'd done little else but eat since arriving in Calabria.

"Take more," Cataldo's dad, Salvatore, insisted. "Look, he doesn't eat anything," he mumbled, helping himself to seconds.

We drank Cataldo's hearty, brick-colored Gaglioppo rosé. Then Cataldo broke out a bottle of his 2013 Cirò Riserva. The wine was fresh, powerful, and, yes, even salty. I offered to pour some for Mom, but she demurred, adding, incredibly, "I drink very little. I always have the fumes of the cantina that come upstairs and make me drunk."

That night I joined Catalado, Giuseppe, and a group of winemakers that also included Francesco de Franco of 'A Vita, another organic producer who was part of Cirò's new wave. I don't remember who drove, but as we headed north for an hour and a half on the ss 106 toward the arch of the Italian boot, I sat in the passenger seat with Giuseppe in the back, leaning forward between the seats. The setting sun enflamed the sky as we sped through miles of citrus and olive groves, heading toward the Pollino mountains that separate Calabria from Basilicata.

Giuseppe announced that this was one of the most dangerous stretches of road in Italy, with the most traffic fatalities. He recited historical tidbits from the back seat, including the etymology of the word *Italia*. The Greeks had used it to describe the Calabrian toe, and the Romans later expanded its definition to refer to the entire Italian peninsula. Therefore, in so many words, he said proudly, Calabria was the original Italy.

Our destination was the well-appointed roadside restaurant Da Lucrezia in the Ionian beach resort town Trebisacce. Dinner was a marathon of seafood: raw prawns drizzled in oil, hand-formed pasta with octopus, eel with peas, and lightly grilled stingray. At evening's end Chef Giuseppe Gatto sat at our table in his chef whites and poured himself a glass of local rosé. Discussion became animated over the subject of the Clupeidae family of fish. Chef Giuseppe described a certain fish as being as long as the distance between an extended finger and thumb, calling it a *sarde* (sardine).

Winemaker Giuseppe, who was an expert local fisherman too, erupted, "It is not possible to call that a sarde."

Hands flashed. Fingers were held up in the air to demonstrate the proper size of fishes and their classifications. We were only about sixty miles north of Cirò, but there was stark disagreement as to what could be called what. At one point winemaker Giuseppe called the local inhabitants "ignorant." It didn't seem to be taken as an insult by Chef Giuseppe, who shook his head firmly. Winemaker Giuseppe turned to me and explained in an aside, "We could go on like this for two, three hours. Every place has its own name for fish. A hundred kilometers away it's completely different."

On the way back home that night, Giuseppe Ippolito took the wheel. Everyone else was drunk or exhausted. I dozed, going in and out of consciousness, and he continued rattling on into the night. He spoke of the idea of Le Calabrie, Calabria's plural name before it became known as one: Calabria. It made sense. Calabria is Italy in miniature, with a mountainous northern border and mountains that run down its spine, all of it surrounded by seas under a relentless Mediterranean sun. It is defined by local traditions and ideas that can be divided, redivided, and divided again into infinity. Like Italy itself, it can be what anybody says it is, I figured, as long as they do not have the misfortune of being from the place next door.

1. Giuseppe Ippolito.

2. Cataldo Calabretta.

2   *Three Gentlemen of Abruzzo*

The landscape around L'Aquila is one of Italy's most stunning, dominated by the jagged and often snow-covered Gran Sasso peaks, the tallest in the 750-mile Appennini mountain chain that runs down the center of the Italian boot. As majestic as they are deadly, the central Appennini serve as the epicenter of some of Italy's most ferocious earthquakes—among them the 2009 quake that leveled much of L'Aquila, killing more than three hundred souls and leaving tens of thousands homeless.

In approaching L'Aquila, as with most Italian towns, you have to pass through outer rings of cheap, soulless, and ugly concrete constructions from the postwar twentieth century to arrive in the Centro Storico with its grand piazzas, medieval palazzi, and graceful churches. Nearly a decade after the big quake, I stopped beside a shaded park of tall pines and walked to the heart of town under an intense July sun, the temperature edging to a hundred degrees. Dozens of great palazzi were covered with construction scaffolding. An equal number stood condemned, reinforced with steel girders and wood beams. Some back streets still looked like bombed-out war zones. The husks of pharmacies and apparel, leather, and lingerie shops appeared as if they had been abandoned years earlier by refugees who fled in the night. The billboard fabric covering scaffolds around the Piazza Duomo hopefully announced, "L'Aquila Rinasce," signaling a revival in progress.

Yet, by the looks of things, the locals were all gone. Where were the groups of noisy children, the flying soccer balls, the gelato? Where were the old men and women? The greengrocers, the markets with the piles of early pears, figs, and tomatoes? Where were the people?

L'Aquila is in many ways a symbol of Italian endurance. For most of its eight-hundred-year history, it's seen sieges, sackings, plagues, foreign dominations, and natural disasters. Built on the bed of ancient lake, it has been ravaged by earthquakes many times only to be rebuilt. How many times had Italy—or Italians—fallen and learned to stand again?

L'Aquila's sheer beauty, its number of opulent palazzi emblazoned with family crests and set around impressive squares, struck me. How could such a small mountain town in the middle of nowhere have come to justify such attention? L'Aquila's golden age was some six hundred years ago, when it became a prime exporter for saffron and wool and an important northern city in the Kingdom of Naples, with ties to Northern Italy, Rome, and far-flung Europe.

For much of the nineteenth century before the unification of Italy, L'Aquila was capital of "Abruzzi," under the Kingdom of Two Sicilies. More than a century later, the region's southern tip was peeled off to form Molise and the rest of it left as Abruzzo. Geographically, Abruzzo lies on the eastern edge of central Italy. But, in an odd administrative twist, proving latitude is sometimes more than geography, the Italian census and statistical bureau still considers Abruzzo a part of the Italian South. Abruzzo is the South's most prosperous region and one of the least despoiled, with more than one-third of its surface environmentally protected as parkland. It supports modern textile and leather industries without looking industrialized, and its verdant hills and valleys are an important font of wine and fruit as well as home to some of Italy's best dry-pasta makers. In recent years its support of federalist far-right politicians, including the separatist Northern League, makes it ideologically a kind of North of the South.

Abruzzo also lends its name to two easy-to-find and easy-to-drink wines: red Montepulciano d'Abruzzo (not to be confused with Tuscany's Vino Nobile di Montepulciano) and white Trebbiano d'Abruzzo, from the similarly named local grapes that dominate them. The wines, like its people, aren't generally the most exciting. There isn't so much of a wine scene here as there are flashes of brilliance—human tremors in its pastoral expanses.

Emidio Pepe is the picture of a dapper, old-school Italian gentleman-*contadino*. Well into his eighties, he is lean and bronzed, with white hair and mustache, and blue eyes that shine with a playful spark that belies his age. In public he is soft-spoken and crisply attired, with his collection of herringbone driving caps and perfectly knotted ties.

In his later years, Pepe is surrounded by females. Two of his three daughters work with him: Sofia, who has been the winemaker for more than a decade, and Daniela, who runs the estate administration. His eldest granddaughter, Chiara Luis Pepe, the high-energy face of the brand, who manages exports across the globe, does a lot of the public speaking, allowing Pepe to smile ethereally and nod.

Now approaching his sixty-vintage mark, Pepe is a staunch traditionalist who has changed little since 1964, when he took over familial winemaking and became the first Pepe to bottle. His white wine grapes are still stomped in large wooden tubs by family members and workers. His red Montepulciano d'Abruzzo is destemmed by hand in his singularly anachronistic and laborious fashion. His wines sell out the world over, and he is revered by young Italian winemakers and urban seekers from Milan to Brooklyn. Pepe is certainly the real thing. But his success is also based on a representation of rural Italy as we might dream it. There's the spry, old patriarch, the beautiful daughters and grandchildren, and a wholesome life on the farm; then there's the delicious wines made with a know-how passed down for generations along with a rejection of modern shortcuts and chemicals. The reality is somewhat more pragmatic, shaped by Emidio Pepe's shrewd bootstraps business acumen, work, and ambition.

On a hillside facing the village of Torano Nuovo, less than ten miles from the Adriatic Sea in northern Abruzzo, the Pepes have built their own hamlet. The old family farmhouse has been reno-vated into a cozy *agriturismo* with a swimming pool, restaurant, and rooms. In a house next door Pepe lives with his wife, Rosa, with an apartment for Sofia and her family. Still farther along the ridge is the coral-ochre facade winery, with tall letters mounted on the clay-tile roof spelling out VINI PEPE. The entire complex is as tidy as any Tyrolean burg.

I arrived at Azienda Agricola Emidio Pepe early one morning as he was finishing a hearty breakfast with his family. At the back of the agriturismo, a pair of young Pepe grandsons in their swim-ming trunks were playing with a garden hose, watering down the terra-cotta terrace. Behind them the country views rolled across vineyards and olive groves toward the Gran Sasso peak of Corno Grande. Inside the house Pepe was showered and looking fresh in a polo shirt and shorts after what had already been a long predawn in the vineyards. His workhand's breakfast consisted of generous portions of prosciutto, pecorino cheese, and homemade sweet cakes made with flour milled from the Pepes' wheat.

I had met Pepe at several wine fairs where he said almost noth-ing, where he just exuded—along with his wines—a legendary old-world elegance. But, on this day, I saw a different Pepe, in his element. What I quickly discovered is that one of the reasons Pepe rarely speaks publicly is his later-in-life fondness for speaking in his mother tongue. Not Italian, but Abruzzese dialect, with its lack of vowel endings and a mashing of words that might as well be Hungarian.

While Pepe chewed the last of his farm breakfast, his daughters and granddaughters—dressed in jeans and summer blouses and wearing stylish sunglasses pushing back their long, brown hair—downed a final round of espresso that excluded the patriarch. His family apparently keeps him away from coffee, believing he is naturally supercharged enough. Daughter Sofia, with her niece Chiara in the back seat, drove me through the family's forty-plus acres of vineyards scattered around the area. Most of the vines were shaped over six feet tall in the Pergola format, topped by a horizontal canopy of leaves attached to a wire grid.

"Grandfather always had the idea of using the vines like a solar panel," Chiara chirped as we walked through a row of Montepulciano pergolas.

The morning breeze blew warm and hazy from the Adriatic, and as I looked west to the horizon, I saw Pepe, stripped down to a white tank top and work shorts.

"Papà is always working," explained Sofia, a broad, easy smile crossing her face. "When he is on the tractor, he is the happiest; he is the strongest man in the world. He is a great observer," she added. "He is always looking, always observing to understand. He always says, 'The plant isn't going to tell you anything by itself. You have to observe it to understand.'"

By the time we walked down the dirt path to where Pepe had been, he had disappeared. We then crossed the road to the vineyards of Pepe's "other daughter," Stefania. Things had not gone well for Pepe's eldest daughter, a career schoolteacher who broke with the family years ago to start her own winery. After the premature death of her husband in a 2011 tractor accident, Emidio and Sofia took on the management of her vineyards. On this morning black irrigation hoses, fed by a nearby reservoir, were laid across the high trellis wires and dripping water between the dirt of vines.

Sofia stared disapprovingly as the drips formed puddles on the hard, white clay that had cracked under the summer sun. "I don't like it," she said. "He turns the topsoil too much and then it doesn't absorb water."

It was a technical point but a major source of father-daughter discord. Though Pepe has always farmed organically, he is an old-school tiller who likes to plow frequently. Sofia is of a newer generation of farmers that believes frequent, superficial plowing kills soil life and broils it into infertile dirt. She prefers a once-a-year, deep "ripping" of soils instead.

Sofia explained that she had banned her father from plowing the estate vineyards, but that he still cared for Stefania's his way. "This," she said, "is something Papà and I fight about."

The nineteenth-century Italian diplomat and journalist Primo Levi summed up Abruzzo and its people as *forte e gentile* (strong and kind). In the Pepe family, the strong part could be upgraded to "stubborn." Meekness isn't tolerated. Pepe himself, I would come to learn, confers respect and responsibility on those who've stood up to him and earned it.

Sofia, who shares her father's blue eyes and fine features, began working with him at eighteen. She wanted to learn to make wine but recalled, "Papà didn't let anyone in the winery. He would say, 'I make the wine.'" Instead Pepe bought Sofia a new salesman's case and told her, "Go sell the wine." For years she traveled across Italy, taking orders. But, gradually, she pushed her way into the winery. For five years, from 1998, Sofia and her father worked side by side.

Joining them was Stefania, who'd earned a master's degree in wine management at the International Organization of Vine and Wine in Bordeaux. She returned home from France with different ideas about modern winemaking, including the use of international grape varieties and oak barrels for aging. Such notions became another source of conflict among the Pepes.

"For years it was like this." Sofia held up her two fists, punching the knuckles together as we walked back to her car.

Stefania tried her way. Pepe found the wine unrecognizable. So she quit, taking with her a share of the familial vines. In the family shorthand, the two words that sum up Stefania are "Chateau Margaux," the famed Bordeaux first growth where she interned, evoking something both foreign and elitist. Pepe became convinced by Sofia's capacity and her respect for the winemaking traditions he preserved, and he handed off winemaking responsibility to her in 2003. But the fact that Pepe "lost" a daughter to independence haunts him and the family. Pepe, who quit school as a young boy to work, outwardly blamed Stefania's misconceptions of his winemaking on her schooling.

"Grandfather doesn't think much of the education system," said Chiara, then twenty-four, who studied business and spent a year at Paris's Sorbonne before returning home to work in the family enterprise. "In fact, he didn't want me to study. He told me the only way to learn is to travel and talk to different people."

As Sofia drove north on a road overlooking the Tronto river valley dividing Abruzzo from Le Marche on the northern side, she reflected on the differences of the two regions. "The Abruzzesi are a little more closed and hardheaded," she said, window rolled down, hair flying in the wind. "Also, in wine, they don't want to change anything. The hills of Abruzzo can be taller and steeper. In the Marche they are softer, like the people. If you look at Montepulciano d'Abruzzo, the wine is more austere, and little by little they open up. The wines from the Marche [also made from Montepulciano] are more delicate and softer."

Sofia has followed her father's philosophy and techniques, with some tweaking. Whereas Pepe relied solely on his taste buds in the cellar and the vineyards, she used frequent lab tests. While Pepe long ago eschewed chemical farming products, she has taken steps beyond organics by embracing biodynamic agriculture and its soil preparations, curative teas, and its timing to the cycles of the moon.

Back at the Pepe agriturismo, the family matriarch, Rosa, was in the kitchen, being aided by the wife of one of Pepe's longtime vineyard hands. The two of them, wearing hairnets and aprons, were busily preparing a lunch of thick tubes of *paccheri* pasta with wild greens and roasted lamb shanks while also getting a jump on the next day's eggplant timbale.

The dried pasta itself was made by a local pasta maker using Pepe's own Senatore Cappelli wheat, an early twentieth-century variety of durum wheat introduced by the Abruzzese Marquis Raffaele Cappelli for its superior quality in pasta and breadmaking. Though use of Senatore Cappelli wheat waned in the second half of the century, with chemical-intensive farming giving way to more productive varieties with shorter stalks and growing seasons, it has made a comeback in the twenty-first century with smaller organic farmers across Southern Italy.

Rosa made lunch for four generations of family and occasional guests, about sixteen people every day. But her smile was as bright as a summer morning in Torano. The kitchen was her domain and her refuge. Her husband, daughter, and others had to wrestle with the caprices of nature—hail and drought and spring freezes and harvest rains, not to mention the familial battles over soil tilling. The kitchen was hers. And it was far more predictable. In the winery Rosa had one role: opening and decanting bottles of Montepulciano d'Abruzzo destined to leave the cellar with more than ten years of age. She poured with a steady hand—and without use of a funnel—from one bottle into another clean one, leaving sediment behind. The bottles were then topped up with the same vintage and recorked with a manual-levered corking machine.

The light walls of the dining room illustrated Pepe's story, adorned with retired farm implements and memorabilia, including posters for Pepe wines in Russia and Japan and a 2015 cover of Italy's *Gambero Rosso* magazine showing Pepe's face and the headline "Mister Montepulciano."

Pepe arrived in his summer work clothes and pointed with a weathered index finger to a picture frame containing one yellowed typed page. On it was a list of wines: a simple report of the minutes of something called "The Friends of Good Wine Club" from Chicago in 1979. "Look," Pepe said in Italian, breaking out of his usual dialect. His eighty-five-year-old voice was as deep and raspy as a vintage car engine. "This was from 1979—America, Chicago." The list was a ranking of Italian reds tasted by the club in February of that year. At the top of the list was Emidio Pepe Montepulciano

1970. "Enh," Pepe grunted for emphasis as if to say, *Look at that.* His finger descended the list, stopping at each of the other nine wines that were tasted—mostly Piedmont wines like the 1971 Barolo from the legendary traditionalist Giacomo Cappellano, and a 1971 Nebbiolo from Giacomo Conterno, along with Biondi-Santi's 1973 "Il Greppo" Brunello di Montalcino.

"I was first before all of these," Pepe said. "Barolo . . . Brunello . . . enh . . . Biondi-Santi! Chicago," he added. "I've been to America a hundred times!"

Emidio Pepe is obviously a man with a lot of pride and no small ego. He rarely drinks the wines of others and talks about few wines he admires outside of those produced by the winery of his late friend and fellow Abruzzo eccentric Edoardo Valentini. "I made better reds," Pepe said. "He had soils and altitude and exposition that are better for the whites. But for reds, I always beat him."

I followed Pepe out the back door and into the old Montepulciano vineyard that sloped down the hillside toward Torano. He explained his neatly proscribed formula "uno-uno-uno" for cultivating pergola vineyards. The canopies of his vines were short trimmed to provide what he says is the optimal ratio of "one vine, one square meter of leaves for one kilogram of grapes." (It takes about one and a half kilos to make a bottle of wine.) As he walked in the shade under the vines, he tied up loose shoots and pulled dried ones that had been cut but left in the wire grid above—the result, he said, of sloppy work during the recent vine pruning.

"Look at this. You don't leave things like this," he complained, tugging on a long brown desiccated cutting and dropping it on the ground.

Chiara, whose father, Giuseppe, works with Pepe in the vineyards, joined us and followed her grandfather's lead in tying up the loose ends. "The workers always make me angry," he cried into the heat of midday, with only me, Chiara, and a few cicadas to hear him. Then, after nearly a minute, he fumed, "The workers are going to kill me!" As we walked back up the hill, he veered from the vines into the rows of greens and tomatoes that Pepe also cared for, along with the family chickens. Perspiring from a morning of work, he proclaimed, "The countryside is my gym—not just a gym for the physique, but for the mind also." As we entered the house for lunch, as if letting me in on a secret, he leaned in toward me and said in a low voice, "You stop, you die."

At the round table set for lunch sat Pepe, Sofia, Daniela, Chiara, and Pepe's Belgian importer with his wife, young son, and baby boy. A kids' table was laid out for the younger Pepe grandchildren. Pepe's daughters and Chiara brought out a platter of layered salumi—prosciutto, salami, and *lonza* (cured pork loin)—as well as another plate of sliced aged sheep cheese, along with baskets of homemade brown bread and bottles of Pepe's green olive oil. The stars of the meal were Pepe's white wines—his golden, silky, rich Trebbianos. We drank the young 2014 with the pasta and the 2007 with the lamb.

There were several conversations going at once, family members came and went, and Chiara's chair got taken over by her younger sister, Elisa. Sofia's husband, Fabio, arrived and squeezed in at the table. Then Sofia set out a bottle of 2004 Trebbiano, a dense, buttery wine that had aged beautifully, with a light, sherry-like oxidation. Pepe was telling me the secret of longevity for his wines; it came from aging them in vitrified cement vats, "like a big bottle." Eventually tension rose around the table when Sofia told her father what she had seen in her sister's vineyard: the soils compacted like cement from too much plowing.

Pepe shook his head and said, "I don't remember working the soil in that vineyard."

"Si," Sofia insisted.

"No," Pepe responded, raising his voice.

"Si!" Sofia bellowed, holding her ground, pointing an admonishing finger at her father.

"No!" Pepe dug in for the last word, and his daughter let him have that.

As the meal wound down and espressos were passed to all but Pepe, I sat between Chiara and Pepe and said something about the Trebbianos.

"In Las Vegas, they sell for six hundred dollars a bottle—the last vintage," Pepe blurted. "Six hundred dollars in a restaurant! In Las Vegas!"

"Nonno," Chiara admonished her grandfather. "What does that have to do with the taste of the wine? What does that have to do with the quality?" She turned to me with a roll of her eyes. "I hate that. He doesn't understand that price has nothing to do with quality."

"Seicento dollari americani . . ." Pepe bragged quietly. He didn't understand what all her fuss was about, but he seemed to have little desire to confront his first grandchild, who had in little time become a force.

I had begun to understand Pepe. Despite others' romantic view of him as a wine purist, he was first and foremost a businessman who had quit school at the height of World War II and, as he put it, "conquered the world" starting with hands and a tractor. Why shouldn't *seicento dollari americani* in the capital of American high rollers be an achievement?

". . . a Las Vegas," he muttered, stood up, and shuffled off for his midday nap.

The next morning, Pepe was already out in the vineyards when I arrived. "Working with grandfather means a lot of diplomacy," Chiara explained. "Sofia has the complete respect of grandfather in the cellar. But in the vineyards, he still wants control."

Chiara led me through the winery that morning describing Pepe's low-tech wine style: few machines, rarely adding sulfites, no pump overs of juices over grape skins during fermentation, no temperature controls in Pepe's vitrified concrete fermenting and aging tanks. "Grandfather says a wine that is fermenting is like a man with a fever: it doesn't want to be moved around."

Later that morning, after Pepe tended to the chickens and other farm chores, he showered and joined me before lunch in a tasting room of the winery to talk about his life. When Pepe began work on the family farm, it was only about fifteen acres. At eleven years old, he quit school to graft vines, tend livestock, and cultivate soils for other people. Some years later he enrolled in a correspondence course to improve his Italian. In 1953, at twenty-two years old, he bought his first tractor with his brother-in-law, plowing fields and harvesting wheat for landowners throughout Abruzzo and Le Marche. "We worked twenty-four hours on that tractor with my brother-in-law," he said. "I worked the night and he worked the day." One night in 1954, as he was trying to repair the tractor, part of Pepe's left hand got caught in a tractor tread, severing much of his middle finger.

"It was in Le Marche," he remembered stoically, looking at the stub that is left. "I went to the hospital carrying the piece of finger to get it reattached, but they didn't know how to do that at the time."

The work took more than a physical toll on Pepe, who eventually realized his agricultural business model wasn't working. "By the time we paid for the tractor, it was worn-out and time to buy a new one," he said. "It was then I understood it was time to find another way to make a living."

In the late 1950s Pepe became chairman of a local chapter of Italy's association of young farmers called Provare, Produrre, Progredire (Try, Produce, Progress), nicknamed the "Three P" club. In 1960 the club sent him on a life-changing, month long exchange program in the Netherlands. It was his first time outside Italy, and Pepe stayed with a family that produced table grapes grown on two-and-a-half acres in greenhouses in the cool, damp Dutch countryside. The grapes, sold in Italy at a premium, were enough to sustain the family. This astounded Pepe. Italy was the land of grapes. It had sunshine, a Mediterranean climate, and infinite natural vineyard slopes. The idea that the flat, humid Netherlands could sell hothouse grapes to Italians taught Pepe his life's most valuable business lesson: "I realized you had to create a market. If you don't create a market, you are dead."

Pepe's father sold grapes to large area producers as well as barrels of wine to bottlers from the North who used it for blending. As a young man, Pepe became a proud agricultural entrepreneur. At twenty-three he bought his first tiny Fiat Topolino 500, and, a few years later, he traded up for a sleek, sophisticated, four-door Renault Dauphine. "People began to say, 'You are spending too much on cars and not enough to find a wife,'" he remembered with an amused grunt.

Pepe began experimenting with winemaking using his father's simple equipment below the family home. In 1964, with grapes from the family vineyards and others he'd purchased, Pepe filled five thousand bottles of Montepulciano wine. "My father thought I was crazy to put wine in bottles," he said, raising his voice to a shout. "He asked me, 'Who is going to buy those bottles now?'" Pepe was driven by a belief in Montepulciano, "a grape that's good and sweet and you can even eat it like a table grape."

"I knew how to make wine already because we made wine in the family. It was good wine. I changed nothing," Pepe said. "The grapes were destemmed by hand and that made wine that was sweet and delicate." In that same year, at thirty-three years old, he married Rosa, a local schoolteacher.

For the first few vintages, Pepe called his new wine label Aurora, named after the predawn hours when he began work, and sold it from the back of a new car: a sleek Alfa Romeo Giulia Super, which he drove first around Italy and then north to Germany. "With a hundred lire in my pocket, at the wheel of the Giulia Super," he recalled, puffing out his chest, "I was the strongest man in the world."

At an early edition of what was called Italian Wine Days in Verona (the predecessor to Vinitaly), Pepe read a brochure on the young Montepulciano d'Abruzzo wine appellation, which was officially declared in 1968. "They wrote that Montepulciano d'Abruzzo is meant to be drunk young. That it's not meant for aging. It was ridiculous! I wanted to age bottles to prove them wrong." Proving them wrong became his life's work. Pepe's first expansion of the winery came in the 1970s, when he created an aging cellar for bottles, stacking more and more aside until half of his production was stored for later release. When I visited Pepe, his cavernous, vaulted aging cellar was full of hundreds of thousands of bottles, and he was buying land from his neighbor to expand underground, on the other side of the road.

I've considered whether Emidio Pepe is a tradition-clinging reactionary or a revolutionary who embraced "natural winemaking" long before the crowd, and have come to the conclusion that he is neither. He is a pragmatist and a perfectionist. He believed in Provare, Produrre, Progredire. But, he'd reasoned, why embrace change if it hurts your product? He resisted time-saving technology like destemming machines not because he was categorically opposed to machines, but because mechanical destemmers didn't do a good enough job for him, leaving bits of broken stems in the must. "The machine breaks the stems, and when you taste the wine, it is tannic and bitter," he said. "Doing it by hand makes the wines vellutato [velvety]." Similarly, pressing white grape bunches underfoot—outside the cellar door in a wooden tub—allows for a gentle pressing that doesn't break stems or crush unripe berries. Unlike many of his contemporaries of the Italian fine wine movement that exploded in earnest in the 1980s, Pepe shunned *barriques*—the standard 225-liter Bordeaux oak barrels. In fact, he never used any wood for fermenting and aging wine. Stainless steel—ubiquitous in about 99 percent of modern wineries—was banished also. Instead he stuck with concrete, which he changed from raw to glass-lined in the 1980s, believing it to be the perfect home for wine.

"With concrete, the taste of the wine was wine; it added nothing like wood," Pepe said. "Capito? I liked the taste of something delicate, not modified by wood. My wife didn't like oak either. Wine is like a human. When you put wine in glass, va bene, it feels well," he went on, adding that steel was too conductive a material for winemaking. "When you put wine in steel, the wine has to build a house around itself to protect itself from the outside, and it loses a lot and produces a lot of tartrates that it needs during the aging process. It's like a man who builds a house for himself and spends all his money."

In the early 1970s—Pepe was not sure of the year—a group of Abruzzo producers organized a trade trip to New York. He was excluded because his winery was too small. "The next week, I bought a ticket and flew to New York," Pepe said. "I found a restaurant on Forty-Sixth Street called Vesuvio. The owner was Neapolitan. He wanted my wine and introduced me to an importer. I've been to the U.S.A. a hundred times!" Pepe reiterated, repeating the number for the first time that day. I nodded in affirmation.

"Enh!" he said.

There was a time, in 1999—when he had two daughters in the cellar with him, and he fought with Stefania over her Bordeaux winemaking methods—that Pepe bought about fifty acres of vine-yard land in Australia after traveling there to present his wines. His thought was to plant Montepulciano and have Stefania take it over. "The idea was to do two harvests a year of Montepulciano." Pepe shrugged. "But no one from the family wanted to go and plant Montepulciano in Australia." Perhaps the thought of staying half a world away from Abruzzo was too much for the members of this clan. Pepe has lived his whole life in Torano, surrounded by females. He was his family's only son, raised among four sisters, and he became a father of three daughters.

We were joined in the tasting room by Sofia and Chiara, and Pepe complained mockingly of not having his own son. "When Sofia, the youngest, was born, when I realized it was another girl, I fainted at the hospital," he deadpanned. "Of course I wanted a male to drive tractors and work on the farm. Now I'm eighty-five years old, I still have to do all this work! If there were another man in the house, I wouldn't have to do it!" He went on, but with a sparkle in his eye. Pepe was clearly in his element, surrounded by women. It gave him purpose. He was still the one in the family who drove the tractor. His legacy and credo was still the sun around which the others orbited. His work ethic pervades the life on the farm and is taught to the young through example. Here, you aren't given a job so much as you have to find something you are good at that benefits the clan.

"I have understood that he who produces something has to find a market to create work," Pepe said. "Young people today don't want to create work; they want a job. The young people don't want to work in agriculture, but the youth unemployment in Italy is 37 percent! School malforms these kids. They come out with no passion and nothing useful to live life. They are afraid to do anything. Afraid to make sacrifices. This is the problem of the school. Traveling the world is the best education. That was my education. That and reading the newspaper."

Sofia poured glasses of seven vintages of Pepe Montepulciano starting with a rich, intense, and woodsy 2010, that drew glycerin legs down the sides of a large, egg-shaped glass. "This is Montepulciano d'Abruzzo Montepulciano," Pepe enthused. "At fifty years old, it will be still be good—va bene."

At lunch we drank other vintages stretched back to a brick-colored 1979. Pepe takes great pride in showing how his wines can age to prove Montepulciano naysayers wrong. To my taste this insistence on old wines and their mystique is a little exaggerated. A Pepe Montepulciano after a mere seven years can be as good as anything sunny central Italy produces. Why wait? But, to Pepe, aging wine is more than important—it's personal.

Lunch was another chaotic and delicious meal, beginning with Ascolana olives (pitted, stuffed with meat, and fried) and fresh ricotta, followed by Rosa's timbale, a baked dish with layers of pasta, meat, cheese tomatoes, and summer vegetables. Yet what I noticed that day more than anything was the way Pepe and his daughters' laugh together. Hilarity erupts around the table in a split second— Pepe, Sofia, Daniela, and Chiara—in a display of Pepe teeth and with Pepe fire in their eyes. Pepe's determination and confidence has passed to his daughters and grandchildren and seems to imbue everything they do. Emidio Pepe is not so much a wine but a sort of biological imperative of the clan.

At the end of the meal, Pepe rested his elbow on the table and held a glass of the 2010 Montepulciano d'Abruzzo in front of his face. The others went on talking, but he stared silently into the ruby liquid. He looked like a man reading his own epitaph. What was he thinking?

You stop, you die.

Without a word he stood and walked to the door. I glimpsed him out the window, shuffling back toward his vines.

Abruzzo's other important wine force belonged to one of the few families living within the medieval walls of the tiny hilltop town Loreto Aprutino, in the southern part of the region. For centuries the Valentini had been landowning intellectuals, lawyers, doctors, and iconoclasts. Edoardo Valentini became an Italian legend over more than fifty vintages beginning in the early 1950s. His son, Francesco Paolo Valentini, who took over with the death of Edoardo in 2006, rarely leaves home. For twenty-five years his Venezuela-born wife, Elena, says he has promised her a honeymoon away from here.

"I'm still waiting!" she teased her husband, smiling, inside the library and office of the Valentini nineteenth-century palazzo at the edge of town. It was a hot afternoon, and Francesco grinned and replied, "People who travel, are those who are not content where they are."

Valentini, lean and energetic at fifty-five, with curly, light brown locks that flop over his brow, looked like an aristocrat farmer but displayed a schoolboy's mischievous sense of humor. He often followed one of his wisecracks or observations with a four-part chortle: "Henh-henh-henh-henh."

The Valentini line emigrated from Spain in the 1600s, arriving in Rome in the court of the Spanish-Italian noble Renaissance family the Borgias. The Valentini name came from one patron, an

Italian duke, who lent it to them. In the seventeenth century, one Valentini ancestor, critical of corruption in the clergy, was exiled to the hinterlands of Abruzzo with some twelve thousand acres of land to administer. Little by little, over four centuries, the Valentini holdings have shrunken to about five hundred acres, given away as daughters' dowries or confiscated during modern pushes for national land reform.

Edoardo, a lawyer, "was the first to interest himself directly in the farm," Valentini said. "The rest were just administrators." Edoardo Valentini achieved a greatness rarely seen in Italian wine. During decades when most of the Italian wine industry struggled to produce anything more than fresh, young, and simple whites, Valentini made extraordinary and age-worthy white Trebbianos along with red Montepulcianos. Most of his tiny production was distributed to wine lovers in Italy.

The elder Valentini rarely discussed his wine methods, other than to say that he used big barrels for fermentation and sold most of his harvest to a local cooperative, keeping the best grapes for his wines. He never permitted visitors to enter his cellar, even friends like Emidio Pepe. To the end he remained decidedly low-tech in his personal and business dealings, sticking to communicating by phone, fax, and handwritten letters.

Francesco Valentini, who studied agronomy and psychology before returning home to work with his father, has kept his father's methods alive, likening the spontaneous fermentations in large oak barrels to "nineteenth-century winemaking." The tall, heavy, dark wood shelves behind him were crammed with books—leather-bound legal volumes, literature, musical scores, and the work of Valentini ancestors, like the nineteenth century–born Camillo Valentini's *The Psychology of Hunting*. On a table in front of the massive desk where generations of Valentini have sat was a bottle of Francesco Valentini's latest obsession. It was not wine.

"Good wine is something you can make in many places: Italy, France, Spain, America," Valentini said. "But olive oil . . ." He shifted his weight forward in his antique desk chair. "Oil is much more restricted. Quality oil comes from the heart of the Mediterranean. Which is Italy. Italy has an infinite diversity of quality for oil," he added, his light eyes glinting. "Of course, we Italians have the capacity to do it badly!"

I know some things about olive oil. I have been a student of it and sometimes olive harvester for nearly two decades. Fraud in oil is rampant. Industrial brands have been caught illegally adding seed oils or using the "extra virgin" label for excessively acidic oils. "Extra virgin" must have a measured acidity below 0.8 percent—an indication of the relatively quick pressing of fresh olives. Some have also stretched the notion of what "Italian olive oil" means. With insatiable worldwide demand for Italian oil, large Italian brands bottled blends from across the Mediterranean and label it "produced in Italy." But when oil is good or even great—picked and pressed under ideal conditions for luminously green color and distinct vibrant flavors—it is just as inspiring as remarkable wine.

Valentini harvested his olives starting in late summer, with machines that shake the olive-bearing branches with sets of pincers. He brought them for processing to the mill of his neighbor Alberto Cerretani, continuing a relationship that began between the two families in the 1970s. Now he and Cerretani had entered into a partnership and were building a new olive oil *frantoio* among his olives to be called Valentini e Cerretani.

It was an oddity. Hardly anyone in Italy was building new olive mills at the time. Though oil was a necessity of life, the cultivation of olive trees had a return on investment that was close to nil. Mills take a cut (in oil or cash) for pressing others' olives, but, in the twenty-first century, it was hardly a business proposition. It followed the same quest for excellence that drove Valentini years earlier to develop a line of vintage-dated pastas with the pasta maker Verrigni from his own wheat. Only this was more personal to him.

"Jesus Christ, before he was crucified, made his walk in an olive grove, not a vineyard," Valentini said. Well, there surely was enough in the Bible to justify the production of any Mediterranean staple from wheat to wine to figs. Valentini seemed to be grasping for confirmation of his new venture that stood well apart from his father's legacy.

"There are a few places in the world that have a terroir that's adapted to high-quality olives," he said. "Imagine that in Abruzzo, we have twenty-five cultivars of olives."

Ask most Italians where the world's best olive oil comes from, and if there are any olive trees in proximity, they will likely point to them. Valentini is, unsurprisingly, a fan of Loretana olives (the local name for what is more commonly known as the Dritta variety), which he cultivates to produce about twenty-four thousand liters annually. He tends those olive groves with methods that could be considered organic, though he is far too proud to seek out such a label. "I don't want to be confined in anything," he said. "I am a free spirit."

As the morning heat rose, Valentini took me to his olive groves and vineyards. But first, with a little bit of trepidation, he allowed me to have a look at the cellars below the palazzo, where his wines finish their primary fermentation. The tight, vaulted brick space was packed with large oak vats dating to 1850, some of which had been refurbished with new fronts. The floors were covered in river stones arranged in square patterns. The place was tidy, naturally cool, as still as an abbey, and smelled vaguely subterranean. It was also the closest I would get to seeing how Valentini wines are made. The Valentinis' resistance to showing too much could be explained in many ways. Valentini once told me that he feared people bringing in yeast spores from other wineries, and besides, he'd said, "a winery is an intimate place—like a bedroom."

"For my wine, nothing has changed since 1800," Valentini said. "Oil is the opposite. For oil, you must use the best technology possible."

We climbed into his Range Rover, and he drove out of town along a rutted road, through an oak forest, arriving at a plateau full of olive trees. In the middle of it was the concrete shell for the mill he would complete with Cerretani for the fall 2019 harvest.

"Loreto Aprutino has the highest density of olive trees in Italy," he said. The trees were small and compact, running over the hilltop of light clay soils and up a facing hill to the south that was topped with vineyards. "The Loretana is a nervous, living sculpture; the trees are not big. Thirty kilometers away, you find oil that is completely different."

Valentini told me that, years earlier, he was motivated not by a love of wine, but a love of nature. Now in the shade of an olive tree he confessed, "For me, wine is the wife; oil is a secret love . . . henh-henh-henh-henh."

He had great ambitions for his move into olive oil, and he spoke about creating a center for oil education with tasting rooms that would attract restaurateurs, sommeliers, and others. "I want to pay the same attention to oil that is paid to wine," he said, hopping back into the driver's seat. "My dream is that restaurants will have oil lists, not just wine lists. The consumer today doesn't know the difference between what is a defect in oil and what is quality. The consumer thinks that oil is a condiment, but they don't really experience the taste, the aromas, the typicity, la bellezza."

The world of Italian olive oil is like Italian politics and much else in Italy—a carousel of opinions and fashion with few accepted truths. Personally, I prefer ultragreen oil that's *pizzicante*, which means it pricks the back of the throat. There is a lot of debate about this sensation: Is it a defect? Or an attribute of freshness?

"An oil that is fresh should be bitter; it should prick, from the polyphenols," Valentini said. "An oil that is sweet is too ripe. It has too much acid."

At times that morning, I had the feeling of being in an olive oil infomercial as Valentini waxed on about the claimed medicinal effects of good oil—antioxidant, anticholesterol, anticancer. I love good olive oil, good wine, and good Mediterranean food. But if a fraction of the claims about their attributes were true, I'd feel half my age when I sprung out of bed in the morning.

"Food is culture. Food is history. Food is also medicine," Valentini was saying as the vehicle rocked up a hillside path. "It's not just sustenance. An oil that you make here should not be like an oil from twenty to thirty kilometers away."

We arrived at a vineyard that sloped gently to the north with equidistant views of the Gran Sasso peaks to the west and the Adriatic to the northeast.

"Trebbiano and Loretana are cultivars that have been here millennia," Valentini said. "They have the same mother—the earth here. They express the same characteristics. They have similar DNA."

Wow, I thought. That was a big claim. Trebbiano itself is a source of genetic debate. It's a family of vines, not one specific cultivar. Trebbiano d'Abruzzo wines can be made with local Trebbiano Abruzzese or the more productive Tuscan version. They can also be made with the Abruzzo's Trebbiano-like sibling Bombino Bianco. Some said that Valentini's wines are made from Bombino—a claim he scoffed at. "It's Trebbiano Abruzzese," he said. But here was Valentini making a connection between two entirely different species from entirely different families of flowering plants. It was like grouping mice and men or eggplant and apples. The only thing that local Trebbiano and Loretana olives outwardly have in common is that they were cultivated side by side for centuries.

"At lunch," he said, "I will give you a glass of Trebbiano and a glass of oil to taste together."

After we drove back to Loreto, I walked down to the Cerretani mill, which was housed in a vintage garage-like structure. The Cerretani family has milled flour and pressed olive oil in Loreto for nearly two hundred years, yet there was nothing striking about the place. Alberto Cerretani used the same modern centrifugal decanters as everyone to extract oil quickly and without exposure to air that would lessen its aromas and flavors. But he was particular about decanting his oil as soon as possible after the olives were harvested. For most of his clients, that meant within a day of harvest. For Valentini, his most demanding client and newfound business partner, that meant within a couple of hours.

Valentini, Elena, Cerretani, and I met at a nearby inn for lunch, where Valentini wanted me to taste his wines and oil with *pasta mugnaia* (literally, the miller's wife's pasta), a traditional Abruzzese dish of wide, hand-pulled noodles in a red sauce that, in this instance, was seasoned with onions, carrots, pork, lamb, oil, wine, and pecorino cheese. When Valentini entered carrying an armful of his bottles, the staff greeted him like royalty, bowing and hustling to get him situated. An oversized Plexiglas wine bucket with ice was promptly set on a side table. Valentini began opening a half-dozen vintages dating back to 1978, the bottle and label of which were covered with ash-colored mold.

A man at least a decade older than Valentini sauntered up to the table as if he knew Valentini, and the two men greeted each other. The man then pointed his phone at Valentini, who flushed with embarrassment.

"Take a picture of the bottle," Valentini implored. He set it on the table and stepped back.

"No, with you," the man directed.

Valentini offered the man a glass of the wine instead, but he shook his head.

"Look, there's a beautiful woman to take it with," he said, offering Elena.

"With you," the man insisted.

Valentini finally relented, awkwardly posing with a hand on the bottle and a forced smile.

The man took his picture, shook Valentini's hand as he said his goodbyes, and went back to his table. Who was it?

"I don't know. I've never met him," Valentini said, and laughed nervously. "Henh-henh-henh-henh."

Just then another sexagenarian approached with a camera and snapped a photo of the bottle.

"The Loretani are a photographing people." Valentini laughed again.

Valentini is not accustomed to public displays. He doesn't even involve himself in the prosaic mercantile aspects of selling his wine. His agent simply allocates it to the world. The Valentinis' lordly secret, it seems, has always been in its restrained quantities of wines made to age gracefully. Valentini skimmed only about 20 percent of his best grapes to make wine; the rest he sold off. After he makes wine in separate lots, there is another cut of what is good enough to make it into his final vintage blend. "I am an assembler," he remarked. "I take six or seven lots and assemble them in the glass." Valentini makes three wines, starting with his most well-known—white Trebbiano d'Abruzzo. He also makes deep-colored Cerasuolo d'Abruzzo rosé from Montepulciano, but in the decade since the death of his father, he only released four vintages of red wine. "The other years," he said, "the wine didn't please me."

His 1978 Trebbiano was still lively yet creamy, recalling a great Burgundy white, with toasted flavors Valentini attributed to the residues of degenerated yeast cells in his unfiltered wines.

"I always smell particular aromas in our wines, like chamomile, hay, and chicken broth," he said. He then turned his attention to the olive oil, pouring about a tablespoon each of Cerretani's oil and then his own into small plastic cups.

Cerretani's oil was green with a pizzicante bite and charged with aromas that seemed to capture the full growing season, from wet spring meadows to the dried grasses in the heat of summer. I then sipped Valentini's oil and closed my eyes. It was like the Cerretani oil but even more so, with the same sensations and aromas only amplified. Yet there was nothing in common with Valentini's wines. Valentini's wines were soft, complex, and discreet. His oil was direct, focused, and in your face. I tasted more oil and more wine but couldn't begin to find the commonality, other than the fact that both were products I could consume regularly for life. I said this to Valentini and challenged him: Exactly where was the similarity?

"There is a similarity when you are working the raw materials of the Loretano olives and the Trebbiano . . ." he offered, his voice trailing off.

Valentini struck me as a man guided both by methodical empirical observation and a kind of poetry that sounded in his head. This may be true of all great winemakers, but in Valentini's case, both the science and the poetry ran strong.

When the pasta arrived, I asked Valentini about his father and what he had learned from him. Had he been a scientist or a poet?

"My father was a scientist and a poet," he said slowly, after pondering the question. "The first thing for him was not to destroy the natural material. Then you made wine."

Stefano Papetti Ceroni was not born into wine or agriculture. He's an intellectual city kid from Bologna—a seat of the industrial North known as home to the world's oldest university and for its streets and piazza's lined by elaborate porticos. As a child in a prosperous and educated business family, he was a voracious reader who devoured everything he could get his hands on. That included his mother's cooking magazines, which had a section in the back dedicated to wine. "I read all the reviews where they talked about the aromas in wine like flowers and cherries, and I said, 'It's not possible to smell all these aromas in a liquid,'" Stefano marveled.

At twelve, he says, he bought his first bottle of cheap supermarket wine and brought it home—"not to drink but to smell," a practice that he continued through high school years. By eighteen, in his last year of *liceo*, wine had become a passion. Stefano enrolled in sommeliers courses and began to travel to vineyards in Northern Italy and France. "But I'd never been in Abruzzo," he explained, "because for people in the North of Italy, where is Abruzzo? They don't even know."

After law school, Stefano worked for a Bologna law firm. In 2001 one of the firm's clients was a leather-goods producer who had won a case against a counterfeiter. One day in spring, he went with a court officer to seize some contraband belts. Also taken to the counterfeiter's site that day was a young woman lawyer whose firm represented a textiles client making a similar seizure. When he cast eyes on Eloisa, Stefano says, he felt as if he had already known her for a long time. "Our Cupid was that court officer," he recalled.

The couple was married in 2005 in Loreto, where Eloisa's mother's side of the family, the De Fermos, kept a palazzo and were once one of the principal landowners. Though the couple frequently took trips to Tuscany, the Piedmont, and Burgundy to visit vineyards and taste wine, it wasn't until 2007 that Stefano's wife said, "Let's go see the family vineyards."

"I had the second coup de foudre of my life when my father-in-law stopped the car in front of the vineyard and said, 'This is it,'" Stefano remembered.

When I met Stefano in summer on the De Fermo farm outside Loreto, he was forty-two, a man with a quiet, studious bearing and gentle gray-green eyes. He wore a loose, rumpled linen shirt and spoke in precise Italian. We crossed the road that runs by the farm—an old Roman road converted to a two-lane blacktop—and walked through his vineyards. He grew a mix of Montepulciano d'Abruzzo, white local Pecorino, and Chardonnay grapes that had been tended part-time by Stefano's father-in-law for thirty years in which he made wine for the family and sold most of the crop.

The land was inherited by Stefano's mother-in-law, Nicoletta De Fermo, from her childless uncle Carlo (also known as Don Carlino), a lifelong bachelor and wine lover who in the 1920s traveled to Burgundy and in 1926 returned with Chardonnay to plant on less than three acres. The rest of the farm was filled out principally with his selection of Montepulciano. "Don Carlino made wine until 1955,"

Stefano said. "Nobody knows why he stopped. When he died in the 1970s, the farm went to my mother-in-law."

When Stefano first saw the vineyards, they spanned more than forty acres, and Stefano began traveling to Abruzzo on weekends to study them. The following year he asked his in-laws for permission to cultivate one hectare—about two and a half acres. The next year he asked if he could take over the rest. His father-in-law was happy to offload the work.

The family employed a crew of workers who had been there decades, working under one old guardian, and Stefano's arrival set up a culture clash. Like many of his generation, Stefano was drawn to biodynamics. It's almost a cliché for wide-eyed, urban newbie farmers to be attracted to the alchemical and esoteric philosophy of the late nineteenth-century and early twentieth-century Rudolf Steiner and his ideas on improving agriculture through soil life. Who wouldn't want to work with the moon, nature, and its cycles and treat your vines with natural herbal teas like nettle and horsetail? Who, like thousands of modern vintners the world over, wouldn't want to create a powerful soil and plant preparation by placing manure in a cow horn and burying it for the winter? The guardian of the farm, not surprisingly, resisted those ideas.

"We fought a lot," said Stefano, who, in the spring of 2009, confronted the guardian and demanded the keys to the farm buildings.

"The farm belongs to my wife's family, not you," he told the man, who grudgingly turned over the keys.

Stefano began unlocking doors. At the back of a storage garage containing a truck caked in dust and cobwebs, he found a small wood door. After inserting the right key, he opened the door and stepped into what he immediately knew was Don Carlino's abandoned winery.

"I found concrete tanks and big oak barrels," he said. "It was like someone left the place fifty years earlier planning to come back the next day and never did."

The guardian was eventually dismissed, and, little by little, Stefano began hiring younger, like-minded assistants. After restoring the two concrete tanks, he brought in new, big oak barrels and a pump and began his first harvest in 2010 with a mere three thousand bottles of Montepulciano he called Prologo. Over the subsequent years, Stefano expanded his production but still used only about half of the vineyard grapes for his wines while selling off the rest. In 2015 he stopped lawyering entirely to become a full-time farmer, commuting weekends to Bologna, where his children attend a Rudolf Steiner school. He made a second easier red Montepulciano without wood aging called Concrete, a relatively dark Cerasuolo d'Abruzzo rosé, a Chardonnay called Launegild that he largely sells in France, and a Pecorino called Don Carlino. He also produced small amounts of wheat, legumes, and oil. "The future of agriculture has to be small quantities and high quality," he said, citing the price of standard wheat at just one euro for five kilos. "That's nothing; it's the price of one coffee in a bar."

Stefano showed rare confidence in his ability to adapt to his new world. While most in his place would hire a trained enologist to run his cellar and the intricacies of winemaking, Stefano took it on himself.

"I don't need a winemaker," he said back in his small, tidy stone-and-brick vaulted wine cellar lined with wood casks. "I have friends who taste with me."

Of course, it helps if one of those friends is Francesco Valentini. The friendship began after Stefano appeared at Valentini's door and asked him to taste his wine. Valentini willingly obliged, as he has helped other young producers around Loreto. The pair have developed a frank relationship, and Valentini often scolds Stefano for selling his wines too young.

During an Easter lunch with a group of friends including Valentini in 2015, Stefano served a bottle of his 2011 Prologo. "When Francesco tasted it, he closed his eyes and said, 'It's the first time I tasted a Montepulciano that's like mine,'" Stefano said. "I was hit by this." He fluttered his fingers in front of his face in a pantomime of tears.

Every week during the school year, Stefano made the commute from Bologna at the edge of Northern Italy's Po River Valley—the foggy, smoggy flatlands that serve Italy's economic and industrial engine. South of Bologna forks the *autostrade* network. To the west the highway runs to Tuscany and Rome. To the east the highway runs to the Adriatic and down the back of the Italian boot, through Le Marche, Abruzzo, Molise, and Puglia.

"When I told grandmother I was moving here, she said, 'What are you going to do in bassa Italia?'" When Stefano pronounced *bassa Italia*, he hissed the double s's in a sign of disdain. "To her, that's what Abruzzo is," he said. "A pretty place with no culture. For me, it was a funny thing to discover Abruzzo. People are closer to Naples even more than are the people from Rome. The language is similar to Neapolitan. Their way of thinking is like Naples's."

The idea of the Abruzzese as somehow being near Neapolitan was strange to me. Outwardly they seemed more like Italy's answer to conservative and reserved Midwesterners. Abruzzo seemed a sleepy, industrious heartland having little in common with Italy's loud, flamboyant capital of confusion.

Stefano's eloquence and his sensibility also seemed alien to this place. He was clearly a northerner who had traveled in the opposite direction of most Italians to find his life's work. Inversely, he sold more of his wines in Milan or abroad than he did locally. "In New York restaurants, De Fermo is better known than in the restaurants of Loreto." He laughed.

Stefano was still a newcomer to Loreto and winemaking. Yet, in spite of that—or perhaps because of it—he approached his work delicately, so as not to impose a style on his wines. The wines weren't as complex or rich as Valentini's and Pepe's. But, like those wines, they had a raw, unvarnished appeal. His Montepulcianos were elemental, almost minimalistic: clean, dry expressions of fruit that reminded me of strawberries in April. They could have been from another time in Abruzzo—if, in that time, their maker had had a bit of equipment and been so careful.

"I know that I won't be rich doing this job, but my life is to be here," Stefano said softly. "I cannot explain why I arrived here, but I am deeply romantic, and I believe it was written somewhere that this place should be awakened."

We sat at a rustic table near a small, open wood door of his cellar, a patch of white light glaring on the cement floor. Outside, the countryside had fallen into its midday silence.

"How many harvests will I have? Thirty? Thirty-five? What can a man do in thirty-five years?" he asked.

I didn't know how many harvests he had left but I was glad he was here, walking softly across this farm as its steward.

"Not a lot of big things," he said, answering his own question with a humility you could taste in his wines. "But a lot of little things."

3. Emidio Pepe with (*from left*) granddaughter Chiara and daughters Sofia and Daniela.

4. Francesco Valentini.

5. Stefano Papetti Ceroni.

3 *The Four Seasons of Tabarrini*

Every place in Italy is south of somewhere else: geographically, psychologically, and culturally. But what about Italy's deep central heartland? To which part of Italy does it belong?

Umbria nestles like an island in the dead center of Italy, the only region that doesn't touch the sea or a foreign border. Wedged between Tuscany and the Roman region of Lazio to the west and Le Marche to the east, Umbria defines itself in part by what it is not. Specifically, Umbria is not Tuscany, the fashionable, worldly, once-upon-a-time cradle of the Italian Renaissance.

In the mid-1980s, when my wife and I first visited Umbria, it was billed in vacation-speak as "the next Tuscany." Amazingly, that term is still tossed around. Comparisons from afar are obvious: the two neighbors resemble each other in their gorgeous rolling hills topped by medieval villages. But the likenesses end inside the walls of those villages and the minds of their inhabitants.

Tuscany, molded six centuries ago by the Medici family of bankers and politicians, is blockbuster, cosmopolitan Italy, with a culture of daily interaction with the works of creative geniuses like Filippo Brunelleschi and Michelangelo and its twentieth-century fashion roster of Guccis, Puccis, and Ferragamos. Its wines have been shaped by an establishment of noble families like Antinori, Frescobaldi, and Incisa della Rocchetta.

Next door lies sleepy, sober Umbria, restrained in its medievality. While Tuscan families were wheeling, dealing, competing, and

67

trading, Umbria, with its graceful, perched towns such as Perugia and Spoleto, was a vassal of the Papal States right up to the invention of the lightbulb and Italian Unification in the 1860s.

After the regional capital, Perugia, Umbria's greatest attraction is Assisi. The birthplace of Saint Francis of Assisi, with its medieval basilica dedicated to the saint (badly damaged by an earthquake in 1997 and restored) and its well-preserved first-century Roman Temple of Minerva, draws international pilgrims and tourists. Yet, like Francis and his old coat, Umbria feels closer to Rome and the South. I've heard it said that, to Tuscans, olive oil is a business, and to Umbrians, it is a religion. For centuries most everything in Tuscany was business, and most everything in Umbria was related to religion.

When I look to the vinous heart of Umbria, I look to Montefalco: a tiny but once-significant hill town that looks out over the Spoleto Valley to Spoleto and Assisi. The wine-growing area is also miniature—only about a thousand acres or just 6 percent of Tuscany's Chianti Classico. Yet what Montefalco lacks in volume, it makes up for in power with Sagrantino, a black, raging beast of a grape that is one of the world's most tannic. Historically it was made into sweet passito and bottled for special occasions or distributed by local families to important people—the local priest, the mayor, the local carabinieri, or a doctor who made a house call. In recent decades Montefalco Sagrantino has made a comeback as one of Italy's most potent dry red wines. Sagrantino is also used to boost the region's second and more approachable red wine, Montefalco Rosso, in which Sangiovese plays the lead role. Over the years, I have been drawn to fresher, lower-octane reds, partly as a matter of taste and partly because I can't put away alcohol the way I once did. But Sagrantino is an exception. Drink a good one, with all its dark secrets and exuberance, and you aren't likely to forget it.

When I look to the heart of Montefalco, I look to Giampaolo Tabarrini—not just my favorite interpreter of Sagrantino, but one of my favorite characters in Italian wine. And Tabarrini is a character: jubilant, eccentric, quick-witted, profane, independent, and exuberant to the point of seeming madness. He has also risen to a level of world renown, from humble beginnings on his family's unassuming farm, on the lower flanks of Montefalco, in a burg of two thousand souls known as Turrita.

I first visited Tabarrini in 2014. He had just turned forty and was eager to enlighten me about Sagrantino. "The trouble with Sagrantino is to understand Sagrantino!" He seemed to shout with his whole skinny body, from his Converse Chuck Taylor sneakers right up to his nearly shaved head, oversized ears, and teeth blackened from coffee, hand-rolled tobacco, and Sagrantino. "Sagrantino has too much of everything! There are a lot of polyphenols. A lot of tannins. A lot of sugar. It is many times over: A lot! A lot! A lot! So how do you balance it?"

Tabarrini insisted that my wife and I stay for a hearty Umbrian lunch made by his small and perpetually beaming mother, Franca. On this and many visits since, a visit to Tabarrini was a joyful occasion. When Tabarrini is around everyone seems to have lots to laugh about.

My wife and I stopped by the Tabarrini winery a few years later on an evening in April 2017. Tabarrini, ever a *fagiolino* (string bean) of a man with paranormal energy and a ten-thousand-watt gap-toothed grin, greeted us up front. With him was Daniele Sassi, then Tabarrini's sales manager and right-hand man, who had the looks of a level-headed accounting associate, sporting ironed shirts, stylish eyeglasses, and unruffled graciousness. Daniele, with his university education, polished manners, and precise way of speaking, was Tabarrini's foil, also acting as his occasional translator and, sometimes, his whisperer.

The old farmhouse and winery faces east atop a small rise above a two-lane country road, and, on this evening, a spectacular, painterly yellow light fell on the distant Appennini mountains. Construction work was going on at Tabarrini. A piece of the hill to the side and back of the winery had been removed and replaced with concrete piers. Tabarrini led us around back, down a dusty drive, and into a cavernous space the size of a train station. I was stupefied. Tabarrini was in the final stages of building his new playground—a cellar that seemed about a hundred times as large as his old one. For now, it was empty. There was a succession of classic ceiling vaults on pillars connected by one long, central alley. In all this extension was about fifty-four thousand square feet—the size of an American supermarket. And it was all for Tabarrini's very modest annual wine production.

Tabarinni twirled and danced throughout the cellar. "I don't think there exists anywhere else in Italy a winery so big for sixty thousand bottles," he said. He was wearing blue jeans and a sweatshirt, his ever-present battered brown leather satchel draped across his chest, containing things like his phone, wallet, and tobacco. He laughed— not just any laugh, but a signature Tabarrini seizure that shook his entire body and sounded like the braying of a ticklish donkey. At the time the European Union was subsidizing half of the costs of winemakers' cellars. No doubt Tabarrini benefited from that. But the dimensions of the work were colossal. It made no sense. *Why would he need that kind of space?*

"With smaller lots of wine, I can take more care," Tabarrini said. Understood. Smaller batches of wine, selected plot by plot, mean more choice for the winemaker in deciding what wine goes into each blend and what does not. "It's like cooking pasta." Tabarrini stood tall, putting extra emphasis on the word "pasta." "If you make pasta for fifty people, you can make one big pot, or you can make the pasta one by one. Making the pasta for each one is much better." He let out a relatively restrained titter as his eyes widened, and he gave me a meaningful look at having revealed one of the laws of nature.

Tabarrini then took us into a side room that was his old winery, full of tall steel tanks. Parked in the center of the floor were a pair of shoulder-height steel cylindrical tubes, just wide enough to fit one skinny Tabarrini. The tubes were closed at the bottom and perforated all over with thousands of tiny holes. "I invented a new fermenting system!" Tabarrini said proudly as he walked over to one of them. "I got the idea from making tea with a tea bag."

I had some idea where he was going with this. Red winemaking— apart from fermenting sugars into alcohol—is chiefly about extracting color, complex chains of flavors, aromas, and tannins from grape skins during a period known as maceration. Fermentation may take weeks, though maceration can last much longer.

During the heated bubbling of fermentation, grape skins, seeds, and other solids get pushed to the top of a vat in one thick "cap." A floating cap can be dangerous because trapped juices in those solids have contact with air, which can, in turn, unleash wine's natural next phase—vinegar. To stop this from happening, winemakers have developed a range of techniques over the centuries. The oldest is traditional punching down of the cap with tools or under foot in what the French call *pigeage*. Modern winemakers are just as likely to "pump over" liquid from the bottom of the vat and spray it over the cap daily. At the end of the twentieth century, robotic mixers called roto-fermenters built into wine tanks came into vogue but dropped out of the scene just as quickly. In the first decades of the twenty-first century, more and more winemakers strived to perform fewer operations during fermentation, with the idea that gentler handling of grape must extracts the best of the fruit without its bitterness.

"My grandfather taught me, the less you touch the wine, the better it is," Tabarrini said, his voice turning reverent.

To illustrate how his system worked, Tabarrini used his arms and legs to partially encircle the cylinder, like the outline of an imaginary vat. Crushed grapes would go into the hole at the top of the cylinder. The free-running juice would filter out into the vat, while the solids would stay inside the steel tube. Thus the whole system did resemble a tea bag steeping in a pot. Tabarrini had tried a homemade version with steel netting but wasn't satisfied. To perfect the dimensions and calculate how many solids versus how much liquid must go into each vat, he worked with an industrial engineer on these prototypes and was looking for a company to produce the system. It seemed like a detour from his work; the project would take years. But Tabarrini's restless mind had brought him here. "Why?" I wondered aloud.

As I said it, his face broke into a smile, his arms flailed like the wings of a pelican taking flight, and he shouted, "Because it means I don't have to do nothing!" He arched his back and brayed. Then he exclaimed with joy, "With this system, the pump will disappear from the winery! There will be zero pumping! Zero punching down. Zero nothing!"

Zero nothing. It was perfect Tabarrini. Extraction technique is pretty dry stuff, but it's key to getting Sagrantino right. Tabarrini is one of the last winemakers every season in Montefalco to harvest his Sagrantino, waiting for grape tannins to fully ripen and turn soft. Most winemakers don't allow grape solids like skin, pulp, and seeds to stay macerating in wine more than thirty days; Tabarrini typically waits six months or longer. By doing little and letting his wines rest first in vat and then in large oak casks, Tabarrini seemed able to tame Sagrantino, giving his wines a rare balance and elegance.

Sagrantino's contemporary image was created by Marco Caprai, the charismatic scion of an Umbrian textile family and creator of the Arnaldo Caprai winery. Caprai brought dry Sagrantino to the world in the 1990s and 2000s—a time when big, opulent wines were in vogue along with aging in new French oak barriques that added even more tannic heft. Caprai nourished the idea that wine didn't get any bigger than Sagrantino, and his efforts drew others to the region, including the Lunelli family of Northern Italy's famous sparkling wine Ferrari.

Tabarrini was well aware that he and the rest of the Montefalco winemakers owed much to Caprai for establishing Montefalco's renown. But the early success also came at a cost. "Caprai was the best and the worst for Sagrantino," he said. "He promoted the wine as the biggest, the most powerful, the most tannic. It's like I said at a wine dinner in Philadelphia: it's like a guy who says, 'I have the biggest dick in the world!'" Tabarrini's face lit as his voice rose. "How many women are going to want it. Really? Think about it," Tabarrini said thoughtfully, moving into his wizened, practical contadino mode. In my mind I could only picture astonished dinner guests who might not have expected a lesson on the limits of male anatomy. Tabarrini leaned toward me, his face almost touching mine, and, as if letting me in on a secret, said, "Most women do not want that—they will be afraid!" In other words, in the wine world, size didn't matter as much as it once did.

"Barolo is super tannic, but the good ones will be smooth in three years," Tabarrini explained. "It's the same story with Sagrantino. You can make wine without exaggerating. And wood—why add more wood to something that is already rich in tannin?" Tabarrini's volume had built to full operatic aria. "Do you add salt to a plate of stockfish?" he asked rhetorically of the preparation of traditional salt cod prepared throughout Italy. Then he answered his own question: "Only if you're an asshole!" Tabarrini's delight over this punch line turned into hyperventilation. Anyone walking into the room at the moment might have mistaken his glee for a medical emergency.

That evening my wife and I joined Tabarrini and his wife, Federica, for dinner at a small trattoria near Montefalco, where Tabarrini recounted his story. The son of a railroad conductor and weekend farmer, Tabarrini was always attracted to life on the farm. But, after high school, he went to work as an account manager at a nearby Mercedes-Benz auto dealership. "My mother was always doing everything to push me off the farm. She dreamed of me in a tie and jacket, and with nice fingers," he said and held up a hand. In the mellow light, I could see the blackened lines, stained from years of handling Sagrantino.

While advancing his business career, Tabarrini continued to help out on the farm. By twenty-six he'd worked his way up to general manager of three dealerships, logging long hours during the week while using weekends to make wine at home. "In 2000, I realized it was impossible to do both jobs," he said. "And I said, 'Why should I come home from work frustrated every night?' One thing is doing something because you do it well. Another thing is doing what you love. Whenever I had time, I was on the tractor." Tabarrini spoke with his father, Nello, who told him, "If you want to come back home it's okay." On the last day of that year, Tabarrini's parents went to a local notary and signed over to their son both the winery and the family's fifty acres of vineyards.

Tabarrini's father and grandfather had created their niche selling wine in bulk to French and Luxembourg merchants who said they were supplying taverns, though no one actually verified what happened to the wines after they traveled north. Tabarrini harbored greater ambitions. In 2004 he released three vintages of Sagrantino, from 1999 to 2001. Then he began the unusual step in Montefalco of individuating three single-vineyard crus, each one an expression of a different terroir. It took only about a dozen years after that for Tabarrini to establish himself as one Sagrantino's best and brightest.

Everyone in the family has defined their role on the farm. His father raised pigs and cured salumi in the pen of the family's small, old house next to the winery. His uncle Angelo was his cellar master. His mother did the cooking. Federica helped in the kitchen and ran the business office. And Tabarrini, like a child at play, kept coming up with new ideas and bottling them.

The Tabarranis traditionally made small quantities of white wine, blending a relatively rare local Trebbiano variety known as Trebbiano Spoletino with Grechetto, an ancient Greek–origin grape planted throughout Central Italy. A similar formula is used in Umbria's south in Orvieto, with their own local version of Trebbiano known as Procanico.

With the 2004 vintage, Tabarrini became one of the first local producers to bottle pure Trebbiano Spoletino, from vines in his uncle's garden. Spoletino was typically planted at the edges of gardens and farms in an antique system called *vite maritata* (married vine), spread by the Etruscans, some of Italy's first winemakers. In this system farmers paired vines with elm, poplar, or other trees. Because grapevines are not parasitic, they could climb up into a tree canopy without killing it.

What intrigued me about Spoletino was its impossibility. Over years of writing about wine in Europe, I had come to see viticulture as a fine and precise craft. To make a quality wine, as the finest French traditions espoused, vines needed to be carefully pruned back to their stubby essence in a number of classic training systems that favored low production and, logically, higher quality. Of course, this worked to maximum effect when the vines were planted on steep slopes of poor well-drained soils.

Spoletino flouted all of that. It was planted on the fertile floor of the Spoleto Valley in an almost negligent fashion, attached to trees that were used to mark farm property lines. Many fine winemakers will tell you that their vines produce an average of two pounds or less of grapes. One Spoletino vine in the maritata system can yield more than a hundred pounds. Instead of taking a few seconds to collect the vine's fruit, harvesters had to use ladders to climb in trees, each vine taking up to half an hour. Most important, Tabarrini's Spoletino, dubbed "Adarmando" for his maternal grandfather, Armando, was delicious, with bright citrus acidity and a range of fruit flavors, aromas, and salinity. When I'd first asked Tabarrini about the vines that went into the wine, he told me, "I don't do anything to them." He didn't treat or trim or do any of the usual pampering that grapevines usually required. "You could drop a bomb on them, and they would still produce."

I returned to Tabarrini at the end of a long, hot summer to better understand Trebbiano Spoletino. I'd tasted many Trebbiano family members from Umbria's Orvieto as well as Abruzzo, Tuscany, and Northern Italy's Soave, but Spoletino seemed to be something apart.

"Trebbiano doesn't mean anything," Tabarrini said after greeting me with a warm hug. He had on flip-flops, shorts, and a polo shirt emblazoned with ITALIA that could have been read at a hundred yards. To him Trebbiano might as well be translated to mean "the local white grape." The appellation that came after was more important.

We got into his truck and drove down to the valley floor. There was a light, warm wind blowing across a parched, brown landscape that smelled of dried herbs and straw.

"I don't like a lot of white wine," Tabarrini said. "I wanted to make a white wine with great acidity because for me white wine should be like a blade, but not an acidity that hurts the stomach."

In 2003 Tabarrini started to get serious about Spoletino. Working with University of Florence viticulture researchers, he identified sixteen of the best vines from his uncle's farm. From them the researchers were able to develop two clones that Tabarrini later replanted in a conventional spur-pruned, cordon-trained vineyard across the road from his winery.

At the base of the valley, in the hamlet of Fratta, small farms grew olives and grains and vegetables, sunflowers, and corn. Tabarrini stopped the truck next to a small plowed field framed by two long rows of what appeared to be unkempt trees with gangly shoots reaching in all directions and along high steel cables between the tree canopies. There were about three dozen trees in all that belonged to his uncle Angelo. The evening sun cast long shadows that provided respite from the day's heat. Above our heads loads of green grape brunches dangled from the tree canopies. Monster Spoletino vines had taken the form of the elms to which they clung. You could see where the vines ended and where the tree foliage took over, neither vine nor tree suffocating the other.

Trebbiano Spoletino had caught on after the simultaneous efforts of Tabarrini and the architect-turned-winemaker Giampiero Bea of Paolo Bea. Some thirty producers now sold what they said was Spoletino, but Tabarrini doubted most of the wine was really from Spoletino. He said he had a simple way of identifying true Spoletino. "The old farmers told me that Trebbiano Spoletino looks like a dick," he casually explained.

I'd never heard of "dick-like" used in ampelography as a description for grape bunches, but obviously I hadn't spent enough time in Umbrian vineyards.

"Look," Tabarrini said. He reached up into a tree and cradled a bunch of green grapes. The bunch was long, and flanking the top part near the stem were a pair of smaller groupings of grapes commonly called "ears" but, in this case, admittedly could be seen as testicles. At the other end of the bunch, the tip was slightly bifurcated into a bulbous head, or *cappella*. The whole effect was of a hanging phallus. "You see?" I saw.

On the way back to Turrita, Tabarrini passed another small stand of Spoletino in the trees of one of his suppliers. The man, his skin rough as artichoke stalk, rode atop a tractor, plowing a field of dark, dry clay. Tabarrini approached him, and the men talked about the difficult vintage that began with spring hail followed by a long summer drought. Tabarrini paused to inspect some grapes with an instructive observation: "See? The dick. This is Spoletino." Back in his truck, he pointed out other vines that were planted maritata. But the grape bunches came to a pointed head that had no bifurcation. "They are not Spoletino. And this is the problem!" His volume dialed up. "If you go to a nursery and ask for Trebbiano Spoletino, you get this. But it's not Trebbiano Spoletino. It's another thing. Some bullshit. Nothing is the same with these grapes—the only thing they have in common is the name. Too many people are trying to plant Trebbiano Spoletino now not knowing what they are doing or what they are going to do with the grapes."

Back at the winery, Tabarrini led me across the road to a vineyard now covered in shade. On the other side of the valley, the old pink stones, terra-cotta roofs, and towers of Spoleto, Trevi, and Foligno were bathed in orange light. Here, on the first slopes above the flatlands, were ten acres Tabarrini propagated mostly from the two clones selected by university researchers. He had high hopes for this orderly vineyard with its cordon-trained rows of Spoletino that stretched eastward and had begun blending small batches of the wine from it with the wine from maritata vines. What he didn't bottle commercially went to the same place as all his wines that didn't make the final cut: to his mother to sell out of the winery in bulk.

77

Yet, in seeing this vineyard, I was disappointed. I had been moved by the free and poetic ease of the maritata vines, which had been depicted romantically by centuries of European painters and written about since Ovid's *Metamorphoses* in the first century to Goethe's *Italian Journey* eighteen hundred years later.

I was glad to learn later from Giampiero Bea that his own experience with conventional planting of Spoletino—sourced, coincidentally, from his uncle's farm—had been a flop. Bea was another serious experimenter in Montefalco, though he was as taciturn as Tabarrini was effusive. He had selected maritata vine cuttings a decade earlier and planted them on a half-acre of prime terroir slope higher up the hill near Montefalco. Since 2004 he used the original maritata Spoletino to make a different kind of wine. Whereas the grapes of most of the world's white wines are pressed at harvest for their juice and the skins discarded, Bea used long macerations with skins (some which were partly desiccated in an *appassimento* drying loft) to make a rich, smoky, and strong "orange wine" style called Arboreus.

Still, Bea has never bottled any from his modern Spoletino vineyard. "I am not happy with the result," he said and wondered if there was not something about the more banal terroir of the valley floor and the influence of the trees that made superior Spoletino. "There seems to be a symbiotic relationship between the vines and the trees." Bea was making plans for a new maritata plantation on a plot of valley flatlands he also used for wheat. But he didn't want to wait fifteen years for a tree to get tall enough to support a Spoletino vine. So the architect and tinkerer in him had come up with an alternative: building treelike substitutes from concrete and bamboo.

"I am searching for an artificial solution," Bea told me. "But I don't know if it's possible."

I hoped that too didn't work. I was rooting for the trees. Yet I was also doubtful about the future of Spoletino, which seemed destined to end up cannibalized by classic Italian infighting, beyond the fundamental argument over the variety's phallic bunch shape. In

2011, after an appellation was created for Trebbiano Spoletino all over Montefalco, both its pioneers, Tabarrini and Bea, refused to participate. To hear Tabarrini tell it, he was disillusioned with the rampant spread of faux Spoletino vineyards, and the loose way in which the appellation was crafted, allowing any type of wine anywhere throughout Montefalco.

"After they made the appellation so big, I said, 'Fine, just make it so that we are not in it. I don't care,'" Tabarrini told me outside his winery, with a triumphant look as he kicked up dust in his flip-flops. He held up his index finger in a signal that another Tabarrini pearl was coming and added, "This is how you win!"

I wasn't sure exactly about what was being won in this battle—perhaps just independence from his neighbors. Most every Italian wine producer I know bemoans the wine bureaucracy. The Italian appellation or DOC/DOCG system intended as a stamp of quality is too often led by peers who are shortsighted, stupid, greedy, or worse. I hear it all the time.

"I am right in the middle of the Spoletino map," Tabarrini cackled. "But I have nothing to do with it!"

As summer night fell, we were joined for dinner by three winemakers from Campania who had driven up from the Naples area in one car. Much of Italy was still on its extended mid-August Ferragosto vacation at the beach, and this night at Tabarrini likely represented the most unconventional wine gathering in the country.

Giovanni Ascione, a former marketing executive whose tiny Nanni Copè winery in Caserta province produced a rare red from another near-extinct grape called Palagrello, protectively cradled a box with that morning's mozzarella. Sabino Loffredo, who created Pietracupa out of his dad's hobbyist winery and now turned out some of Italy's most improbable but stunning white wines, wore a deep tan, a few days of stubble, and dark aviator glasses, a look that betrayed his previous life as an Italian cruise-ship fitness coach. And Luigi Tecce, known for his intense Taurasi reds, was reserved as a professor and dapperly dressed in a sky-blue blazer. We sat on the stone terrace in front of Tabarrini's winery at a long table draped in a white cloth and set with traditional ochre and deep-blue hand-painted Umbrian ceramics. Above us, from an iron shade pergola dangled bulbs to light the area Italian-style—which means as bright as a dentist's office.

Federica, as usual, wore her bemused grin, on this evening with an oversized black T-shirt with the word CHAOS in large white letters, which summed up the unpredictable vibe I'd come to expect in Turrita. Tabarrini's dad sat at the head of the table and fetched platters of his own cured pork salumi: *capocollo* (shoulder), *lonzino* (tenderloin), salami, and prosciutto. Ascione carved up his oblong ball of mozzarella the size of a Christmas roast. We drank Tabarrini's fresh and lip-smacking Adarmando 2012. Tabarrini's mother brought out a delicately layered eggplant parmigiana, and we shifted to Loffredo's signature mineral-driven Greco di Tufo called "G" 2010. As I recall this meal—and here we are, still at the beginning—I am amazed at the number of dishes we went through that evening. We took small portions and ate and drank slowly. Tabarrini and the others got up between courses to smoke.

The second part of the meal turned to red wines as we ate Franca's handmade tortellini in broth followed by tripe in a deep, dark red sauce of wine, onions, and garlic that tasted like it had stewed as long as one of Tabarrini's Sagrantinos. For this course Tecce opened a string of vintages of his Taurasi, named Poliphemo for the cyclops Polyphemus in Homer's *Odyssey*. It was a rich and musky wine from one of the deep South's blackest grapes, Aglianico, and Tecce's wines varied almost anarchically and expressively from vintage to vintage.

As midnight approached, Nello Tabarrini excused himself and shuffled off to bed. As a final course, we ate tiny roasted quail the Tabarrinis had bought from a young local hunter, the birds laying in a dish with heads fallen to the side. They fell apart at a slight touch, and we ate with our fingers, cleaning the bones with our teeth.

Tabarrini turned off the lamps above the table. A breeze cooled the air, and the lights from the other side of the valley sparkled and flickered. The smoke around the table suddenly had a sweet, familiar scent—a joint was making the rounds, and Tabarrini's laugh came on faster and higher-pitched in the moonless, star-filled night.

The next morning, after a rest at a small inn in Montefalco, the Campania crew and I had breakfast at a café with Frederica and Tabarrini, who had something to show us—the product of another Tabarrini family story.

A decade earlier Nello Tabarrini spotted a vine that had grown to the size of a tree being used for shade on the terrace of a summer villa in the unfortunately named town of Bastardo, about five miles southwest of Montefalco. He struck up a conversation with the owner, a woman nearly his age. She complained of the vine's shagginess and of having no one to trim it. Nello offered to do so in exchange for some cuttings. Tabarrini showed the cuttings to researchers at the University of Florence, who identified it as Grero, a near-extinct blending grape that was dark and acidic.

"I said, 'Okay, I'll plant one hectare of it," Tabarrini explained as he drove Federica's Fiat back from Montefalco. It was nine in the morning, and he was clearly already revved for the day. He let out a laugh so forceful I thought he might lose control of the car and send us careening down one of his neighbors' vineyard slopes.

To keep his project a secret from curious neighbors, Tabarrini had the cuttings grafted in France. Coincidentally, Perugia horti-culturists were also researching a grape identified as Grero, found on the estate of the retired Italian TV host and 1960s-era beauty Aba Cercato, on the outskirts of medieval Todi, eighteen miles southwest of Montefalco. In 2013, after a few years of experiments, Tabarrini began making the first-known single-varietal wine with Grero, a late ripener like Sagrantino that he harvested beginning in late October. The results surprised even him.

"It makes a wine that doesn't look like anything else in the world!" His grin stretched between his ears like a laundry line. "It is not a lot of alcohol—the highest alcohol I had was only thirteen percent," he said. "It's got higher acidity than Barbera, a color as dark as Sagrantino, and zero tannins."

Back at the winery, Tabarrini explained as his friends arrived how he hoped to release his first Grero wines in early 2018 under the label Piantagrero—an apt play on words from *piantagrane* (troublemaker). He planned to release four vintages, including about three hundred bottles each of 2013 and 2014 and about thirteen hundred bottles of 2015—all of it was presold to importers and distributors, most of it in wood cases that contained one bottle each of the first two vintages and three bottles of the third. For each year Tabarrini had a local animator draw a comic strip–type cell telling the story of his new wine and the vintage. At the same time, in those cases, Tabarrini would also release three hundred bottles of the 2016 vintage. The problem was, in 2016, he was unable to produce the wine. Spring frosts and snow had killed the flowers on his Grera vines; thus there was no fruit. But that wouldn't stop Tabarrini, who eventually corked, sealed, and labeled the 2016 vintage using empty bottles.

"My U.S. importer asked me how much the bottle of 2016 would cost," Tabarrini said to his small audience that morning. "I told him, 'Same price as the others.'" He let out a peal of laughter that was exceptional even for him. "Then he told me, 'Okay, fuck you, I'll take it.'"

Tabarrini's dream was to have his empty bottle on a wine list. In those moments my esteem for his creative capacity leapt to another level.

He poured from a bottle of his 2015 Piantagrero. From the first taste, it was wildly off-putting. No tannins meant no bite. At first sip it reminded me of an adult version of a kids' drink—goofy grape? It was fun. But was it wine?

There is a saying in the Italian wine world that the first thing a businessman who buys a winery invests in is marketing; then he invests in a cellar, and finally the vineyards. A contadino, on the other hand, does the opposite, starting with the vineyards and ending with the marketing. Tabarrini was a contadino who had followed the formula through to its third phase and was now taking marketing to its ironic, Warholian extreme with his 2016 empty bottle. If the highest-level aspiration of great winemakers was to capture the vintage and bottle it, Tabarrini's idea was as true as it was audacious.

For a wine to have merit, people have to enjoy drinking it. But here Tabarrini was playing a different game of rarity and novelty. He showed us prototypes for the label of the empty 2016 bottle of Piantagrero. On it was a caricature of broad-eared and bestubbled Tabarrini grieving with his Tuscan enologist Emiliano Falsini, who was hugging a drooping vine as snow fell in a sky with the first swallows of spring.

In early November I drove across the Appennini in an insistent rain. As I approached Turrita in late afternoon, the sky opened to let in golden light. The wheat and hay fields were dark with freshly plowed wet clay. Vineyards were aflame with the yellows and reds of the last leaves clinging to browned vines. I knew that, after harvest, Tabarrini would be working in his cellar on his latest obsessions. I was eager to see what those obsessions might be.

Daniele greeted me up in front, and as we walked down to the cellar, he informed me coolly, "Now, you are going to see something psychedelic."

In the new wing of Tabarrini's winery, the floor was slick as glass. A dozen pairs of columns held up ceiling vaults extending down the length of the winery in freshly painted white. Each of the first few niches held a pair of modest-size oak barrels on red-painted wood stands. The cornices of the columns each sheltered lights that illuminated the architecture. The walls and the lower parts of the vaults were dramatically up-lit in layers of white light, as were the arching vaults that crossed the central alley.

Tabarrini, in ripped jeans, a zip-front jacket, and exceptionally thick stubble, was intently standing over a man who was seated at a small folding table, tapping on a computer tablet. Tabarrini looked up, took the tablet, and approached me, grinning like someone who has learned a great secret and was about to confide it.

"Watch this," he said. He tapped on the tablet, and the winery changed colors—the whole central line of vaults was bathed in a deep-gold light. He looked at me, his face mirroring my open-mouthed astonishment. I had never seen Tabarrini quieter.

"Now this," he said, and the place lit up in alternating swaths of blue, violet, and green. He was as transfixed as a kid with a new toy. Another tap, and the vaults lit up red, white, and green, in the colors of the Italian flag. Tabarrini now let loose. He folded over with laughter. He returned the tablet to the technician, and we wandered down the hall of the winery, taking in the changing kaleidoscope of colors that seemed infinite.

"This was all developed by an Italian company," Tabarrini said proudly, and then, with degrees of awe and irony, added, "It's the same system they use in discotheques."

As was expected vintage 2017 provided no occasion for partying. It was a somber, small harvest following frost, hail, and drought. Tabarrini's yields would be less than half his typical harvest. Because of the heat, many producers in Montefalco and across Italy figured the grapes would ripen early and therefore began harvesting early. Tabarrini waited until his normal harvest times, in October and the first days of November. It had been a risk. Longer hang time of grapes means more phenolic maturity—greater complexity of wine—but only if fall storms don't swell the grapes until they burst, turn vineyards to mold factories, or otherwise shred the crop.

"Everybody was saying this year we should start earlier," he said. "It's bullshit. I waited, and what happened? The vines started growing again in October!" His laugh sputtered like an old car engine. It was a phenomenon he'd never witnessed. Drought had shut down the vines, which seemed to revive as temperatures cooled. "I asked my father, 'Do you ever remember the vine shoots growing in October?' He told me, 'No, but look at the figs.'"

Tabarrini led me up the stairs and out of the winery, where a fig tree fanned out near the family chicken coop. The fig tree had the last of its fruit—large, plump figs—months after the late-summer fig season.

"They were bigger in October than the figs of summer," he marveled. "It was so dry that all the trees stopped working—the vines too. They just froze. When the plants finally got water, there was plenty of energy and then the trees started to work again."

When we returned to the cellar, Tabarrini walked over to a waist-high steel tank that contained all his Grero for the year. "It's a disaster," he said. He seemed more amused than sad. He was, I'd determined, in love with the grape even as he was learning its recalcitrance. Grero was a winemaker's nightmare, owing to the loose clusters that contained relatively few berries—only about a quarter of those from Sagrantino. Production wasn't just low; it was abysmal. In bad years it was even worse.

Tabarrini beamed. "It's totally unproductive," he said. Looking down at the miniscule quantity of wine, his body shook with delight. "This is the most crazy wine for me this year." He unscrewed the steel tank lid and drew some liquid out with a glass wine thief that he dripped into a wineglass. The one mouthful I tasted was like the others I'd tasted before: disorienting. The color didn't match the flavors. The wine in general didn't match anything in my wine memory bank.

"It has higher acidity than my white wine," Tabarrini said. He wasn't laughing but wore a look of wonder. "It embarrassed me. It's like a blend of a white wine and a red wine, though which white and which red I don't know."

It was clear to me that Grero had become more than a novelty—it had become a mystery that grabbed Tabarrini's attention and would pull him in deeper and deeper.

A couple of vintages later, he and Federica identified twenty-five red grape vines in the middle of their Spoletino vineyards as Grero. His Grero had been planted at the same time as some nearby Spoletino, and someone had apparently mixed up one batch of vines. But, to Tabarrini's delight, the grape bunches on these vines were full, bearing four to five times as much fruit as his other Grero.

"They produce like a normal variety," he said. "Less than Sangiovese, but more than Sagrantino." He was baffled. Why would Grero surrounded by Spoletino perform better? "We did everything the same in the two vineyards. It was the same soil. The same everything. So what is the difference?" After talking with several agronomists, Tabarrini developed a hypothesis: "Pollen!" Grapevines are typically self-pollinating, meaning that each plant has male and female flowers. For some reason Tabarrini's Grero vineyard wasn't producing enough pollen to fertilize its own berries. Apparently his Spoletino had pollen to spare.

"Maybe this is not the right way to say this," Tabarrini said, letting me in on his secret. "But Trebbiano Spoletino is able to fuck the flower of the Grero and make it more productive!"

He was planning experiments for 2021 that dealt with blowing different kinds of vine yeast into his Grero vineyard. I am still waiting to learn what *that* will create.

Over many years writing about wine, I have come to love the self-taught eccentrics, the outliers and inventors, *i matti*, the crazy ones who make wine more than a business—they make it a living, exciting culture. I came to appreciate Tabarrini for that. But I also have come to know him as a wise man and a caring human being. Plus, his mom is one of the best Italian cooks around, making his place one of the best to find yourself at mealtime.

When I think of Tabarrini, I can't separate him in my mind from his family: his wife and three generations of Tabarrini that eat together and help keep him earthbound. I think I have shared more meals with the Tabarrini than just about any other wine family north of Sicily, and I've never felt like an intruder. The Tabarrinis have a way of embracing anyone who is around at mealtime and making them feel like a member of an extended clan.

In mid-February Montefalco is as cold and lifeless as it gets. In 2018 I drove there for the annual Anteprima Sagrantino, marking the release of the 2014 vintage with a series of tastings and lots of discussion about Sagrantino's place in the world. My first stop was to check in with Tabarrini. This time his news was about Sagrantino. Since the early 2000s Tabarrini produced three single-vineyard Sagrantinos. The richest of them, Colle Alle Macchie, comes from the kind of vineyard you would expect it to come from: high elevation with pure clay soils and a hot, sunny southern exposure. As I'd once written about his Macchie wines, "You could try to tar your roof with it, but what a waste." Now that seems an exaggeration. The wine has evolved into something that is big but not brutish; think of a large man with a concert pianist's fingers. At its best it is full of beauty, agility, and nuance, all of which improve with time.

Tabarrini's architectural wonder of a cellar still looked almost empty. Wearing a down jacket to protect against the chill, he led me to one five-thousand-liter steel tank containing his 2017 Colle Alle Macchie. Normally fermentation of the wine finishes in a few weeks, but, to his astonishment, this batch was still fermenting more than three months after harvest.

"I called Emiliano a week ago," Tabarrini said of his enologist. "And I said, 'Emiliano the Macchie is still fermenting.' Emiliano said, 'At what temperature?'" Most red wine ferments above 20°C (68°F). Below 15°C (59°F) would be rare. "I said, 'Less than 9°C [48°F],'" Tabarrini said. "He said that is not possible! But it is!" Tabarrini's body convulsed in laughter.

He opened a valve in the side of the vat and poured some of the thick, murky, deep purple liquid into a pair of glasses. It was as cold as beer from a bar tap, still slightly sweet, and full of fermentative carbon dioxide bubbles. In the winery kitchen, Tabarrini's mother was whipping something up. A new uncut prosciutto cured by Tabarrini's father was laid out on a table. Tabarrini hoisted it on its side onto a *morsa*, a steel and wood stand for slicing. Balancing the leg with his left hand wrapped in a kitchen towel, he held a long, round-ended prosciutto knife in his right and carefully sliced away the skin and fat at the widest part below the haunch.

"This is the best," he cooed, "the first slices of prosciutto." After he cut through the fat, the red of the cured meat appeared, and he gingerly slid the knife back and forth—teasing thin, nearly transparent slices from the ham. "The thing with slicing prosciutto is to never run—you must go slowly," he counseled, as serious as I'd ever seen him. "When you cut, you should be able to see the blade underneath. That means the slice is thin. And prosciutto needs to be thin. Salami can be thick. Prosciutto no."

He held out a pair of slices draped on the knife's edge, offering one to me and the other to his father. I don't think I'd ever tasted the first slice of prosciutto and savored the never-refrigerated range of flavors, the fat and meat melding with herbaceous and animal aromas.

"Look how the prosciutto cries when it is fresh," Tabarrini said of the beads of fatty moisture on the knife. "When you buy a prosciutto in the market and you cut, the fat separates from the meat. That is because the pigs don't exercise. They don't move. Here, our pigs move; they eat pasta leftovers and vegetables. They eat what we eat." Tabarrini fed the slices to those who came in for lunch—Federica; their son, Filippo; and Daniele. Cellar samples of wine were passed around, which we drank with a main course Carciofi alla Giudia, the classic Roman-Jewish recipe for fried artichokes.

As midafternoon sunlight broke through the churning clouds, Tabarrini, Daniele, and I took a drive. Tabarrini's Sagrantino vineyards were green with winter weeds and muddy from days of rain. We drove past an old two-story house near the top of the rise in the hillside, the ground-floor windows of which were boarded up. The house had belonged to Tabarrini's maternal grandparents, serving as both home and bodega from which his grandfather Armando sold wine and other farm products; now Tabarrini, Federica, and Filippo lived on the second floor.

"It looks abandoned," Tabarrini said. "I like it that way because it looks like no one is here."

Indeed, there was no sign the place was inhabited. No thought had gone into the yard; there were no flower beds, no gate. There was just a chest-high cement shrine with the words *Ave Maria* painted at the triangular top. Even the shrine was empty. Tabarrini explained that his grandfather had built it while incarcerated during the fascist period for his refusal to testify against an antigovernment neighbor. "It had a Madonna inside, but somebody stole the Madonna right from there," Tabarrini lamented. "Can you believe it? The Madonna!" To hear Tabarrini tell it, nothing was safe in the countryside—not even livestock or curing prosciutto.

He veered off the road, onto the edge of his eight-acre Colle Alle Macchie vineyard, where the tires sunk into the mud. We got out of the car and walked, Tabarrini in white sneakers that seemed to glide over the wet, heavy earth.

"When I was twenty-two," he told me, "I used to bring Federica up here at night. She was only sixteen or seventeen, and I said, 'This place will be our future.' Sagrantino needs sun; Sagrantino needs wind," he cried out. He pulled his pouch of tobacco out of his shoulder bag, rolled a thin smoke, and lit it. "If Sagrantino is green, it's lost."

Like all of Tabarrini's vineyards, this one was what he calls "essentially organic but not on paper." After years of being certified organic (and collecting the Italian subsidy that came with it), he dropped the certification. "Organic is all about money," he said. "When the inspector used to come, he never got out of the car to look at the vineyards." He drew on the cigarette and shook his head. "For us it also dangerous!"

It was the first time I'd heard anyone use that description for organic agriculture. Dangerous? "Because one day, something will happen!" Tabarrini howled into the wind. "There will be scandal about organic. And you would be in the middle." He walked toward the car and trampled the last bit of tobacco and paper underfoot. "You can shit in the snow," he cried, "but one day the snow will melt, and everybody will see the shit!"

That evening, the eve of Sagrantino's Anteprima, Tabarrini threw a party in his winery for other Sagrantino producers at a long table. The guests included locals from century-old estates like the gentleman farmer Filippo Antonelli of Antonelli and the young, long-maned Francesco Pambuffetti of Scacciadiavoli, as well as outsiders like the boyish-looking Alessandro Lunelli of Trento's Lunelli family; the wide-eyed and personable Chiara Lungarotti of Lungarotti, twenty miles northwest in Torgiano; and Peter Heilbron, a soft-spoken Italian-German ex–beer executive who created a natural oasis at Tenuta Bellafonte.

The only "rule" of the evening was that everyone wear a hat. Tabarrini began the evening in a black fedora, slicing prosciutto for his guests as he had done that afternoon. By the time Federica's handmade vermicelli in red sauce was served, he was hatless, affectionately draping himself over his guests and pouring their bottles. We drank Sagrantino after Sagrantino into the night, with Tabarrini cajoling, gesticulating, cursing, and laughing. He argued with Lungarotti about the location of some of her vineyards, using corks to illustrate the terroir. While motioning to make a point with an expensive but delicate German wineglass, the stem snapped in his hand, sending its crystal bowl and contents crashing and splashing. He illustrated to his guests how to eat fresh, wild *Rapunzolo* (Rapunzel) radishes, tilting his head back and placing the long greens, doused with fresh oil and salt, on his tongue.

Lungarotti gazed at him in wonder, then turned to me and said, "In all of Italy, Sagrantino is the wine that talks most about the person who makes it. Sangiovese talks about the terroir and soil, but Sagrantino talks about the person. And Giampaolo he is—how would you say it?—possessed."

The evening finished in the cellar, lit an unearthly violet as Tabarrini and others took turns making circles on his self-balancing scooter. Tabarrini traded a straw sun hat for a loose beret, and that sent him directly into a state where he seemed to be channeling a raucous rabble scene from *Les Miserables*.

The next morning I walked the frozen, cobbled center of quiet, medieval Montefalco to one of my favorite public piazzas in Italy: a wide-open circle at the height of town dominated by its thirteenth-century palazzo comunale. On the top floor of the palazzo in the Sala Consiliare—which is painted like a nineteenth-century gift box, with plaster decorations in red, blue, and gold—was a very quiet and serious tasting of scores of Sagrantino for the international vino-scenti. I took a seat at one of the long tables facing front as young sommeliers filled a series of glasses of the 2014 vintage for me. After a night of drinking into the wee hours with Tabarrini and his fellow merrymakers, it was sad to drink alone in silence, with our spittoons and small bags of breadsticks—like Sunday morning in church after a Saturday night feast. It was also a big mountain for my taste buds to climb, with Sagrantino seemingly still emanating from my pores. Within a half hour, my teeth and gums were tarred. After a few inky versions, I'd had enough.

I thought about what Chiara Lungarotti had said the night before. Tabarrini was possessed. But his wines, even his Colle Alle Macchie, were not the most extroverted of Sagrantinos. They were lively and intense, but at the same time precise and melodic. He was one of the few who seemed to understand this beast and shaped it into his cry from deep in Italy's heart.

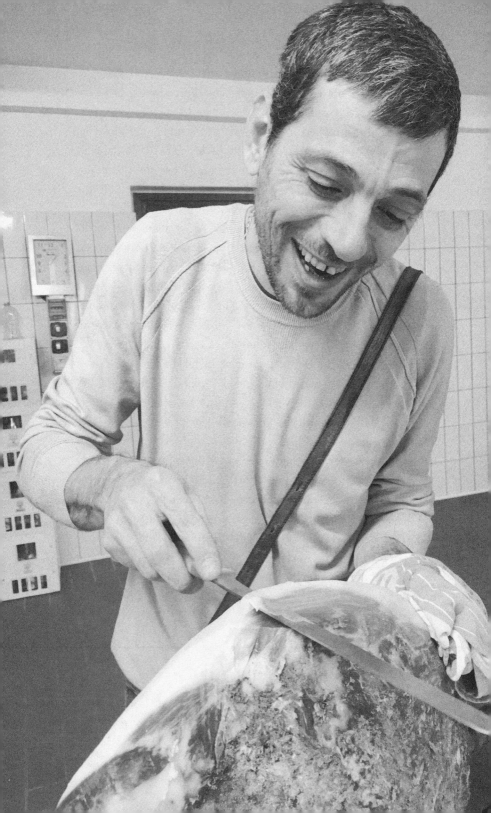

6. Giampaolo Tabarrini.

4   *Three Musketeers of Campania*

The Naples area of fifty years ago lives in my mind as a collage of memories—of black-haired people with theatrical faces, daring noses, and well-cut clothing. Of the intimate sounds of home kitchens and loud voices that rose and fell, making melodies even in anger. Of ancient streets in which salt breezes mingled with the scents of almond cakes, frying fish, motor exhaust, and nutty espresso. Of Naples's baroque architecture and the mysterious courtyards of once-opulent palazzi. Of the tired lime stucco that clung to the old buildings and the men who gathered mornings in front of cafés, including one man who had no legs yet moved around in a child's red fire engine, from which he held court. Of the endless banners of laundry and bedsheets on the line, the rainbow-colored beverage and ice cream kiosks, and the general stores with their baskets of soccer balls and stovetop moka pots. Of the barrels of fat olives from the *salumerie*, the fishmongers' clams on ice, and the fruit sellers' gigantesque Sorrento lemons.

I had no awareness of the awful slums here that had bred cholera, illiteracy, and violence. Nor did I have a way of knowing that, for Naples, the worst was yet to come in a decades-long explosion of organized crime, heroin, urban violence, and mountains of stinking, uncollected garbage. When I've returned to Naples since then, it has taken hours to adapt to its gritty denial of modernity and norms—the cop with the louche, unshaven mug or the military tank parked near the port with a gunner on alert in the turret. Yet, on a

95

random street at any given time of day, it can seem that nothing has changed in half a century. One thing that has changed, however, is that now wines from the Campania countryside are good enough to bottle and send north—and around the world. Wines like white, rich, and floral Fiano di Avellino and crisp Greco di Tufo and the thick-as-blood Taurasi reds made from Aglianico.

In the fall of 2017, at harvest's end, I set out to visit the three musketeers of Campania—Ascione, Loffredo, and Tecce—I had eaten and drunk with that one summer evening at Tabarrini. My first stop was to see Giovanni Ascione in Caserta Province, a destination about which I was mildly apprehensive. Caserta is not only home to the Versailles-like eighteenth-century Royal Palace of the Bourbons, with its colossal gardens and fountains, but is also the stronghold of the murderous and toxic waste–dumping Mafia, the Camorra.

Driving north along the highway from Naples in a light morning rain, I took in a landscape that would probably be shocking to most Western eyes. Shoved together in the mess were graffiti-covered cinderblock shacks, tin-roof shanties, makeshift mechanic garages, small factories, tiny gardens with tomato plants and peppers, and tired laundry soaking up the drizzle. Fig and olive trees sprouted from pavement cracks next to piles of tires and garbage and smoldering fires. In the South the sun can go a long way to cover blight. But, on this day, there was only a gray smear of a sky. I buoyed myself with the thought that, in Italy, beauty has a way of sneaking up just around the corner.

An hour later I pulled into Vitulazio—a neat, orderly agricultural burg of about seven thousand people with fruit-colored stucco houses, hedgerows, and small squares. Giovanni and I met at a café called the Manhattan Lounge Bar. It had all new, slick fittings, including a big flat-screen television showing the morning news and a gleaming back bar stocked with a wide range of liqueurs, local wines, and Champagne.

A loosely bound group of men sat at the bar with their morning espressos, helping themselves to the cream-filled pastry *cornetti*, chatting with the owner, or lazily glancing through the sports pages as one would leave and another show up and exchange cheek kisses with the others. The scene could have been anywhere in middle-class Italy. We were only thirty miles north of Naples, but it could have been three hundred. We stood at the end of the bar and stirred the foamy *crema* atop our espressos. I mentioned to Giovanni just how clean and civil his hometown seemed. Giovanni was a compact, charismatic man with a gray buzz cut and dark puppy-dog eyes rimmed by round glasses. His personable face, covered with grizzle, seemed to want to bend itself into a smile.

"Yes," he replied. "It's clean and civil, but it's the border."

"The border?" I asked. "Of what?"

Giovanni gave me a grave look that lasted a few seconds longer than I felt it should have. Then he said in a near whisper, "Gomorrah."

Neapolitan writer Roberto Saviano's famous 2006 exposé on his hometown's bloody Camorra crime and drug gangs with roots deep in local families had been titled *Gomorrah*. A movie and a television series followed the book, along with credible death threats. At the time of this writing, Saviano was living nomadically under police protection. In the aftermath "Gomorrah" had also become shorthand for some of Italy's most casual and brutal violence. And the town of Caserta, just fifteen miles southeast of where we stood, was the epicenter.

A quarter mile away, behind a modern electric gate, sat the Asciones' modest half-acre. The two-story 1960s-era house built by his parents was ringed by an orderly garden full of citrus, pomegranate, prune, and pear trees and patches of wild *friarelli* (broccoli rabe). At the back of the lot sat the Nanni Copé winery, no bigger than a two-car garage and as colorless and sterile as a laboratory.

We sat at a white table that matched the walls of a small office, and Giovanni found a map in an out-of-date guidebook to orient me.

"Caserta is divided in two—the north of Caserta, where we are, is agricultural. And the south is industrial and commercial, really part of Napoli."

With a pen Giovanni drew a large circle around Naples that extended well beyond its borders into Caserta province. "Napoli has grown with a kind of Los Angeles effect," he said to describe the sprawl. "These are a hundred comune [towns] that are really part of Napoli . . . that's a hundred places with criminalità."

Next he drew a heavy horizontal line through Caserta province following the lower branch of the Volturno River that, to him, divided the north and south of Caserta. "It's two different languages, two different cultures," he said. "The south with the city of Caserta is part of Napoli. Some of them even have telephone numbers with Napoli prefixes." He slowly repeated the part about the Napoli telephone prefixes while giving me a look that implied the fatefulness of the distinction between Naples's old 81 code and Caserta's 823.

The foreignness of Casertano, the local dialect from Caserta, was another metaphor for the separateness of the two worlds. When he watched the movie *Gomorrah,* he said, he relied on the Italian subtitles: "I couldn't understand anything without them."

"If I go into a bar and I hear someone speaking Casertano," he added, "I am afraid. I leave the place."

I found it strange that the southern part of Caserta, which included its famous Royal Palace, had grown relatively prosperous. I had grown up with the moral maxim that poverty creates crime and crime creates poverty. But Southern Italy seemed to confuse the rule: wealth can't be extorted from nothing, and it's not easy to base criminal activities around artichokes or grapes. Crime feeds off business activity and generates more opportunity for more crime.

"Most of the people—three hundred thousand—are not criminals," Giovanni said. "But the culture is a total acceptance of criminalità. Totale!" He said it with a dramatic flourish.

Around the turn of the millennium, a swath of Naples and Caserta province had come to be known as the "terra dei fuochi" for all the illegal dumping and midnight fires of illegal trash. "Here," Giovanni said, pointing to the more sparsely populated Vitulazio and the northern part of Caserta Province, "the hills are poor, but they have kept their traditions."

Vitulazio is not known for wine production but for most every other manner of agriculture from fruit to dairy cows to now-diminished tobacco. Most of the vineyards lie in nearby hills that produce smooth, low-acid reds from Casavecchia, a once-forgotten vine rediscovered by a nineteenth-century farmer near Roman ruins. In the twenty-first century, the wines got a boost with the creation of the Casavecchia di Pontelatone appellation.

Giovanni's wine interest, however, was fueled by Pallagrello Nero, another old variety recently returned from the dead. He began his career in wine in 2007, at the ripe age of forty-three, when he bought two small vineyards. One was a six-acre plot of Pallagrello (with some Aglianico and Casavecchia) on sandstone soils at the eastern edge of the Pontelatone appellation. Outside of Pontelatone he bought another couple of acres of Casavecchia that he replanted with Fiano.

Giovanni's microproduction is about ten thousand bottles classified under the regional appellation as Terre del Volturno—half sold in Italy and the rest sprinkled through about twenty foreign countries. Most of it is his red called Sabbie di Sopra il Bosco (literally "Sands Above the Woods"), from his mixed Pallagrello-dominated red vineyard. "It was a dream to make wine from my soil," he said. "Pallagrello is a wine of major class. It has tantissimi polyphenols and tannins with finesse and incredible elegance."

Words seemed to roll off Giovanni's tongue, but if he sounded like a well-educated, expert marketer, it's because he was one. He was born in Vitulazio to a pair of educators. His mother was a school principal, and his father a middle school teacher who worked summers analyzing and classifying tobacco. After business school in Rome in the 1980s, Giovanni embarked on a brilliant career, becoming marketing director for Renault in Italy, then managing the Ford account for Ogilvy and Mather before leading an Italian public relations agency and finally his own production company.

Around 2000 Giovanni was living in Tuscany and writing as a hobby for *Bibenda*, the publication of the Italian Sommeliers' Foundation, about mostly foreign wines from California to Burgundy to New Zealand. Wine became his obsession, he said. "I decided to change to another life and produce wine. Today maybe I earn a tenth of what I earned fifteen years ago." He explained his life change this way: "I don't believe in reincarnation. I believe you have to do everything in this life."

There is little to see in Giovanni's winery: a few stainless steel tanks in which he ferments his wine and a few oak barrels from Burgundy he uses to raise them. He harvests early, for lower alcohol and more acidic freshness, and uses gentle methods, pumping over the wine himself during its fermentation. For his whole operation, he has one assistant—a local *ragazzo* he calls his "eyes" for when he is with his wife and kids at their apartment in Rome.

Morning melted into afternoon, and Giovanni suggested we hunt down some lunch provisions. We got in his SUV, and he drove outside of town, stopping at a family roadside fruit stand for some pizza. Made in a wood-fired oven, the pizzas were completely different from Naples style. They were cheese-less versions, stuffed with ingredients like tomatoes or broccoli rabe and sausage and wrapped in brown paper.

He loaded the pizza in the trunk, and we continued southeast along a two-lane road lined with small farms. The car filled with the aromas of baked crust, sausage, and cooked tomatoes. Giovanni announced our next stop by painting circles in the air with his right hand. "La mozzarella," he exclaimed, stretching out each syllable like it was a string of melting cheese. "Laaa mozzzzzzzaaarrrrrr-rellllllllllaaaa. Mozzarella is very important." He struck a professorial tone. "The two great mozzarellas in Campania are from Caserta and Salerno. These are the two great rivals."

Good, fresh buffalo mozzarella—not the industrial supermarket fakes that come shredded, skimmed, or molded into rubbery blocks—is one of the food world's simplest but baroquely sensual products. Its white, fleshy spheres suspended in salty liquid are to cheese what Naples-born Gian Lorenzo Bernini's sculptures and fountains are to Rome's civic architecture. Water buffalo, which probably have been domesticated in Southern Italy for a thousand years, produce extra-rich, tangy milk that gives mozzarella its fleshy consistency and subtle flavors. Though great buffalo mozzarella is made throughout the South, mozzarella di bufala Campana is the gold standard.

"The mozzarella of Caserta is stronger." Giovanni made a fist and pumped it in front of his chest. Then, he unfurled his fingers and fluttered them in the air. "The mozzarella of Salerno is more delicate." He explained the difference, saying Caserta buffaloes are traditionally milked once a day and therefore make more concentrated milk. In Salerno their counterparts are milked twice a day, providing a more diluted milk. "Caserta mozzarella is wilder, more aggressive," he said. "I prefer it."

"Aggressive" is not a word I would associate with mozzarella—at least not in a good way. It reminded me of the scandal a decade earlier in which traces of poisonous dioxins (produced by illegal burning of plastics and other waste) had infected grazing areas and were found in buffalo milk in Caserta. The government recalled mozzarella, public outrage led to boycotts and the quarantine of agricultural zones, and testing was stepped up. Even if the mozzarella was cleaned up, Caserta—which was nicknamed the "Triangle of Death"—was not. Giovanni, of course, doesn't buy from just anywhere. Caserta mozzarella producers tend to purchase milk from farmers, and, naturally, he doesn't trust the dairies in the southern, more corrupt part of the province, with their Napoli telephone prefixes.

He pulled into a parking lot in front of a drab, modern box of a building emblazoned with red and green plastic letters that spelled out *Caseificio La Baronia*. "I buy my mozzarella here because I know the owner and I know the milk comes from the hills around here," he explained.

We made our way around back, to the staff entrance, where we covered our shoes with disposable booties and donned shower-cap-style head coverings. The production area was one large room filled with steel vats and a half dozen men who did the physical work of mozzarella making. They were all clad in white and wearing aprons, plastic clogs, and ball caps. I watched a pair of men who were huddled over a shallow, waist-high wooden tub, kneading curds into a coherent paste. They took turns stirring the paste into a smooth, velvety mass before two of them hoisted it into a large plastic container.

We were greeted by the owner, Alfonso Cutillo, who opened the *caseificio* (cheese dairy) nearly three decades earlier with his cousin. Cutillo, the ex-mayor of Pontelatone, is a tall, middle-aged man, with dark, heavy lids and meaty hands. Suited up for work, he was a little soft around the middle of his apron and had a series of chins. He excused himself to go back to a long, narrow steel basin filled with a milky white liquid and faced off with a rounder, shorter man who wore his cap backward, their four hands beginning an elaborate dance. While Cutillo held up unformed slabs of white cheese, his partner's fingers pulled off (in Italian the verb for breaking off pieces is *mozzare*) pairs of mozzarella balls and dropped them in the *salamoia* (salt water brine) below. Cutillo paused from his work to pull off some small pieces of warm cheese for us to taste. The mozz was deliciously creamy but lacked the salty tang that comes from brining. "Mozzarella has three to four days of life at this top quality," he said.

Giovanni and I would eat that morning's mozzarella within hours of its creation. After stocking up at the shop in front, we headed back to Vitulazio. The sky had turned a brilliant blue, and the sun accentuated the stands of oak and walnut, the fruit orchards, the olive groves and plots of tobacco. Giovanni reached into the back seat for the cheese bag and pulled out a smaller plastic bag filled with four small *bocconcini* (egg-sized balls of mozzarella). While more or less steering the car, he managed to unknot the bag and invited me to dig in as part of an improvised antipasto. I took one of the bocconcini in my fingers and bit into it—a shot of warm liquid ran down my chin. Just a little time in its brine had brought out all the subtle mozz glory. There was a hint of hay flavor to remind you that it was made on this earth and not by heavenly *putti*. It yielded just enough in the mouth to prolong the sensation of cream oozing over the tongue. Back at Giovanni's family home and his modern, bright kitchen, we ate a simple lunch accompanied by his Nanni Copè wines.

Organized crime was one of Giovanni's preferred subjects because, in his multifarious life, he was not only winemaker, writer, and photographer, but he also managed to work for Libera Terra, the twenty-first-century nonprofit that repurposed land confiscated from convicted mobsters by the courts. Founded by a crusading Catholic priest and an Italian judge, Libera Terra runs cooperatives across Southern Italy that use the lands for producing organic wine, pasta, beans, canned tomatoes, jams, and olive oil. Giovanni supervised winemaking under the group's Centopassi label and drew on his corporate experience to act as a strategic planner. While farmland and vineyards were not a mob profit center, they were a way for mobsters to display their success—and maybe launder some money on the side. For communities in the South, agriculture is an important source of employment, and Libera Terra kept those properties from being abandoned.

"The Mafia, Camorra, and 'Ndrangheta are completely different things," Giovanni said of Italy's three principal crime syndicates based in Sicily, Naples, and Calabria, respectively. He used a long, serrated, and dangerous-looking pizza knife to slice into a ball of mozzarella, which bled white as it split into quarters. He divided the pieces, ground salt over them, and drizzled on some of his newly pressed, opaque green oil. "The Mafia always has had a pyramidal structure with one capo who ruled. When there was a war, it was to decide who would rule," he said. He lifted a forkful of mozzarella.

Anyone living in Italy since the early 1990s recognizes the names of Giovanni Falcone and Paolo Borsellino—the Sicilian anti-Mafia prosecutors both assassinated in bombings by the Corleone-led Sicilian Mafia in 1992. In death the popular lawmen were treated as martyrs. Public outcry had punishing consequences for the Sicilian mob.

"After Falcone and Borsellino," Giovanni said, "the Sicilian Mafia was so broken by the state, they realized they couldn't continue. They had to go underground to be tranquillo. There was no more violence in the streets. Their children went to universities and became lawyers or went into finance. On the other hand, the Camorra was never pyramidal. It's always like mushrooms in the forest, popping up everywhere. They never have had one capo and so they are always at war. It's criminal gangs, and many of their capos are less than thirty years old. They are always at war with each other. They die young."

We ate the pizza with our fingers. The broccoli rabe was a deliciously bitter complement to the seared fat and flesh of the sausage. The cooked tomatoes, the last of the year's crop, made me long for summer even before winter had begun.

"'Ndrangheta is a middle structure." Giovanni remained matter-of-fact, as if he were relaying a recipe. "They are clans and they have territories." He poured vintages of his red Sabbie di Sopra il Bosco. They were easy drinking, fragrant and fruity, with layers of spice and acidity that complemented the meatiness of the sausage and the October sweetness of the tomatoes. "My idea is to make feminine wines," Giovanni said. "Red wines, not black ones."

It seemed an odd statement juxtaposed with a description of the Italy's often violent criminal pantheon. We chewed and sipped in silence.

"Now," he continued, "'Ndrangheta is the most important of the organizations and the most rich. They are everywhere. They are in everything." He poured more red wine as he rattled off the activities of the Calabrian mob: "Arms in the Middle East, finance, drugs, trash collection. Also supermarkets, stores, and restaurants."

For dessert Giovanni brought forth a wedge of Conciato Romano. Conciato is one of the world's oldest cheeses, which was believed to have been created by the Samnites, an Italic civilization in the Caserta region that battled the Romans. Conciato is the un-mozzarella. Aged in clay amphorae for up to two years, it is an extreme cheese, with a wet, moldy exterior, the aromas of a sheep barn, and a pungency that can bring you to tears. Fitting of Caserta, it is a cheese devoid of all subtlety. Aggressive to the point of sensory violence, it stomped Giovanni's delicate wines and left them lying lifeless on our palates.

That afternoon we headed east in Giovanni's truck, up into the Appennini foothills to his Pallagrello, pergola-trained vineyard. Harvest had just been completed, and the leaves were browning. But the grasses and wild fennel underfoot remained resistantly green. Some miles to the southeast were the gray, calcareous peaks of Mount Taburno rising up from the Volturno Valley. To the north were the rugged Matese mountains that separated Campania from the east coast of Italy and tiny Molise.

Giovanni heaped praise on the pergola system as ideal for the heat of Southern Italy. He ridiculed officials of the European Union who disfavored it as overly productive. "The people who decide these things are ignorant!" He pressed the fingers of his two hands together, crossing his thumbs, and rocked his hands back and forth in a gesture of *what the . . . ?* "Pallagrello is an extraordinary grape," he said. "Every territorio has a vine that best expresses the place. Here, there isn't a better one."

Pallagrello was once grown throughout Campania but was now relegated to this corner of Caserta. And many of those vineyards, Giovanni said, were owned by people who knew nothing about wine.

"Look at my neighbors," he shouted, turning and pointing around the vineyard slope. "This one is a lawyer, that one is a pharmacist, another is a notary. There's a business director and a surgeon. They have money and they hire enologists to make concentrated wine that doesn't express Pallagrello." Giovanni's hands flew, animating his disgust, like a Pulcinella character from Neapolitan commedia dell'arte. "They know un cazzo [dick] about wine," he cried. "There's no contadino here!" He lowered his voice and, with a shake of his head, in a moment of ironic self-mockery, said, "Even I am not a farmer." Then his voice rose again, and he howled skyward, "And I am crazy!"

The A16 Autostrada cuts across the ankle of the Italian boot, climbing into Campania's mountainous Irpinia region around Avellino. It was there that I met Sabino Loffredo at a roadside café, and he embraced me like he embraces everyone: like a long-lost cousin. In the two months since I had last seen him, he had grown a thick black beard streaked with white. The name Irpinia comes from *hirpus*, which means "wolf" in Southern Italy's extinct Oscan language. Sabino's newfound pilosity indeed gave him the look of one.

We downed espressos at the bar. He stopped outside to light a cigarette, took a few drags, and headed to his truck. I followed him through an industrial tangle of automotive and metalworks plants that first sprouted here in an era of investment after the cataclysmic 1980 Irpinia earthquake. On the other side of the highway, we climbed through forest and vineyards to tiny Montefredane and its expanses of Fiano.

Sabino's haphazard Pietracupa winery is perched at about 350 meters in altitude, and it was as I remembered it from a visit years earlier. Behind a small iron gate stood a faded, white postwar house, the yard around it littered with old vats, wood pallets, and scattered machine parts. A loading dock in back partly sheltered winemaking equipment and fermentation tanks from rain. Through a wide opening I saw a confused mix of exposed brick and cinderblock walls dimly lit by bulbs dangling from wires above steel tanks, casks, and clutter.

"It is a mess," Sabino observed in his broken English. "A *very*, *very* mess." And that was the thing about him: at forty-eight, Sabino made gorgeous white wines in the most pitiful of conditions.

Antonio Capaldo, chief of the region's largest and most innovative winery, Feudi San Gregorio, praised Sabino's Fianos on more than one occasion as the best in the region—above his own. But he added, "Nobody knows how he does it." Which is strange because Sabino doesn't exactly have secrets. He is as transparent as he is proud of the fact that most of his winemaking equipment is twenty years old and out-of-date. "Every time an enologist comes into my cellar, they say, 'How can you make wine here with this?'" Sabino's voice—a baritone colored by tobacco, coffee, and wine—had a casual and ironic southern lilt. He lit a cigarette and ranted about enologists always trying to sell winemakers equipment they don't need.

We got in Sabino's truck to take a ride around his vineyards. Sabino said goodbye to his dog, Gaetano—a gangly, spotted mutt, genetically somewhere between a sheepdog and a collie—and drove down the narrow road for about a hundred yards, when he looked in the rearview mirror, slammed on the brakes, slapped the wheel with his palm, and cried out, "Figlio di puttana [son of a whore]!"

He kicked open the truck door, and there was Gaetano—a large, affectionate missile of hair, paw, and tongue—who had found a way out of the winery fence and was trying to climb in. Sabino fumbled for his phone and called his father, Giuseppe, who arrived in his small Fiat about five minutes later to take Gaetano back to the winery.

"I am sorry," Sabino said. "Gaetano is like a child. It's a very problem! It's a *very, very* problem."

On the left side of the narrow, unstriped blacktop was a wooded area, and on the right were vineyard slopes that fell downhill toward the valley below. I noticed that a wide swath of the woods had been incinerated by fire. "This happened last year," Sabino said with an indignant shake of the head. "Most of the fires are made by shepherds. If it wasn't for the firemen that arrived, it would have burned my vineyards."

I knew from my years of traveling to Sicily that shepherds were more than just pastoral artisans. They could be ruthless arsonists set on burning woodlands for grazing, and vineyards were sometimes a casualty.

Sabino stopped the truck in the road. "In fact, we cannot say who it is who does this," he said with a grave look, momentarily sounding judicious—an attitude he couldn't keep longer than a breath. "But the shepherds—they break your balls. It is always them. Who else has an interest in doing this?"

He turned his truck south and drove down the hill, onto another road of patched asphalt and tar only wide enough for a single car. The road divided Montefredane to the west from Prato di Principato Ultra to the east, the two rural burgs with a combined population that barely topped five thousand. Stopping the truck, he waved his right hand toward Montefredane. "Here," he said, "it is all Fiano." Then he nodded his head in the opposite direction, out his window. "And here it's all Greco di Tufo."

What, I wondered, was the difference between the two? I imagined that local contadini had figured out the geology of their terroirs long ago and discovered which vines paired with which soils. After all, didn't *everything* in old-world vineyards have a reason?

"The difference?" Sabino shook his head. "Nothing. No difference. Montefredane is Fiano, and Prato is Greco. That's it. In fact, I planted Greco in Montefredane." He shrugged. "My idea is to have all my white wines in Montefredane."

He parked, and we got out and walked through a Fiano vineyard that had been harvested a month earlier. The limestone and sandstone felt soft underfoot. Under the late morning sun, he peeled off his down jacket, exposing the dark T-shirt he wore underneath.

Sabino harvests early—first Fiano, then Greco for his two basic monovarietal whites that are bottled six months after they ferment. "I prefer the grapes green for freshness and elegance," he said.

"I speak for my personal taste—yellow grapes make something richer and heavier that I don't like. I want to make a photo of the vintage. I don't want to cover the vintage with my idea of how to make wine."

When Sabino is convinced of the quality—"when the vintage is perfect"—he leaves wine from small parcel selections in the tank for at least two years, then fills about a thousand bottles each of limited editions called Greco G (from Greco) and Cupo (from Fiano). "Everybody wants my Cupo," he said in a monotone. "Yesterday one of my importers called and said 'I need one hundred twenty bottles.' I said, 'You can have eighteen.'"

Sabino's white wines are indeed as dramatic and memorable as the landscapes of Campania. His Fianos come on like a hit of sea air in spring—robust, floral, and expansive. His Greco wines are all zip and lemon spice. Both finish with the bitterness of Southern Italian almonds, and, with age, the wines seem to scavenge stone and metallic memories of the vineyards in which they grew.

"Anyway," Sabino said as we headed back to his truck, "I don't drink white wine."

He spoke as offhandedly as someone might express a lack of fondness for sushi. But here was a man who built a career on Fiano and Greco di Tufo. One of Southern Italy's cult producers of white wine—and he didn't drink white wine? "I don't know why," he said. "Of course, every day I taste my wines—that's different. But for the last eight years, I drink red wine."

It might have started with his buying more than four acres of Aglianico from his uncle a decade earlier. That vineyard—more than a half hour's drive to the northeast—had perhaps gotten Sabino thinking in other directions. "My idea is to make an Aglianico with the elegance of Pinot Noir," Sabino told me. That was not an easy task. Aglianico is a black, leathery grape with very little in common with ephemeral Pinot. Still, Luigi Tecce had found more than brute force in Aglianico—as had younger producers farther south in Basilicata, around Monte Vulture.

Sabino drove down to the valley floor, crossing under the autostrada and through industrial parks, to arrive in Atripalda, a bustling Avellino suburb. It was lunchtime, and the traffic crawled slowly on the two-lane road that ran in front of the Trattoria Valleverde Zi' Pasqualina. Sabino was on the opposite side of the road as the trattoria but noticed a parking space not far away. He edged the nose of his truck into oncoming traffic to take it, simultaneously waving his arm out the window. A young woman in a sun-peeled Fiat with a busted headlight stopped inches from him, blocking his path. She stared coldly through him as if she knew him or at least knew his type, with his aviator shades and grizzle.

"Women—they are prepotenti [bullies] in the car," said Sabino, looking every bit the agitated wolfman. He gesticulated his frustration with his left arm as his right arm made a series of quick, short, sharp moves between the wheel and stickshift. The engine roared as the truck swung left, then right, finishing the turn into the parking space backward, all in front of the woman in the Fiat. She never blinked.

At Zi' Pasqualina there is a Pasqualina who cooks with her daughters in their dark sweatshirts and worn aprons. Sabino strode into her kitchen, where the women embraced him like a prodigal nephew. We sat in the wood-lined fifties-era dining room, and we ate hot bean and escarole soup with Sabino's wines.

Sabino is an accidental winemaker. His father was a pension administrator who made wine to sell to local restaurants at the family's property in Montefredane. His mother was a high school gym teacher. At university Sabino studied law briefly but grew bored, switching his studies to physical education. After graduating he went to Great Britain to learn English, working in a Brighton Pier fish-and-chips joint, where he quickly ascended from prep cook to waiter to assistant manager. Then, in 1996, he landed what seemed his dream job: fitness instructor on an Italian cruise line off the coasts of South America and Europe.

As Sabino tells it, there were days on end where his only responsi-
bilities were opening the ship's gym in the morning, closing it in the
evening, and giving a few personal massages booked by big-tipping
female passengers. Life was good, and he rarely gave a thought to
wine. Then, one day, two years into his traveling life, when Sabino
was on a cruise docked in Rhodes, he went with his then-girlfriend,
a cruise singer, to the beach on a rented motorcycle. On the way
back to port that evening, he took a turn on the bike and was hit by
a gust of wind, throwing the couple into a drainage culvert. Sabino
was the more severely injured, his back broken. He was flown back
to Naples for emergency surgery.

"My doctor said, '99 percent of people after an accident like that
stay in the wheelchair,'" Sabino said. During his months-long con-
valescence, he accompanied his father on his trips to Montefredane.
"I went into the vineyard, I went into the winery, and my passion
was born," he explained. "It was my destiny. I believe in destiny."

After the soup, we ate hearty plates of roasted potatoes and
peppers covered with fried eggs and sampled some of Sabino's
first red Aglianicos. In contrast to the near-perfection of his whites,
the reds tasted like incomplete experiments, studies that were just
taking form.

"When I started to make wine, I didn't know anything," Sabino
said, balancing a green pepper on the end of his fork as it cooled.
"I started at zero. For me, wine was white or red. I was like a child.
When you don't know anything about something, you don't speak.
You just listen."

He worked with his father's enologist and toured Tuscany, Burgundy, and Champagne, meeting producers and tasting. From the
beginning Sabino recognized that he liked wines that were nimble
and spirited. He understood that, with refrigeration and a small
amount of sulfites, he could block the naturally occurring secondary
fermentation (or malolactic fermentation, which converts sharp
malic acid to creamier lactic acid) and keep his white wines lean.

His breakthrough came in 2004 when his 2003 vintage of Cupo was awarded "three glasses" by Italy's *Gambero Rosso* guide.

"It made me understand the possibility of this terroir in the vintage," he said. "Everybody spoke about 2002 and 2003 as shit vintages. But if you taste the wines from here—not just mine— they are fantastic." He began to trust his instincts, which told him not to borrow money or invest in new equipment. "I have three pumps, all twenty years old, and an old filter and press," he said. "I realized I didn't need anything else." With his 2006 vintage, he severed ties with his enologist to work solo and began exporting. He assembled land and vineyards by buying from his cousins. He arrived at around twenty acres from which he produced about fifty thousand bottles. He had no interest in growing larger.

"I want to make a wine at the right price; fundamentally I am a socialist," he said glibly. "Also, if I am bigger, I don't have time for my wife, my family. For me, freedom is fundamental."

After lunch we drove toward his Aglianico vineyard, which was in full harvest. Sabino stopped at a dive on the way called the Bim Bum Bar, to buy espressos for his harvest crew. In the truck Sabino complained about his fellow producers in Avellino—how they couldn't work together and how some followed hack enologists who peddled yeasts that imparted tropical flavors to their wines. "Here the mentality is stagnant, like swamp water," he said, an unlit cigarette dangling from his lips. "Nothing moves."

That evening, as night fell on Montefredane, I returned to Sabino's winery. His harvesters drove in a flatbed from his Aglianico vineyard filled with a couple of tons of grapes in small, plastic harvesting baskets stamped with the cheer of Avellino's once glorious and now amateur league soccer club: Forza Lupo (Go wolf). The men stacked the cases on the loading dock, then dumped the grapes into the mouth of a destemming machine that pumped whole berries through about fifteen feet of fat winery hosing, up to the top of a steel vat and into its open lid. Sabino, at the top of the ladder in a pair of shorts and an insulated vest over his T-shirt, was bent over the vat, shouldering the hose and directing flow of the fruit. His father, Giuseppe, used a pitchfork to move the piles of stems that were spat onto the concrete out of the way. His dog, Gaetano, wandered between the men, who took breaks to drink from plastic cups, pouring from a wine bottle marked Greco 15 in grease pencil. It was an ordinary scene made extraordinary by the fact that it was orchestrated by one of Southern Italy's most acclaimed winemakers. Between the grinding of the destemmer and the clattering of the leaky, blackened pump resting on a steel handcart, the noise was deafening. Where the hose attached to the pump, a steel clamp was missing, in its place a mass of sad, brittle, yellowed packing tape.

That night another wine illusion shattered. Many perfectionist winemakers I admired developed winery techniques that were gentle to the point of midwifery, their role being simply to assist in the birth of new wines. They used only quietly purring peristaltic pumps, or forewent pumps altogether in their gravity-based wineries, where grapes simply dropped down from the level above. But here was Sabino, guided by lupine impulses, using all the delicacy and craft of a prep cook on the Brighton Pier.

A light rain began to fall. The men, sweaty from their work, smoked and bantered in a dialect I couldn't recognize as Italian. Finally, when the Aglianico filled the tank, the din ceased. Leaving the winery that night, I followed Sabino's truck down the hill toward Avellino. A neighbor's dog bounded after it, leaping and barking furiously in the rain. Sabino gunned the engine, and the dog sprinted about a hundred yards and then stopped, his tongue hanging low as he turned toward home. That hound had recognized Sabino's truck and gone after it. I like to think he sensed something about the driver, that maybe he had sniffed out an Irpinian wolf in man's clothing.

For the third musketeer, I drove east of Avellino along winding roads that took me deeper and higher into Irpinia's mountains, arriving at a place that seemed forgotten by the modern world, with its hushed towns and the remnants of once-great castles. I found Luigi Tecce at his familial home on a hilltop, where the comune of Paternopoli meets Castelfranci and Montemarano. Here the Tecce clan had once made their own hamlet of scattered houses. The place was startling in its stillness, with none of the sounds of man or machine, only the calls of morning birds and the barking of Luigi's collection of adopted stray dogs.

Alien to the setting was Luigi himself—a rail-thin and elegant dandy here in the middle of a nowhere he rarely leaves, sharing his family's house with his two unmarried sisters. With his neat, short-trimmed hair and gray stubble, he wore blue jeans with a light sweater and a bright floral-print scarf hanging loosely around his neck. His eyes were covered by bulbous, cinematic dark glasses, creating a look that was more *cosmopolita* than contadino.

Yet Luigi is a modern master of Aglianico, here in his vineyards that lay at about six hundred meters in altitude. It was a few days before his harvest, and he led me across the road to a plot of about two and half acres of century-old Aglianico vines that stood above head height. They were planted side by side in pairs that were braced by one shared chestnut post, the vines resembling small trees. "It is called a raggiera," Luigi said of the system, which looked like nothing I'd ever seen, *raggiera* referring to the shoots growing like *raggi* (spokes) off the central trunk. It is from this old vineyard, planted in sedimentary soils mixed with spewed volcanic dust from Mount Vesuvius, that Luigi makes his Poliphemo. Twenty years of working this and other vineyards—that now totaled twelve acres—mostly by himself left Luigi, at forty-six years old, tired, "Stanchissimo!"

"I never had an enologist, no chemicals, no technology," Luigi said. He was neither as demonstrative as Giovanni Ascione nor as easygoing as Sabino Loffredo, but quietly eccentric, with a fire that seemed to burn just below his skin and flare occasionally. "To make a traditional product takes three generations—three generations of knowledge," he said in a raised voice. "Someone who is an intellectual or a businessman can't become a natural producer from one day to the other!" Luigi let out a weary sigh with his whole sinewy torso. "To learn these traditions takes time."

Time and tradition are more of his paradoxes. In spite of growing up on this hilltop and spending most of his life here, his methods are largely self-taught. His father died suddenly from an aneurysm, and it was only then, at twenty-six, that Luigi turned to working the vineyards. "I invented everything by experimentation," he said. To him there is no contradiction. He insisted he gleaned things from his forefathers by a kind of generational osmosis: "I learned unconsciously from being around my father and grandfather." When I pressed him about this, asking how that would have helped him as a young man with no one to teach him about wine, he held his arms out to the side as though laying his chest bare and said poetically, "I closed my eyes and looked backward."

We crossed the road and went around the back of the family house to the winery he built with the help of a few friends. Outside a dozen of his once-abandoned mutts swarmed him. His cellar, in contrast with Sabino's, was a crisp white box of Teutonic-like precision. He used *tini*, old conical chestnut casks, for fermenting his Aglianico along with big oak barrels for aging. He used little equipment—a handbasket press, a pair of state-of-the-art gentle pumps, and hand tools. All of it, even the floor, was as clean as an Italian grandmother's Sunday tabletop.

"When things are disorganized, you can always blame something else," he said dryly, removing his bulging shades to reveal big dark eyes. He climbed a stepladder next to a *tino* half-filled with the season's first grapes, fermenting on their own yeasts to be used as a starter, or *pied de cuve*, for the rest of the harvest to come. With one foot in a sporty designer sneaker balanced on the edge of the cask, he used what looked like a long white plastic garden hook to press down on the cap of grape skins.

When he finished with this operation, he descended and rinsed the tool off in an industrial sink. We walked outside toward a smaller, old farm building where he aged some of his wines, partially in

Burgundy barrels. He paused to hand-roll a cigarette and point out the building's rustic outer wall that displayed the local terroirs with its mash of sandstone, limestone, fossils, and silica. As Luigi dragged on his roll-up, I listened again to the morning under a darkening sky. A breeze rustled in the olive and pomegranate branches across the road.

As a young man, Luigi left his home to study at university in Naples for the simple motive of avoiding Italian military service. He studied economics and for two years became the personal assistant of an Italian legislator in Rome. "When I was young, I had the illusion of change—of the left," he said. "But Italy won't change. Ever. It's like *Il Gattopardo*." This was a reference to Sicily's emblematic 1958 novel, Giuseppe Tomasi di Lampedusa's *The Leopard*. "Everything needs to change, so everything can stay the same." An election upset put his boss out of office, and Luigi returned to the family farm and tended to the livestock while his father cultivated corn and wheat and sold grapes from the small, century-old vineyard. Then, in 1997, the Tecce world was rocked by the sudden death of Luigi's father, who was only fifty-eight.

"My father was the center of our family economy," he said. "My mother and my sisters and I depended on him. We had no money in the bank. But we needed to eat."

Luigi, the eldest of three siblings, turned his attention to what his father had been doing: grape farming and selling fruit from his small vineyard. Eventually he replanted the other vineyards that he bought from his cousins and began experimenting with making wine for himself and his friends. "I didn't ask for money from the bank," he said. "I didn't ask for money from the state. I didn't ask for money from anyone. I worked poco a poco [little by little]."

With a couple of dogs in tow, we walked to his younger vineyards, which he'd planted a few hundred yards down the road, as Luigi recounted how he'd become intrigued with the world of wines and in 2001 enrolled in a sommelier course in Rome, where he tasted Barolos, Bolgheris, Bordeaux, and Burgundies. Up until then the only wine Luigi had known was the potent, slightly sweet, familial wines he had grown up with.

"The first time I tasted Pinot Noir, to me it didn't taste like wine," he confessed. "To me it was like drinking dirty water!" But, as Luigi's palate broadened, he developed his own elegant ideals of what kind of wines he could make on his familial terroirs: "Here, it's a particular version of the South—the South of the mountains," he said. "We have the alcohol of Puglia and the acidity of Trentino."

His younger vineyard, which now produce his simpler wine, Satyricon, was regimented in rows of cordon-trained vines sloping down to the northwest and a horizon filled with a collection of peaks locally known as Monte Tauro. This morning the peaks came in and out of view as the sky churned brilliant blues, grays, and black.

Luigi's first commercial wines were produced with the 2003 vintage, including about eleven hundred bottles of his Poliphemo. On the back label of them, he put what he calls a "provocation"—a testament to the purity of his winemaking. The labels to this day read:

Selected Yeasts	NO	Deacidified	NO
Enzymes	NO	Clarified	NO
Malolactic Bacteria	NO	Filtered	NO
Added Tannins	NO	Gum Arabic	NO

"My label upset people, but now this has become a fashion," Luigi said, venturing into an another area of conflict. While he adheres to a method that most everyone considers "natural," he abhors most natural winemakers and their wines. "I hate the natural wine label. Defects don't make a wine natural. I always made wine for me and my friends." He shouted into the wind, "The world of natural wines fa schifo [sucks]. It makes me crazy—it's business."

Luigi is also a thinker but—another seeming paradox—doesn't like intellectual wines. To him, work, the kind of hard work that tires a man to the bone, is the first requisite of winemaking. Not a label, a manifesto, or a concept. "Intellectuality follows work," he told me perhaps three times that day. "My first idea was to produce the best grapes possible. Intellectuality accompanied that but it didn't make the wine. I am very critical of this intellectual chic where work follows ideas," he said, then he winced and spat out the rest of his thought: "Like all this natural wine, biodynamic, Steiner."

On the way back up the road, Luigi took aim at another fantasy that disturbed him: wine as a symbol of power, wealth, or class. "Twenty years ago, there was an illusion of wine as status. You had doctors and lawyers who planted vineyards. Bruno Vespa [the popular Italian television journalist] planted vineyards in Puglia, Ferragamo was in Tuscany, Simply Red on Etna. But there was no soul to it and too much emulation. Chardonnay in Sicily?" he hissed. "For what? What sense? It's like taking Burgundy to Africa!"

We walked back to what had been his grandparents' house but that Luigi uses as an office and kitchen. On the way he pointed out other houses once occupied by aunts and uncles and cousins that are now empty. He sighed. "It's a society that's disappearing little by little. There are few births and a lot of emigration."

Inside the kitchen, with its old, white-painted wood cabinets, he put a music disc in a small stereo player. The music was by his friend the Irpinian folk singer Vinicio Caposella. Though Caposella was born in Germany to Irpinian parents and now lives in Milan, he claims Irpinia as a source of folkloric inspiration and soul. He is also the artist who drew the childlike version of the cyclops Polyphemus that adorns the labels of Luigi's Poliphemo.

On a table with a white cloth protected in Italian *nonna* (grandmother) fashion by a sheet of clear plastic, Luigi set out bottles of his Poliphemo from all the way back to 2005 and opened them. Standing at the counter, he chopped tomatoes and vegetables and layered them on rounds of thin flatbread—frying them in a heavy iron skillet to produce a kind of pan-fried pizza. Then he cut up slices of local Capocollo and bacon-like pancetta, set out a plate of red bell peppers in oil, and joined me at the table.

The aromas of the meat, the frying smoke, and the singed bread opened a hunger in me, and Luigi's wines were as expected: powerful, with a kind of leathery rusticity that normally would make me envision a much different producer—older, built like a vintage tractor, and certainly not a dandy. But his wines, which also varied greatly from vintage, were also leavened by a rakish acidity and scents of eucalyptus.

"Aglianico is a wine of energy and light, not a heavy wine. That is the vision I followed," he said defiantly. "Many Taurasis have explosive power but don't last long in the mouth." As we drank more, he confided his inspiration. "I always thought of Mohammed Ali: dance, dance, dance. He was energy and light. Ali is for me one of the great men of the twentieth century."

Though he'd never been to America, Luigi could quote cult American literary figures like Charles Bukowski and John Fante. Luigi himself could be as prophetic as a Steinbeck character. More than perhaps anyone I'd met, he embodied the melancholy of the deep rural mezzogiorno—so rich in history, beauty, and bounty, but poor and empty in modern times.

"To make a great wine, you need terroir, vineyards, and people," he said when we'd finished his antipasti. "The South of Italy has grande terroirs, grande vineyards, and the sun and the air, but the people don't have enough pride. The difference between a contadino from Tuscany and a contadino from Irpinia is that, in Tuscany, they are proud of their nonni [grandparents] and their past." He raised himself up from his chair. "Here the contadini have shame still."

Luigi stood at the counter again, sliced some porcini, and sautéed them in a pan with olive oil. In another skillet he grilled a steak. With a large antique marble mortar and pestle, he ground up crystals of sea salt as the smells of autumnal forest and cooking meat filled the kitchen. Dogs quietly began to appear at the open door and under the table. I was appreciating a relatively light 2007 Poliphemo, and Luigi spoke of the vintage, with September rains and the snow in October before the harvest. Like many potent Italian wines, Aglianico needed the time to age, for the raging exuberance of youth to calm. "These wines need at least ten years to mature," Luigi said. "Before that, they are neither babies nor adults." As he flipped the steak, his thoughts seemed to turn dark.

"I am the last one," he murmured.

I wondered what he meant by that: the "last."

"The saddest thing of my work is that when I die, it's all over," he elaborated. "There is no one to continue. Finito."

It was sad. What was happening to the Italian countryside? Where were the barefoot *bambini* to have their feet dipped in wine? Neither Luigi nor his sisters had married or multiplied, the latter being necessary for creating future generations of sensitive winemakers. Luigi was adamant that passing down traditions took generations, but he had no future to pass anything on to.

He placed the meat and mushrooms on a plate, and we cut off pieces with our steak knives. "The work is tiring. But to make something that can be drunk in San Francisco and Seoul and Copenhagen is truly a great satisfaction," he said of places he might never go.

We chewed. We drank.

"If people didn't appreciate my wine . . ." he said and quietly set down his utensils. He drew his right index finger across his left wrist and then his left index against the opposite wrist. ". . . I would slit my wrists."

It was an awkward moment. How do you respond to that? I turned back to the wine, and he shared pieces of meat with the dogs.

After we drank coffee made in his stovetop moka, and he smoked another hand-rolled cigarette, Luigi wanted to take a drive. "The South of Italy has layers of history like a torta," he said, and he wanted to show me some of the local slices of that cake. But, first, as we headed to his German station wagon, he confided, "I hate to drive."

"Oh?"

"I just don't like to be at the wheel of the car," he said.

On another day under different circumstances, I might have begged off getting in the passenger side. But, from Tecce's winery's perch, the world now shone brilliantly. The troubled sky of the morning had been replaced by a canvas of Vermeer blues, and I was sated by Cyclops wine.

"The only place I love to drive is Napoli," he continued. Another Tecce contradiction.

"Why would *anyone* choose to be at the wheel in Naples?" I wondered aloud.

"Because five hundred years ago," Luigi responded, "before the invention of the automobile, Napoli was the fourth largest city in the world."

"And so?"

"Therefore," he concluded, "it makes no sense to follow traffic laws."

So he was an anarchist, I surmised: like all the other drivers in Naples, he thrilled to the chaotic split-second decisions, the competition, and the tests of wits.

"In Napoli, if you are aggressive, you will be respected," he explained. "If you are careful, people pass you, and if you are a chicken, you will be eaten!"

As Luigi drove, windows down as we wound through country roads and a landscape cut by the Calore River, his mood seemed to lighten. "Historically, Napoli was a Greek city and Irpinia was Italic," he said. "When Napoli was Byzantine, Irpinia was Longobardo [Lombard]." The topic seemed to bring him joy. "In the 1500s all the nobles from here went to Napoli."

I was awed by the way Luigi could move from wine to architecture to literature, geology, and history. We stopped at the stunning hilltop Abbey of San Guglielmo al Goleto, where the only other beings were afternoon swallows, and where he riffed on the pagan symbols in the Lombard medieval church buildings. Then we hiked to the hilltop Fort of the Rocca San Felice, with Luigi narrating as enthusiastically as one of those museum headsets: "The original architecture is Longobardo, but it was finished by the Angevins and the Aragonese."

When we descended from the castle outlook, seemingly the only people in town, we passed a medieval stone house whose old hand-cut stone lintel and columns had been replaced by an anonymous concrete doorway with a white modern aluminum doorframe and glass door. Luigi looked at it and turned gloomy again. "In the 1950s to 1970s," he said, "everyone wanted to be modern. Everyone dreamed of an American apartment with a TV and a big fridge and a white floor to escape this poor and sad past. But they threw out everything—architecturally, culturally—to be modern." He went on: "I remember when I was little, there was a woman who went around in a truck to sell plastic furniture and Formica and take away the old furniture. It was"—he gave a weighty shrug—"the conquest of plastic." The conquest of plastic. There is little sense in romanticizing the past, but it was a term I would come to think about almost daily and would never forget. We got back in his car, and, when Luigi reached the main two-lane, he gunned the engine, roaring through a stop sign and soaring upward to his lonely lookout.

7. Giovanni Ascione.

8. Sabino Loffredo.

9. Luigi Tecce.

5 Back on the Etna

There is something awe-inspiring about life on one of the world's most active volcanoes. About the landscape's black soils, dark basaltic energy, and surreal lava formations, which were once believed to have spilled out of the mouth of Hades. About the life that takes root in the fissures of lava stone and erupts in dizzying spring colors. About the way generations have mined the tongues of this hardened magma, called *sciara*, to pave streets, erect churches and buildings, and stack in the countryside for terracing vineyards, olive groves, and fruit orchards.

I've been traveling to Mount Etna—or, to many Sicilians, "the Etna"—for more than thirteen years. In that time I have been all over the mountain, seen the mildest spring to snowy winter, experienced all four seasons in one fall morning, and stared down into its sulfurous maw. At certain places and times, the mountain has seemed desolate, forbidding. At others, it's felt as lush and generous as this world can be.

I've developed friendships over long midday meals that lasted past midnight with reds from Etna's Pinot-like Nerello Mascalese and darker cousin Nerello Cappuccio, and whites from its slate-meets-citrus Carricante. I've drunk rustic homemade versions made by mechanics, field workers, and poets; avant-garde wines interred years in amphorae; sophisticated wines that recalled Tuscany or France; and, more and more frequently, wines that justly reflected the place with explosive energy, purity, and elegance. I feel lucky to have had a front-row seat to Italy's most dramatic wine renaissance.

127

In the relatively short span of two decades, Etna wines have gone from forgotten—sold locally in plastic jugs or to tourists in tacky black bottles—to become the hip "it" wines of the Italian South.

On my first wine explorations on Etna in 2008, I'd stumbled into a young wine scene taking shape, particularly on the mountain's northern slopes, where a collection of non-Sicilian *stranieri* joined by a new generation of locals were repurposing many an abandoned *palmento*, the rustic lava-stone-vat wineries that boomed here in the late nineteenth century. That heyday had come at a time when the rest of Europe's vineyards were devastated by the phylloxera louse epidemic, and the continent needed Etna's wines from grapes grown in naturally resistant volcanic sands. The subsequent decline coincided with waves of emigration and the modern post–World War II push to tractors and commercial farming that favored more productive flatlands of other parts of Sicily.

Etna's north face is red country, and I first arrived at a time of experimentation for Nerello. The scene gathered most Friday nights in tiny Solicchiata, at a hole-in-the-wall bar known as the Cave Ox. There, young owner Sandro Dibella would serve up tastes of wine from as nearby as neighboring Passopisciaro or as far away as Burgundy's Vosne-Romanée, while his father grilled sausages on a frail metal barbecue on the sidewalk.

I once thought my attraction to Etna had something to do with my own ancestral connection. The pistachio-producing town of Bronte on the mountain's west side is, after all, the cradle of Camutos, and my paternal grandfather emigrated from Bronte to New York as a laborer in the 1920s. But Luigi Camuto died long before I was born, the family ties are thin, and I found nothing in Bronte that pulled me back—not the way I was drawn to the austerely rugged north face and its views over the Alcantara river valley or to Etna's balmy, white wine–producing east side facing the Ionian Sea. Over time I've come to realize that Etna draws people to her, regardless of roots. Some have settled in to make wine; Etna has a way of hoarding your attention.

Returning in the early spring of 2018, I was eager to take stock. I came for the eleventh edition of the Contrade dell'Etna, a loosely structured daylong *en primeur* showing off the previous harvest's vintage, still in vat or barrel. I had attended the first Contrade dell' Etna, when a few dozen winemakers crammed into the Passopisciaro winery of Roman-Tuscan eccentric Andrea Franchetti, who vacationed on Sicily in 2000 and bought his first vineyards from a local contadino who was happy to unload them. Throughout Italy a *contrada* is simply an area in a cadastral recording system—a type of subdivision that had nothing to do with delineating vineyards. But, from the start of the twenty-first century, a new generation of Etna winemakers had latched onto it as if it were a Burgundy- or Barolo-style designation for wine crus. It was a complete bastardization, but it was something. It had a cool-sounding ring to it on this new frontier.

Now, as I drove up through the Nerello-growing towns from Linguaglossa to Randazzo, the sides of the road exploded in vivid yellows of tall broom, mustard, and fennel-like ferula, the violets and blues of spiny thistles and calamint, the oranges and reds of daylilies, and the pink buds of prickly pear cacti. There were fewer abandoned terraces and fewer fallen-in roofs. More vineyards had been restored, and more old *palmenti* given new life. Sandro Dibella's Cave Ox had long ago moved up the street to become a spacious trattoria and pizzeria with a large wine list and walk-in climate-controlled cellar. The number of wine producers, vineyards, and production had more than doubled, though Etna still produced less than a million and a half bottles. If Etna needed a symbol of its newfound status, it had come in 2017 when Alberto Aiello Graci—a friend from my early days—lured Italy's most esteemed winemaker, Angelo Gaja, to form a partnership with him for making wine on Etna's lesser-known hot, dry southern slopes.

This trip was far more posh than earlier ones. Now I stayed in Linguaglossa, at Shalai, an antique frescoed palazzo that had been transformed by the Pennisi family—to be exact, sons of the local grocer and butcher—into a modern boutique hotel with a Michelin-starred restaurant. On my first morning at Shalai, I breakfasted with Alessio Planeta, CEO of his family's formidable wine company, Planeta, which, in the twenty-first century, had systematically marched from its home in western Sicily across the island while studying and cultivating local vineyards.

Alessio and his siblings and cousins first came to Etna's north face with the idea of making white wine, inspired by the pharmaceutical-entrepreneur-turned-winemaker Giuseppe Benanti's iconic white, called Pietramarina, from Etna's eastern slopes. The family bought vineyards and an old palmento in Contrada Sciaranuova at more than eight hundred meters in altitude, believing that if Etna could make great whites on warmer, wetter slopes, it could also produce even better at cooler, higher spots.

At fifty-one, Alessio, ever the dogged manager, wore the same wrinkled, blue cotton blazer I have always seen on him and lamented that now there were few vineyards left to be bought on Etna. However, he said, there were still few vineyards here compared with the nineteenth century, when vines flowed down the mountainsides to the seaside wine shipping port of Riposto. "There are a lot of interesting people arriving—not all of them will make the most interesting wine in the world, but that is normal. So what?" He carefully swirled the espresso in its cup. "The real power of Etna is that it is a postcard that people remember. It's there—*boom!*—in your face." With his free hand he roughly sketched out the contours of the mountain. "It's an emotion you don't forget. When I started, every wine list had the Piedmont, Tuscany, Veneto, and then everywhere else. Now you cannot have a wine list in Rome or Milan without Etna. This is incredible. For Sicily it is a revolution."

That morning, outside Randazzo, Andrea Franchetti stood erect in front of Castello Romeo, a pink turreted and frescoed eighteenth-century confection of a marquis's palazzo that looked like it could have once hosted balls out of Sicily's literary bible: di Lampedusa's

The Leopard. A great lawn ended in a pair of tall palms and the villa's double staircase; arrayed on the grass were open, white shade tents under which more than a hundred Etna producers poured their wines for a few thousand people who arrived in waves.

At nearly sixty-nine, Franchetti's features had softened. He still looked like a faded movie star with dark tortoiseshell sunglasses balanced on his Roman nose, his thick wave of slightly-askew brown hair combed over his brow, and a seersucker jacket covering his broad frame. Franchetti was one of the first stranieri to have stumbled upon Etna in the 2000s, after first stumbling into winemaking in Tuscany. He was the maestro who created this event, and he and his boyish grin were in their element. "Etna was nowhere ten, eleven years ago," he said. "Now, producers come from Northern Italy to see what's going on, and some of them start making wine here. I ask myself why."

We continued the conversation one morning later that week in his more-or-less-renovated Passopisciaro winery. "Etna is pristine," Franchetti began. "It lends itself to emotion." Wearing a moth-eaten sport jacket, he sat slouched on an old leather sofa. He growled his words carefully, like chords in a jazz composition. "And people are not stuck up. You see, the new, young sommeliers who really sell the wine in Italy, they don't want to be involved in the academy. They want to come to a place that's fun. They have tattoos and a lot of power."

Franchetti has a knack for obliquely riffing on subjects, trying out words and seemingly unassociated memories and ideas until he arrives at a linguistic pearl charged with greater meaning than what he set out to say.

"Wine used to be serious for the knowledgeable and erudite," he mused. "James Bond ordered Chateau Lafite, so you showed off you knew stuff."

Franchetti has led the life of a novelistic character, beginning with his happenstance birth in New York, where his mother, the expat heiress to the South Carolina Milliken textile fortune, traveled so as to have her child in an American hospital. His father was an Italian baron from one of the rare Jewish families admitted to the Italian aristocracy in the nineteenth century. Franchetti grew up among parties and the art world of 1960s Rome. One uncle was a leading modern gallerist; another, by marriage, was the American expat artist Cy Twombly. Franchetti quit high school, bicycled and hitchhiked his way to Afghanistan, wrote some magazine articles, and played bit parts in Italian low-budget noir films. But, for the most part, he led a prolonged, drug-fueled adolescence until the age of thirty-two, when he decided to put on a tie and travel to New York to import Italian wine. Six years later he returned to Rome to marry and start a family with his old girlfriend—a Sicilian aristo-crat who had served years in prison for her activities as a student radical during a violent period of Italy's Red Brigades.

Franchetti had once sold a Twombly painting and used the pro-ceeds to buy land and a ruined house in Tuscany's Val d'Orcia. In the winter of 1990, he left his family in Rome for a weekend of solace in the country and never went back. Knowing nothing about agriculture, he launched Tenuta di Trinoro. Inspired by Bordeaux's maverick *garagistes* and their thick, dark wines, Franchetti created his own limited-edition wines based on Cabernet Franc. While vacationing on Sicily, he nosed around for a place to make wine and arrived on Etna because of the cooler, high-altitude climes. "The Etna," he explained, "is all about moving away from the heat because we are in Sicily."

The wines he'd tasted here were rough, rustic, and still fizzing in the bottle. And, of course, Franchetti wasn't content to only work with Nerello. For his signature wine, called simply "Franchetti," he planted an intimate terraced amphitheater near his winery with an odd-couple grape pairing: Bordeaux's inky, late-ripening blending grape Petit Verdot alongside Lazio's Cesanese di Affile, a subvariety of the workhorse grape that fueled Roman trattoria house reds.

When I first met Franchetti, he looked down on Nerello, which produced thin and pale wines compared to the ripe Bordeaux he loved. For his first Nerello vintage on Etna in 2001, he admitted to illegally smuggling in a barrel of his best Tuscan Merlot to toss into the blend. Franchetti eventually made peace with Nerello, though by that time he'd stopped drinking altogether. Now Franchetti sampled wines by sniffing, observing, and tasting (and spitting).

It was late morning, and the sun hit the courtyard out the window, lighting it white as swallows darted between his farm buildings. Reflecting back on the changes on Etna, Franchetti said there was still a lot of mediocre wine being produced here. But, more than the changes to wine, he seemed fascinated by the social changes— specifically in a new generation that had come of age in the last decade.

"There's a new thing going on where the kids sit outside the bar and of course look at the girls going by. But now they not only look at the girls, but they swirl the wine and use important words like 'primeur' and 'cru.'" Franchetti's mood brightened. "You have these kids saying things like: 'This 2012 is really Etna.' *That*," he said, "is terroir. It's like Bordeaux. There's enough money on the mountain that they don't have to go to Milan or Paris or London. They can stay here and make a living." He sat up now, looking as though he'd shed the weight of his years. "People don't need to emigrate from here anymore—it's a place that has been saved because of wine."

That afternoon I drove west to Randazzo through the *sciara* of the 1981 eruption, formed by magma that had flowed within a mile of town. In Randazzo's center the streets were deserted and the shops closed for Italy's Liberation Day, which marks the fall of Mussolini and the end of Nazi occupation. One place was open for lunch, and a crowd of young people in their twenties holding wineglasses gathered around barrels on the black sidewalk, even spilling into the street.

Il Buongustaio is a family salumeria run by Pippo Cala, his wife, and their son and eldest daughter. Everybody in Etna wine, I later learned, knows Pippo, and he knows everyone in Etna wine. Pippo and his wife, Letizia, stood behind a deli counter filled with salumi and cheeses, slicing meat and preparing sandwiches and salads while their kids circulated through the front room, serving and filling the glasses for the five café tables. Floor-to-ceiling shelves in that room and another behind it were packed with a vast curated selection of bottles of wine—not just from all over Etna, but also across Italy and France, from Campania to Champagne.

I stood at the counter, suddenly ravenous, and asked Pippo for a bit of everything and a glass of red wine. He nodded, waved in the direction of some empty tables, and dangled a piece of mortadella my way at the edge of a long knife. I sat at one of the café tables, and Pippo's fresh-faced son, Giovanni, brought me a tall tulip glass. He pulled a cork out of an already-open bottle of one Franchetti's Etna Rosso Passopisciaro crus and poured it into the glass, making sure that I approved.

Pippo was a slight man with short, thick silver bristles that sprouted evenly from his head. His wife was fleshier, with a thick mane of chestnut hair in which she nested a pair of round black sunglasses. The couple wore their years well alongside what I imagined were their resolute personalities. Their children seemed to have inherited the naïve self-confidence of living at the center of the fixed world of the local salumeria.

Within seconds of having my glass poured, Pippo's daughter, Denise, brought a bowl of fat, spicy green olives and toasts smeared with black olive paste. She wore black jeans, white sneakers, and a T-shirt silk-screened with the words of the American poet and Instagram star Robert M. Drake: "But dear, don't be afraid of love, it's only magic." Another message was tattooed down the underside of her right arm.

"Vino e buono?" she asked.

I discreetly read the spiraling script of her tattoo: "My family is everything."

The Calas brought various plates: Nebrodi prosciutto, salami imbedded with pistachios, sheep cheese laced with walnuts, and conserved tomatoes bathed in oil and oregano. The family worked with and around each other with the instinctive flow of an Italian soccer team. Everyone did a bit of everything, and during lulls in the action they sat outside in the sun, ate, chatted with regulars, and drank wine.

As I drained my glass, Giovanni arrived with a second bottle—the same wine but an earlier vintage. "Try this," he said. He poured and left the rest of the bottle on the table. A young couple arrived, both of whom had the stark Greek features common in Catania. The man was husky, with a beard and dark T-shirt, the woman svelte, with long, black hair and a camisole. They ordered sandwiches and a bottle of white from the refrigerator on the wall near the entrance. After the wine was poured, there was a lot of sniffing and swirling and tasting followed by discussion. The young man declared that something was wrong with the bottle, a Benanti Etna Bianco. The nose was good, his partner agreed, but, in the mouth, there was something off, incomplete. The two younger Calas arrived, poured their own glasses, swirled, sniffed, and tasted. It was strange, everyone agreed. Somehow I was invited into this scene and poured a taste. Indeed, behind the aromas, the wine was strangely soft in the mouth, lacking the knife-edge acidity I expect from Carricante, particularly from Benanti. The wine and glasses were whisked away and another bottle from another vintage—correctly chilled and with new glasses—was brought to the table. This one, after general swirling, sniffing, and tasting was deemed *buono*. It was a mundane scene, but a revelatory one. Franchetti was right: this attention to detail in service and tasting, along with the idea of what a wine should deliver, didn't exist here or anywhere else on Sicily a decade earlier.

I paid a pittance for my meal and walked up the street, noticing something else: the Calas never stopped talking. As I turned the corner, the sounds of Pippo and his family echoed off the lava stone, melding with chatter of the afternoon swallows.

In my travels to Sicily, I have learned two of the Italian South's greatest riches. One is its splendor—nature augmented by thousands of years of cultural layers. The other is its humanly genteel pace, as slow and long as a summer afternoon. In other words, beauty and time. Beauty can be marred or destroyed by greed, ignorance, and apathy, though Etna remained relatively unscarred. Time, however, is more fragile. It can be hijacked by the bitterness of frustration, failure, and poverty that plagued Sicily and the South for centuries. It can also be eroded by the creeping demands of modern success.

Success on Etna meant that winemaking friends had less free time in general and for each other. In the early days of the Etna wine scene, winemakers made few appointments. "Come by when you get here" was a common refrain. You either found them at their house or winery, or you asked Sandro Dibella of their whereabouts. Since time became a limited resource, it needed to be sliced and apportioned—not just to the rhythms of nature and the cellar, but also between trips off-island as well as visits from importers, enologists, journalists, and tourists.

So it was even with Frank Cornelissen, who started with nothing and became Etna's zealot with an avid following. Frank, a former mountain climber turned day trader turned wine importer, left his life in his native Belgium to make wine on Etna's north face in 2001, arriving about the same time as Franchetti and another influential *straniero*, the Italian-American importer-cum-winemaker Marco De Grazia. In those first years, each of them brought a different perspective. Franchetti's was to make lush Super Etna wines free of rules. De Grazia, who helped develop a modern wine scene in Barolo and brought it to the United States in the 1980s and 1990s, saw the mountain's varied terroirs as an iteration of the Piedmont or Burgundy. Frank, on the other hand, seemed to be chasing something mystical. He wasn't so much making wine as he was making manifestos against the modern world. He shunned even manure and organic treatments in his vineyards and banished sulfites or any other additives from his cellar. The results were rough, cloudy, and sometimes began turning to vinegar in the bottle. His white wines, made with long skin contact, like red wines, often went beyond the hip hues of "orange wines," popularized on Northern Italy's Slovenian border. They were something else altogether.

His long days of work were a form of self-flagellation that Frank believed would pay off in beauty. When I first met Frank, he was making wine outside and in the cramped spaces below his Solicchiata apartment, where he lived with his then-girlfriend from Japan, Aki. Frank's tasting room had been his kitchen. When I'd first sampled Frank's wines, they walked a tightrope between nectar and swamp water. When his wines were good, they could be great. When they were not good, they were often undrinkable. Frank's extreme natural method and convictions developed a cult following in Japan and, soon after, the West.

His base wine was a simple, affordable red called Contadino, a primitive and slightly fizzy nonno-style garage wine. But he made his splash with Magma, a red from century-old high-altitude vineyards that was left to ferment and age in amphorae buried in lava sand. The wine was sold in Burgundy bottles, the name hand-painted by Frank in Japanese calligraphy and sold for an astonishing two hundred dollars in Lilliputian quantities. I once watched a couple of English-speaking stranieri order a bottle in a restaurant in Linguaglossa, and what poured out was not red but cola brown. They seemed surprised but did not reject it.

What I've always respected about Frank is his critical self-doubt. At a time when wine lovers were being romanced by amphorae, Frank was turning away from the trend. One step ahead of his public, he acted at times as the natural wine world's Dylanesque apostate. "I think if you know what you're doing, you can make wine in anything," he once told me in that vaguely northern European accent. "Plastic, it doesn't matter."

In the decade that followed, Frank's wine had become cleaner. He had also married Aki, with whom he'd had two kids. He had moved his winery to an air-conditioned warehouse down the road in Passopisciaro, where I arranged to meet him one afternoon at four. Frank was never one for punctuality and arrived at seven.

During the intervening three hours, he'd sent a series of text messages expressing frustration at being tied up in his lawyer's office. He later explained he had been signing contracts to buy more vineyards for his wine business, which had grown from 20,000 bottles to 110,000 in little over a decade—from five people working full-time to twenty-four, from about twelve acres of land to sixty.

Frank hadn't changed much. The first thing I noticed about him was his shock of white hair and matching beard. His chiseled features had sharpened, and his eyes now shone intently from deepened sockets. He had put a layer of meat on his bones but was still thin as a vine post and as intensely deliberate as I imagined the first Benedictine monks on Sicily must have been a thousand years ago.

Frank's winery was filled with fiberglass vats for raising his wines and polyethylene tubs for fermenting. Frank now even used the plastic to ferment Magma. A small room of buried amphorae— once an important symbol of his revolutionary winemaking—was now used for overflow and small-batch experiments. Of those relics he said indifferently, "I don't care—a container needs to be neutral that's the only issue." Neutrality, he told me, was the reason he now preferred fiberglass. Because he made his wines without preserving sulfites, they were naturally prone to sherry-like oxidation in porous containers like wood or clay. But he believed steel was too hermetic, producing the opposite effect of reduction that stunted a wine and brought skunky flavors. He was still searching—more than a decade and a half of vintages behind him had challenged his original beliefs.

"There is no black and white in wine, as in life," he said. "There is a lot of gray. Absoluteness about wine doesn't bring you a lot of good."

Frank pulled a couple of clean glasses off the drying rack above a sink in the corner. He then went over to one of his fiberglass tanks and poured tastes of golden-colored wine—many shades lighter than his wines of the past, which blazed as orange as those roadwork warning signs on Italian freeways. The wine, Frank's MunJebel from the previous harvest, was dense and menthol and far more straightforward tasting than his past works. "I stopped making orange wines because they were just about technique," Frank said. "I always just wanted to basically make wine from ripe grapes and no wood." Now, to protect his wines and keep them pure, Frank used light filtering and pumped and bottled in an oxygen-free environment by using tanks of inert argon gas.

We then sampled some of his 2017 reds, including his succulent, fruit-driven Contadino and a rich but refined Magma. Frank explained that these were significantly fresher and more balanced than the similarly hot vintage of 2006, when his grapes "basically boiled on the vine" and made wines taste old from the start. "We're much better now at reading the vines," he said. "We've got a better sixth sense to know what the vintage is going to do."

Frank's sense of what is "natural" goes far beyond the usual shorthand for "organic" or "biodynamic." He had come to Etna in search of a pristine environment and conducted his work and bottled his wines in accordance with the zodiac-driven biodynamic calendar of the late Maria Thun. Yet there was something that bothered him about methods of biodynamics and other natural systems. His aversion, it seemed, was that, in establishing their own creed, they violated some greater mystery.

"I don't like the fact that, in biodynamics, you try to become God yourself by scattering crystals in the vineyard to stimulate photosynthesis and deciding what the vine needs." He walked back over to the sink and rinsed our glasses. "I don't want to do that. It feels awkward or wrong," he continued, setting the glasses on the drying rack. "That's for God—or the bigger programmer—who already sees what will happen in the vintage."

The sun dropped, casting an orange glow over Passopisciaro. I followed Frank in his truck east to Solicchiata, where he turned down a road to lower elevation and then peeled right along a dirt track where we bumped along until we reached a clearing. We were in the middle of Nerello vineyards that Frank and his crew had recently planted after clearing more than four acres of forest and scrub. The vineyard was divided into two parts by dry lava-stone walls built by Frank's crew. On an upper plateau were classic *alberello* (bush-trained) vines, now looking like small, upright claws and planted in precise formation with 110 centimeters (43 inches) between each. Below, on a larger piece of land stretching east, were perfectly linear rows of cordoned vines between chestnut poles and taut steel wire. The geometry here was 90 centimeters (35 inches) between each vine in a row and 2 meters between each row. It was a conventional setup for a tractor and a far cry from his steep, century-old alberello vineyards used for Magma nearly three hundred meters higher up the mountain.

"People always misunderstood me," Frank said. "I've always liked things clean, orderly."

The vineyards here were surrounded only by thick forest. The evening was still; the only sounds were warbling robins and the tapping of a woodpecker. Frank explained his long-term vision: to use these vineyards for base affordable wines that would allow him to grow his company. He wanted to leave a legacy for his kids. He did the math. At fifty-seven, he said, "I think I have twenty-five harvests to go, and then I have another five years talking bullshit like old people do before the kids throw me out." Night set in, and the birds fell quiet, as Frank looked over his vineyard, lit only by a half-moon.

Frank and I met for a late dinner that night at Shalai. He had cleaned up and wore an iridescent blue shirt and blazer.

"When I came to Etna seventeen years ago, I came with a bike as my only transportation," Frank said as we ate an appetizer of raw red prawns in olive oil that tasted like a day by the sea and no doubt came from that morning's great fish market in Catania. "I always wanted to make the greatest wine in the world. But the first ten years were absolute survival."

We drank an old example of Frank's—a slightly vinegary but drinkable Contadino 2004. "This was the first wine when I became part of the territory," Frank said. "It's got high volatile acidity, but it's still fresh and good. My first three vintages were an intellectual approach."

Frank talked about his two children, now six and eight, and of the demand for his wines that was now double his current production in places like Paris, New York, and Tokyo. "I want to be a custodian of these lands and vines and traditions," he told me. "I want to put everything in trust so my kids can't sell the land, so they can only buy but can't sell. My children will never have the same experience I had," he lamented. "I hope they do something dangerous, like some sort of Alpine mountain climbing and come within an inch of losing their life."

As a father I found this hard to listen to. But, then, Frank had never been the protective or coddling type.

"Then," he said, "they will understand."

Plates were cleared from the table. More fish courses arrived. Frank opened a bottle of his Magma 2014 and poured. I was stunned first by the color and clarity. It was ruby, reflecting the low light in the room. The wine tasted at once subterranean and ethereal. Frank explained that it was the first wine he had filtered. We ate and drank and drank some more, ending the evening with a creamy and evolved Valentini Trebbiano d'Abruzzo, made at a time when Frank had first come to Etna.

Frank had once seemed to be at war with an invisible enemy, with the way things were and the way they were not—and perhaps himself. Now he had changed. His wines were no longer militant, but seductive. They weren't so much trying to change the world as find a place in it. "When you start with nothing, anger is half your energy. Now," he said as if realizing it for the first time, "I am more about the joy."

In the early years of Etna's new wave, the stranieri, with their imported ideas, were joined by two Sicilians—both cultivated young men who learned from the foreigners and synthesized their ideas in their own winemaking.

One was Giuseppe Russo, a classical pianist and the son of a Passopisciaro charcoal seller and grape grower who died suddenly in 2003, leaving Giuseppe to decide whether to sell or cultivate the family's vineyards. At the time Giuseppe was finishing work on a rarefied book, *L'Impossibile Idillio* (*The Impossible Idyll*), about Wagner's music in Luchino Visconti's 1973 film biography *Ludwig*, about nineteenth-century King Ludwig II of Bavaria. The quietly intellectual Giuseppe left music and writing to become a farmer, selling wines under the Girolamo Russo label.

The other new-wave Sicilian on the north face was Alberto Aiello Graci, who hailed from a prominent Catania construction family and had studied economics, worked in a bank in Milan, and returned to Sicily to manage his mother's family resources. Alberto, who is as serious about opera, literature, and history as he is about business and wine, came to Etna to buy and plant vineyards in 2005, after selling off the family's vast grain holdings in Sicily's interior.

In the years I've known him, I've watched Alberto renovate and equip an old palmento for his Graci winery in Passopisciaro—though he kept its second story untouched as a sort of time capsule, complete with blackened and decrepit chestnut casks and a worm-eaten wooden lever press fashioned from a great oak trunk. I've watched him expand, like when he bought the abandoned winery, villa, and vineyards next door and was as awed by their mystery and significance as the patrimony of the family who'd owned it: that of Ettore Majorana, the Sicilian nuclear physicist who in 1938 inexplicably vanished after boarding a ship for Naples. I watched him get married in 2016 in Linguaglossa, following the wedding with a lavish, candlelit reception with an after-midnight dinner for two hundred in his cavernous winery. I'd also seen him grow into a leading ambassador for Etna and Sicily, a point man who helped convince outside winemakers to locate here. As a student of history, Alberto believed that Sicily flourished through open exchanges as it did under the relatively liberal two hundred years of Arab rule beginning in the tenth century. He believed outside competence and competition would benefit all.

His biggest catch was Angelo Gaja, Italy's most exalted wine name and the man who had brought his native Piedmontese Barbaresco and neighboring Barolo into a modern age with French ideas a half-century ago. The Graci-Gaja courtship had unfurled slowly. The elder man visited the mountain several times. Alberto suggested Gaja could make wine on Etna. Eventually Gaja proposed his first joint project in the twilight of his career.

It was obvious why Gaja had chosen Alberto: he was young, honest, energetic, smart, and locally connected. When Alberto went about looking for a vineyard spot, he chose it on his terms—a new part of the mountain for new wines and exploration. The two men bought about twenty acres under vine on Etna's hot, dry southern face while planting another ten. There, in the hills northeast of Biancavilla, was a seemingly endless network of worn asphalt and dirt roads with scores of kempt family farms, olive groves, and vineyards that face the center of Sicily. Because of the dryness—it gets a quarter of the rainfall of the north face—the area was known to produce some of Etna's most concentrated grapes. Yet, while some winemakers bought grapes here for their Etna reds, no name had staked out this ground.

"Life," Alberto said one morning in the spring of 2018, "is about searching for what another may not see."

We were walking in another unexplored part of the mountain in Bronte on Etna's western flank, where soils were generally viewed as too hard and shallow for viticulture. But Alberto had found an old vineyard of a little more than four acres in a contrada called Tartaraci that had once been part of Admiral Horatio Nelson's duchy, Maniace, awarded to him in the early nineteenth century for his help in squelching uprisings in Naples. It was planted with red Nerello Mascalese and Nerello Cappuccio and a bit of Grenache, along with white Carricante and Grecanico. Alberto had offered it as a wedding present to his bride, Mirella Buscemi, a pharmaceutical chemist, who was now expecting the couple's first child. The vineyard sat on a plateau—"a terrace on the sky," Alberto called it. The old alberello vines looked like squat, immovable root stubs between the occasional fig, olive, or cherry tree.

Alberto is an earnest man with fine features, boyish Catanian good looks, and thick, black curls. At forty-three he was also the picture of a stylish Italian businessman, wearing blue velvet eyeglass frames and a Cartier watch. As I watched him march through the vineyard in his wingtip boots, I noticed a newfound sureness to his gait. He was at the peak of life, yet his neck and shoulders had grown stiff as a piling in the Venice lagoon, as if carrying a weight much greater than his own.

Back in Passopisciaro, across a small, rarely traveled road from the Graci winery, lay the gently cut Arcuria vineyard, the heart of his estate, which gave its name to a red wine. For a modern wine-maker, Alberto used old techniques: fermenting in conical oak vats, or tini, without adding yeasts or controlling temperatures. Though he'd shared a high-altitude vineyard with Frank, his wines always hewed to a vision of precision and restraint.

On this day the winery was filled with boxes of wine wrapped together on shipping pallets. He set a bottle down on his wood table and opened it. Called Sopra il Pozzo, this 2015 vintage was the debut of a new wine made from a plot whose grapes had long intrigued him: the highest part of Arcuria, at the vineyard's southwestern tip. When Alberto poured the wine into a pair of glasses, I was immediately struck by the faint color. It was halfway to a rosé. Next came the smell: as delicate as faded rose petals. "Very few red wines in Italy have great transparency, great fluidity, and great complexity," Alberto was saying. But I wasn't really listening—I was busy tasting one of the most ethereal wines I'd ever tasted anywhere. Drinking it felt like drinking a glass of wind.

At lunch we were the only diners at Terra Mia, a small family-run restaurant buried in the vineyards of Solicchiata. We drank some of Mirella's Tartaraci red, which was rustic, solid, and earthy compared with Alberto's diaphanous achievement. Over dishes like a salad of fennel, oranges, and pork roasted with artichokes, Alberto retold

Etna's modern wine history in broad strokes, from the Barone di Villagrande's Nicolosi family, who had made wine for centuries here and essentially wrote the rules for the Etna wine appellation in 1968, to Benanti in the 1980s, all the way up to today.

"For me it is very important to be open. Etna is open. A lot of people brought value here coming from the outside," he said. He seemed defensive—surely from the resistance he had encountered from some quarters. "Angelo can bring something else. He can put a light on Etna."

Not everyone accepted this beatified image of Angelo shining a light on the mountain. Alberto's hopeful, cosmopolitan reasoning fell apart in the proud hearts of many fellow Sicilians who seem to carry the island's history of conquest inside them with resignation and shame.

In an oft-quoted passage of *The Leopard*, the protagonist, Don Fabrizio, the Prince of Salina (played by Burt Lancaster in Visconti's 1963 film version), reflects at a time when Sicily is being absorbed into a united Italy, "For over twenty-five centuries, we've been bearing the weight of superb and heterogeneous civilizations, all from outside, none made by ourselves, none that we could call our own."

Salvo Foti represented a one-man viticultural resistance to the idea of outsiders calling the shots. He is a Catania native whose edge may be due to the fact that his parents left him to be reared by his contadini grandparents on the mountain, while they went off to join Sicily's professional diaspora in northern Europe. As a youth he studied enology in Catania, and in the 1980s his ideas were bankrolled by Benanti, for whom he created Pietramarina: Etna's great white, which tasted like a glass of volcanic minerals, flowers, and fruit licked by the sea and that only got better with long aging of ten or twenty years. His I Vigneri wine company and consultancy proudly employed "thirty indigenous workers," local men who use only traditional methods starting with alberello vines tutored to chestnut posts. Anything else he viewed as a shortcut, flimflam, heresy—an affront to the mountain itself.

For as long as I've known him, Salvo has been fueled by a resentment of non-Sicilians who spoke of "discovering" Etna. After all, he had been toiling here years before, when the mountain seemed his alone. Though he too has made wine for Etna stranieri—notably, for more than a decade, for the British pop star Mick Hucknall of Simply Red—Salvo's team did all the work his way. Which, he believed, was the only way on Etna. Despite European Union sanitary standards banning the use of some ancestral methods in the production of commercial wines (or perhaps because of them), Salvo defiantly and openly used an old, restored lava-stone palmento to make an "illegal" rustic red. His message was clear: He was a proud Sicilian following a higher law of island tradition.

I met Salvo one gray morning at the bar in front of the church in Milo, the center of Etna's white wine making on the eastern face above the Ionian. From there we walked up to Salvo's farm, A Caselle. At fifty-six Salvo seemed to have mellowed—perhaps due to his own success and the fact that his two sons, aged twenty-three and nineteen, had settled down to work with him. In 2015 Salvo sold his family's house and vineyards to buy this old farm, and he continued to plant up the hillside.

"Everybody wants to come to Etna and say, 'Etna sono Io' [I am Etna]." He spoke in a tone that was ironic but resigned. Salvo's hair and beard had turned a silvery white, and his jeans and sweatshirt hung loose on his skinny frame. "It is all egotism. People arrive and say absurd things. It's a moment of . . ." Salvo stopped himself, his teeth showing through the tight line of a half-smile. He held his right forearm upright and twirled his hand and fingers in the air and said, ". . . va bene." I interpreted this to mean "bullshit." He had more to say that was fighting to get out.

"I don't want to go to the Langhe to make Barolo," he blurted, a direct reference to Gaja. "Why does Barolo want to come here to make Etna?"

Milo is known for producing some of the best Carricante whites on Sicily, with piercing length and energy, aromas and flavors that have been likened to spring lilacs and autumnal apples, and the dryness of crushed stone. A Caselle is Foti's Carricante laboratory, with small parcels meticulously worked. For Salvo, alberello vines not only provide 360 degrees of shade from the sun and open ventilation in the wind, but they are also a potent natural and social symbol.

"Alberello has to be cared for vine by vine, not from an air-conditioned tractor. It is the only system here that is in balance." He bent down, pinched a few leaves and small purple flowers from a wild *nepitella* (calamint) plant, and brought them to his nose. "The only problem is that it can't be mechanized. Every hectare takes fourteen hundred man hours per year."

Salvo's I Vigneri team is composed of men from families who have been cultivating vines on Etna for generations. It is a seductive aspect of Etna that vineyards on the eastern slopes are often tended by workers who grew up on the eastern slopes, and that the north face is worked by locals who've known only those vineyards. In a world in constant flux, it gives the place a soulful sense of gravity and continuity. It is also a flattened social structure with labor treated with dignity, not as a commodity. Yet, at times, I wondered if Foti's charming provincialism veered into darker, closed-minded territory.

"The biggest problem is not cultivating the vines, but cultivating the people," Salvo said. "You can't have Romanians or Polish people work in alberello because they don't have this experience. The territory is made by people who live this experience, who cultivate, who work in it." We walked to the edge of the vineyard and looked back over it. "My grandfather used to say, 'It's not your vineyard, it is your sons'." The more Salvo spoke, the more I realized he wasn't a run-of-the-mill xenophobe, but rather the champion of a romantic, imaginary world that extended over these 460 square miles of Etna.

We crossed a high road and entered another vineyard of more than seven acres that Salvo had planted as part of a joint venture with the California venture-capitalist-cum-wine-producer Kevin

Harvey of coastal California's Rhys Vineyard. The natural slope was gentle, with long and wide terraces filled with volcanic gravel and dust that went from red to black in color. Foti picked up a handful of the earth and nodded to the upper slopes of Etna, currently shrouded in low cloud. "It's sky soil," he said. Tens of thousands of chestnut vine tutors followed the hillside that slanted toward Milo, and, behind it, a thin line of the Ionian.

Harvey had been sniffing around Etna for some years by the time he met Foti. After the men became partners in their Etna wine label, Aeris, Salvo once followed him out to the Santa Cruz Mountains, where he was shocked by the separation between patron and workers. "When I went to California, the workers were all Mexican. They didn't greet the owner, and the owner didn't greet the workers." Foti hung his head and shook it as he related this.

Perhaps forgetting I was American, he continued and offered up a piece of what was to him a piece of truly startling evidence.

"They don't even eat together," he said with a grin of sad wonder. "It's another system."

On the east side of Etna is another hardheaded Sicilian contradiction. His name is Cirino Alfredo Biondi. Ciro is also a man of the world, moving as comfortably in his skin in London or New York as he does in his hometown of Trecastagni.

The Biondi family has been growing grapes and making wine on the east side for generations. They began exporting wines to the United States in the early twentieth century, when Ciro's great-uncle, Salvatore, formed half of the Biondi & Lanzafame wine *négociant*. A hundred years later, when looking through some old letters in the winery, Ciro discovered that Biondi and Lanzafame were not only business partners, but also lovers. Following the death of Ciro's grandfather in 1960, wine production stopped. Ciro's father found a government clerical job in Catania and sold off their grapes.

In 1999 Ciro was a midcareer architect, working mornings, as he still does, for the local branch of Italy's emergency services corps, the

Protezione Civile. He began to restore family vineyards, partnering
with a childhood friend whose family also had Etna vineyards. "My
father said, 'What are you going to do with all these grapes?'" Ciro
recalled. For a decade he used Salvo Foti as a winemaker, then, for
a few years, the young Piedmontese enologist Cristiano Garella.
Finally, he took charge of the winemaking with his nephew and
estate manager Manfredi.

By 2012 the company's finances were in disarray. The partners
stopped talking, and Ciro decided to split and form a new company
with his British wife, Stephanie Pollock. But first he had to get
back about two thousand gallons of his wine sitting unattended in
the winery. The wine in question was barrels of the first two vintages—2010 and 2011, of a red single-vineyard cru from a Biondi
family ancestral vineyard called Cisterna Fuori. In a furtive operation at four in the morning, Manfredi snuck into the winery with
a spare key he still had and loaded up his truck.

Ciro and Stef lived in a modest apartment in Trecastagni and aged
their wines in the cramped, dusty cellars long used by the Biondis in
their old palazzo in town, producing about twenty-seven thousand
bottles of red and white wine a year. But the center of their world
was Cisterna Fuori—their five stunning acres of vertical vineyard
terraces planted with Nerello Mascalese and Nerello Cappuccio,
rising to the edge of an extinct crater and facing the big blue of the
Ionian. The rest of Ciro's modern-day fief—rented or purchased
from family members—is no more than a five-minute walk up
the road. All the vineyards are kept like a grandfather's meticulous
garden in alberello format with chestnut tutors. Many plots never
succumbed to phylloxera and have continued to flourish without
American rootstock.

Below Cisterna Fuori, near the two-lane road, was the Biondi
"winery," which is really no larger than a carport with some steel
tanks and a pneumatic press. It was attached to an old red two-
story palmento that had been gnawed by time right down to the
very stones. Up one charmingly decrepit external staircase was a

small apartment, in the kitchen of which the Biondis spent more and more time.

I stopped by Cisterna Fuori one evening and found Ciro with his pair of young bull mastiffs, the barely adult Arthur and the puppy Elsa. At fifty-eight Ciro was built as solidly as his dogs and stood with excellent posture. As long as I'd known him, the crown of his head had been shaved, and now he also sported a white Hemingway beard emphasized by thick black-rimmed glasses. As we walked up through the Cisterna Fuori, punctuated with the occasional cherry, pear, or fig tree, he pointed out some small neglected strips of land at the edges. There was one tiny, overgrown plot at the base he was planning to buy from his cousin, and another from his sister.

At the northern edge of the vineyard a narrow blacktop road climbed the hillside, across it a small parallel plot of neglected-looking cordon-trained vines. We walked through a tear in the chain link and made our way to the back of the vineyard, where there was an abandoned stone storage shed. Ciro explained that he was planning to buy this plot from yet another cousin. He looked around in the evening light, which had begun to leach all color from the landscape. Suddenly he froze, crouching in the vines and motioning for me to do the same.

"I am trying to hide from the other neighbor," Ciro whispered. "I don't want him to know I am buying here until we close."

A hundred yards above us, a man walked toward his truck. In the Trecastagni countryside, you could hear everything: the footsteps in the beaten gravel, the opening of the car door, the diesel engine coughing as it awoke, the shifting of the gears, and the tires rolling downhill toward a point near us. I understood the secrecy. Ciro didn't want anyone nosing around in his business and doing or saying anything that would undermine his sales contract, which in Italy in general was bound to move slowly but in Sicily in particular could take an eternity.

As we waited for the truck to pass, I looked at Ciro. He wasn't easy to conceal. With his light blue cotton shirt, faded red slacks, and shiny skull, he looked like a coastal lighthouse. The truck stopped in the road about fifty yards away.

"Buonasera, Ciro!" the driver called out.

"Oh well." Ciro shrugged and stood. He walked toward the truck, calling out, "Buonasera, Signor Torrisi!"

At hearing Ciro's call, his dogs, who were roaming the other end of the plot, bounded straight for him. "No, no!" he cried, but Arthur, the adolescent mastiff built like a small horse, ignored his master and jumped up on him in a spray of volcanic dust.

As we walked back down to the old palmento along a dirt track rutted by truck tires, Ciro reflected on a question an American winemaker had recently asked him: "If you had to make wine somewhere else where would it be?"

"That is an interesting question," Ciro said slowly. "I never thought about it before, so when he asked, I thought about the question for a while. And then I realized the answer. The answer is, nowhere else because I am not making wine. I am not making wine," he repeated with an emphatic shake of his head as he splayed his hands outward and hunched up his shoulders. "I am keeping the land. Wine is just a byproduct."

Before dinner we drank a bottle of Ciro's easygoing Outis white. Outis, Greek for "no one," was a way of humbly labeling his base wines with a reference to Odysseus's encounter with the Cyclops Polyphemus in his cave (located by other period scribes as on Mount Etna). Ciro prepared fava beans and readied a tiny grill on the balcony for *polpette* (seasoned meatballs) wrapped in lemon leaves. Eventually Stephanie arrived from her part-time English teaching job, and soon after came the lawyer Piero Portales, a large man about Ciro's age with a big smile and shaggy hair, along with his young winemaker, Giulio Castorina. Portales bore gifts in the form of a large wedge of local pecorino cheese and what looked to be a commercial tin of tiny anchovies in oil.

As owner of Masseria Setteporte, Portales was the man who had sold part of his vineyards and land to Gaja and Graci. Portale's father founded the farm in 1968, selling grapes and bulk wine. When Portales took over in 2002, he began by shipping grapes to his friend Michele Satta in Tuscany's Bolgheri and later produced his wine on Etna's north face at Marco De Grazia's Terre Nere winery. In 2014 he began vinifying on site in a large open shed on a shoestring budget. Portales's two sons ran a restaurant in Catania and weren't interested in winemaking, so Portales sold off much of his land and kept the oldest alberello vineyards for himself.

We sat at the wood table for hours talking, eating, and drinking. Then drinking some more. We spooned the sweet and salty anchovies on the polpette, which had picked up the scent of citrus oil—a collision of Sicilian flavors that called for seconds and thirds. We drank a couple of vintages of Cisterna Fuori, an exuberant, earthy blend of fruit and spice and a touch of minerals smuggled out of the underworld. Portales told stories about the sale to Gaja, about how Alberto, his longtime friend, had hidden the partnership until the end. Portales only learned of Gaja's identity from a local reporter. The reason for the discretion was obvious: Gaja didn't want his name and reputation getting in the way. Alberto had sworn his silence. It was business. But the maneuvering had obviously stung Portales. In Sicily there are more important things than business, and the affair had wounded his pride and left him feeling something like a cuckold.

After dinner Ciro opened a magnum of Portales's 2008 red wine clumsily labeled with an antique map of Sicily and the generic name Nerello Mascalese. It was strong and slightly cloudy, with a touch of vinegary volatile acid, but it was delicious. With each glass it grew even more so. It took us until well past midnight, but we drained the bottle. I tried to imagine it with a beautiful label and Gaja's name on it. Portales was no marketer.

"The problem is that we are in Sicily," Ciro said. "And we always have to have someone come from the North or outside to tell us we are doing a good job."

I'd heard it often, many times from Ciro himself. What is it about such a storied island that has left it so fragile?

We walked out into the first hours of morning, down the narrow steps of the palmento. Luckily I was traveling on foot to a small motor-court hotel down the road. A few steps away from the winery, there was a drop in the terrain and the grove of eucalyptus. In the middle of it, under the moonlight, was a pile of construction debris and the husk of an old rusted-out Fiat wagon that had been overtaken by vegetation. Ciro explained his plans for excavating a new winery on that spot. I'd heard him talk about it for what seemed like years. "You will enter into a glass box, and there will be a tasting room," he said, sketching out the design in the air with his hands. "And inside the tasting room, you will see into the winery."

I looked at the eucalyptus trees and the old, rusted car. Then I looked at the old palmento behind us, at the gaping wall cracks and the PVC tube that brought electricity through a hole in the wall that looked like it had been made with the punch of a fist—at the pair of balconies above made of flaking cement and rusted iron and looking like they might give up at any moment.

"Anyway, I have to have a dream," Ciro said and laughed.

I wondered whether the winery would ever be built and what it would be like. Yet, in that moment, it didn't matter. Ciro's ambitions—keeping the land and making wine with another slice of vineyard here and there, and perhaps a cellar he would draw himself—all seemed so close. Cirino Alfredo Biondi, perhaps better than anyone I'd met on Etna, seemed to have mastered his life— and, just as important, the South's gift of time.

10. Alberto Aiello Graci.

11. Frank Cornelissen.

12. Salvo Foti.

13. Ciro Biondi.

6 *The Volcanoes of Vulture*

Nothing much happens in Barile. After the sun reaches its daily zenith, the three thousand denizens of this town at the instep of the Italian boot disappear from sight as if in a southern slumber. The streets are left to roaming cats and lounging dogs. There wouldn't be a reason to pass through here if Barile didn't drape halfway up the eastern flanks of one of Italy's most compelling natural wonders: the dormant volcano Monte Vulture, which, from certain angles, appears to rise up from Basilicata's plains like the silhouette of a vulture in flight. Its inner core is full of life, having collapsed tens of thousands of years ago into a geological sinkhole, or caldera, filled by the green Valle dei Grigi and a pair of vast and deep spring-fed lakes.

Barile's dominant group of settlers, as in most towns of Vulture, arrived about five hundred years ago with a wave of Christian Albanian refugees fleeing the Muslim Ottoman occupation of their homeland. In addition to taking up cultivation on these fertile, dark soils, these Arbëreshë settlers dug a honeycomb network of *sassi* (cave dwellings) in the volcanic tuff stone. The troglodyte societies of Basilicata are now famous because of the three-thousand-year-old city of Matera, dug into a river canyon about sixty miles southeast of Barile, but they were hidden from the rest of the world until the relatively recent days after World War II. The man who brought them to light was the antifascist doctor and writer Carlo Levi, who was exiled by Mussolini in the 1930s to Basilicata and observed the wretched poverty, lack of sanitation, pestilence, and lawlessness of a people guided by a murky fusion of Christianity with primitive superstitions. In his 1945 book *Christ Stopped at Eboli*, he likened Matera's caves to Dante's *Inferno*. The resulting scandal created programs in the 1950s to resettle Basilicata's cave dwellers in modern apartment blocks and houses. When the Italian poet and filmmaker Pier Paolo Pasolini filmed his *Gospel According to Saint Matthew* in the early 1960s, he used Barile's sassi as a setting for ancient Bethlehem, and, to portray Palestine, he chose Matera, which was also used forty years later in Mel Gibson's *The Passion of the Christ*.

While Matera's sassi have seen a touristic renewal as a UNESCO's World Heritage Site and a new generation of boutique inns and restaurants and bars, Barile's caves have remained abandoned and overgrown, or used in the making and storing of the area's best-known product: its potent Aglianico del Vulture red wine from its layered volcanic soils. Surrounded by orderly olive groves, wheat fields, vineyards, and grazing lands, Barile's population has been, like that of most of Basilicata, in steady decline for nearly seven decades—this despite modern efforts to keep new generations here, like the pair of factories in nearby Melfi that make Fiat cars and Barilla pasta.

"Dynamic" is not a word that had been used much for either Barile or Aglianico del Vulture, which never quite achieved its hyped potential as Italy's *next* great wine terroir. Then came Elena Fucci. At thirty-seven she carried herself with a theatrical charisma that, by 2018, had put her at the center of a new, informal group of eight young, smart, and hip organic producers—called Generazione Vulture—demanding attention in the southern wine wilderness. The key was in using Vulture's altitude and slopes to make wines with balance and elegance. Italian critics were already primed and ready for the prophesized coming of great Vulture wines. A few had already hopefully christened the area the "Barolo of the South."

I arrived in Barile on a Saturday afternoon in June and met Elena and her husband, Andrea Manzani, a Florentine engineer who was drawn south by love, giving up his old life for wine and Elena, who, after a morning working in her winery, wore bright-red lipstick and large bauble earrings, her dark eyes encircled with kohl. With her black Cleopatra bangs, green sneakers, and Gucci purse, she was a gypsy-like force of nature. A tiny woman, she seemed to nearly leap up in the air as she walked.

Andrea was her foil: ambling, laconic, and casually assembled, with rumpled jeans and a winery polo stretched across his broad, well-fed frame. When he spoke—at about half the speed of his wife—a wry grin crossed his wide-open, bearded face. "I am the slave of Elena Fucci," he said, introducing himself and holding up his wrists as if they were manacled. Then he shifted from Italian to English and added, "Human rights, goodbye."

Andrea drove us in his truck up through the heights of Vulture at thirteen hundred meters and then deep down into its caldera, its lakes lined with deep-green forests. Here we visited the white medieval Abbazia di San Michele Arcangelo, constructed above its ancient grotto church carved into a lakeside cliff. The landscape was as pristine as it was deserted, and that seemed to explain the conundrum of Vulture in a world where wine was linked to images. If Etna were a postcard, Vulture was a snapshot never developed.

The next morning I arrived at Cantina Fucci from a tight asphalt road, past the town's artificial-turf soccer stadium at the eastern edge of Barile. Here at about six hundred meters in altitude was a four-hundred-year-old bright-ochre farmhouse where Elena had been reared with her two younger sisters and where she and Andrea now lived. Attached to the house was a small, modern, and utilitarian winery built with recycled wood and concrete. The world of Fucci looked over Contrada Solagna del Titolo, a tidy patchwork of Aglianico vineyards and olive groves. The Fucci family worked about fifteen acres of vines that would be a picture of an uninterrupted rolling landscape were it not for the two-lane highway—the infrequently traveled Strada Statale 658 that bisects the contrada and its vineyards before disappearing into a tunnel on its way to the regional capital, Potenza. Down a slope and across the highway was the other half of Contrada Titolo and the modern headquarters of Paternoster, Vulture's near-century-old legendary winery that was now owned, to the indignation of some locals, by northerners from the Veneto.

Elena, with Andrea in tow, appeared with her hair in braids and wearing a straw cowboy hat and an open denim shirt with a white T-shirt silk screened with a very large, very red pair of lips. We walked down a dirt road through the nearest vineyards and into a plot of about 150 vines, each supported by a tepee made from three cane shoots. It was a style of cultivation I'd never seen before, but I could see it provided shade and ventilation for fruit, like Sicily's alberello. The system, called *a capanno*, is almost extinct but traditional to Albanian-Italian Arbëreshë growers. The vines resembled small, vigorous trees with leaves as large as pumpkin foliage and displayed their tiny green bunches of Aglianico. At the back of the vineyard was an old man, hunched and barely five feet tall, who walked toward us, the picture of determination in his baggy green work pants, sagging vest, and tall rubber boots. He moved slowly, holding himself upright with an aluminum cane. He was wearing dark-rimmed glasses, the top of his head shaved to a stubble, and his ears stuck out like a pair of side-view mirrors.

Elena called out to him, and when he arrived she threw her arms around him, introducing him as her ninety-three-year-old grandfather, Generoso, who had been tending the vineyard since dawn. After a few minutes speaking with his granddaughter in dialect, Generoso turned and walked back to the winery, where Elena's dad, Salvatore, would drive him the half-mile to his apartment in town.

The Fucci were descended from Arbëreshë settlers and for centuries had been *mezzadria* sharecroppers here in Titolo. In the 1950s Generoso, dreaming of a better life, left his family here to make his fortune in Venezuela. For over a decade, he worked as a gardener and ran a coffee and lunch cart in Caracas offices, saving enough to return to Barile in 1964 and buy the land his family had toiled over. Generoso sold his Aglianico harvest to wine négociants, who shipped the grapes by train to northern regions, where they were used to fortify thinner, weaker wines of the day. He also insisted his son and daughter become educated at university, and both became schoolteachers.

"My grandfather didn't want his children to have the same life of sacrifice," Elena said, as we walked farther south, past cherry, fig, apricot, and pear trees and through rows of cordon-trained vine-yards. Elena had grown up on the farm, imagining herself leading a cosmopolitan life somewhere north of here. In 2000, when Elena finished high school and Generoso turned seventy-five, the family discussed selling out.

"I said, 'Yes, sell, sell. I will go to the university and I won't come back; there is no one and nothing here,'" she recalled. Then her father found a prospective buyer for the farm, and Elena looked into her future and blinked. "I said, 'Papà do you have to sell the house too?'" She remembered harvests in her childhood, playing in the vines, eating apricots, her mother preparing eggplant from the garden. "I was born here. I understood that I was tied to this place. I realized I would lose everything—that I would have nothing."

So she changed her life. She enrolled in enology and viticultural school in Pisa and immediately began experimenting with twelve hundred bottles of a wine simply named after the place, Titolo. In her second vintage, Titolo was awarded the coveted "three glasses" by Italy's ubiquitous Gambero Rosso wine guide—a rare honor for both Basilicata and a novice. By 2004 Elena had enough confidence to multiply her winemaking tenfold, and by the end of the decade, she had borrowed money from her parents to begin building her new winery with a simple business plan: "One grape. One wine. Doing it well."

In 2011 her life took another turn when she was pouring her Titolo in a pan-Italian wine fair in Northern Italy and Andrea stopped by her booth. At the time he was a construction engineer living in Modena and working on a project refurbishing the railway. He took

Elena's business card, and a long, long courtship began. "He wrote to me on Facebook for six months." She laughed. "I didn't respond."

Andrea persisted, and Elena finally answered. In September 2011 Andrea traveled south for the wedding of a friend in Rionero, less than three miles from Barile. He bought a dozen red roses and phoned Elena to say he was in town. "I said, 'I am not here. I am in Rimini at the beach,'" she recalled, her dark lashes fluttering. "And he took his car and the roses and came to Rimini—six hundred kilometers [360 miles] in a day!"

For Andrea the lifestyle of a tractor driver, winery hand, and export manager at Elena Fucci was a big change from his previous city life, but it seemed to be one that suited him well. When I asked him to describe life in Barile, he waited until Elena was out of earshot and whispered about his fellow Barilesi: "They eat. They sleep. They eat. They sleep."

Elena had strut ahead to a cut in the hillside that showed the different strata of Vulture soils—a geological lasagna of lava stone, pebbles, and ash. As we stood there, a tiny two-door Fiat drove up, and out stepped Elena's father, Salvatore, a smallish bear of a man, who insisted we all go for a ride through the vineyards. We squeezed in, and Salvatore crossed over the highway tunnel and into another part of Titolo. As the car bumped down a skinny vine row, the shocks strained, my guts churned, and I squeezed the handle above the passenger door to keep my head from bouncing against the roof.

Salvatore, a retired high school mechanics teacher, was sixty-five and very proud of his daughter. But he wanted to give some perspective, to impress on me the years of toil the family had spent here. "After the war, a worker was paid one liter of olive oil per day," he told me. "In the 1960s there was a big emigration, and all the vineyards were abandoned. It wasn't always like this with everybody swirling the wine and smelling." With his free hand, he held the stem of an imaginary wineglass that he twirled in front of his nose. At the same time, he gunned the tinny engine up a rutted incline, and the car shuddered. "People here sold the grapes, and they starved."

Elena, unfazed by her father's driving, leaned forward and put her head between the front seats. She explained that the wines she had tasted here when she began were "molto old style," meaning they were throat-burning rustic, tannic, and bitter, with a good dollop of residual sweetness to make them more palatable. "Aglianico needs to be ripe," Elena said. "If it's too green, the tannins are so strong, you risk wasting all your work."

After that, the "molto soft" touch that she and her like-minded pals of Generazione Vulture deployed in the winery resulted in wines that were fresher, less aggressive, and more approachable when young. As Barolo had done decades earlier, she and her compatriots dreamed of advancing the idea of cru—that wines from a specific place, altitude, and soil could give different, noteworthy, and recognizable results in wine. "We think it's a strength to explain the differences," Elena said. "The old generation saw differences as a problem. They wanted everything to be the same."

Late that morning I tasted different vintages of her Titolo, including an experiment in clay amphora and her occasionally produced longer-aged Riserva. Coming from Barile's higher altitude and its particular soils gave her wines more fresh acidity and minerality. I have drunk Titolo often, and there is always a lot going on in the glass with its collision of bold fruit and wild spice, depth and lightness.

"It's important for me when you taste our wines to feel the volcano," she said.

Volcanic wines are trendy and hyped with, for some, an almost magical appeal—as if the volcanic ash and broken-down lava in soils could translate themselves into a powerful, and even empowering, nectar. On this point I am agnostic. Italy has lots of volcanic origin soils that produce wines varying from spectacular to spectacularly awful. But to feel the volcano in a wine? It's hard not to feel it once you've stood face-to-face with her.

At midday Elena, Andrea, and I got in Andrea's truck and headed south to join Barile's other volcano. Viviana Malafarina was Elena's close friend, another dynamo but with a cooler, more cerebral style. She was a statuesque Genoa native who, with no formal wine training, had managed to take the lead in winemaking at Basilisco, the local outpost of Campania's deep-pocketed Feudi di San Gregorio winery.

We stopped at a small clearing above Basilisco's oldest vineyard, appropriately named Storico, about five acres of mostly ungrafted eighty-five-year-old Aglianico vines trained a capanno. Beyond the vineyard a rolling, open landscape of wooded areas, plowed fields, and neatly ordered stands of olive trees stretched for five miles to the small, ancient cliff-top town of Ripacandida and its nearby modern windmills, which reached into a blue sky dotted with meringue-like clouds.

Viviana, in dark braids and a flowing white blouse and jeans, had set a linen tablecloth and place settings on a weathered wooden picnic table shaded by a white rectangle of sailcloth tethered to the branches of holm oak and olive trees. She'd laid out helpings of fresh mozzarella, ricotta, and tomatoes and lit a wood fire in a primitive drystone barbecue pit. Elena brought a basket of red-skinned garden apricots, a bottle of her fruity and herbaceous olive oil, and a bowl of her father's *cruschi*, Basilicata's mild and nutty-flavored Senise peppers that are sun-dried and then fried in olive oil. While cruschi are typically crushed and used as a seasoning, I couldn't get enough of them in their whole, crunchy glory, eaten like chips with a glass of wine. In this case the wine was Basilisco's sole white, called Sophia, a restrained, mildly floral-scented Fiano.

Andrea set lamb chops and sausage on an iron grill over the embers and poked and turned them in a heady cloud of fat and woodsmoke until they were browned. A German sedan parked on the dirt road and Feudi di San Gregorio's young president, Antonio Capaldo, who had driven down from Rome, stepped out of it. I had known Antonio for some years. More than three decades earlier, his family had established Feudi as an investment in their native Irpinia following the earthquake of 1980. Feudi had grown into something more than a modern success. It was arty and edgy, with just the right vibe of the moment. A champion of organic agriculture, Feudi was based in a technically perfect, ecofriendly winery designed by the Japanese architect Hikaru Mori and her Italian husband, Maurizio Zito, and topped by a glass-and-steel Michelin-starred restaurant.

Under Antonio and his codirector, the Friulian agronomist Pierpaolo Sirch, Feudi made wines from mass-market to boutique, expanded across Italy to Tuscany and Puglia, and brought together unlikely partnerships. He'd financed the Milan sommelier-turned-winemaker Federico Graziani to make wine with Salvo Foti on Etna, including a crazy white blend of German, French, and Italian varieties from the mountain's highest-altitude vineyard. And, at Feudi's home winery, he'd created a line of Champagne-method sparklers by pairing Southern Italy's enological everywhere man Riccardo Cotarella with Champagne's cult grower-producer Anselme Selosse.

At forty-one Antonio had a quick, toothy smile, a light beard, and a slightly uncared-for look in his rumpled polo and khakis. He still carried himself with a trace of the swagger of his former life, studying at the London School of Economics followed by years as an international strategic planner for McKinsey & Company, where he was named partner in his early thirties and then abruptly quit. In 2009 Antonio astonished his high-flying colleagues when he told them he was returning to the vineyards of Southern Italy. Now, after nearly a decade of working in wine, Antonio had been humbled by another reality in which disruption didn't come from competitors and markets as much as from the whims of nature. It was fitting, somehow, that Viviana—whip-smart, intuitive, curious, and assertive, yet knowing nothing whatsoever about Basilicata or winemaking—would disrupt Basilisco, giving the region what Antonio calls "a needed external shock."

Over the picnic lunch, Antonio recounted how Feudi arrived here in 2001, when his uncle bought about twenty-five vineyard acres in Barile to see how the local Aglianico compared with the Aglianco-based Taurasi wines from Irpinia. "There was no particular focus," he said. "It was just to show different places for Aglianico." At the end of that decade, when he took the reins of Feudi along with Sirch, the men decided to probe deeper into the region and bought Basilisco, a twenty-year-old company housed in an impressive historic villa at the southern edge of Barile, along with more vineyards.

Like many southern entrepreneurs of his generation, Antonio's mind was ever focused on the future and its opportunities, but his heart was rooted in the lore of a southern past. When an idea appealed to both, it grabbed him. In Vulture he sensed an underappreciated chance in an Italy mostly unspoiled by modernity. Over time he even grew to prefer Vulture's Aglianico: "It's possibly more intriguing than in Irpinia, I am afraid to say."

About a year after Antonio took over at Feudi, Viviana blew through the door by serendipity. From girlhood Viviana had a knack for foreign languages, and, at university, she specialized in Slavic tongues. But her career got off to a dreary start, teaching Italian language and history in the long, subzero winters of Ukraine. One summer she discovered the yacht world of the Mediterranean, where her languages came in handy as a chef, sailor, and stewardess and where she could earn in a month what she had previously earned in a year. She then worked as a guide on luxury river-barge cruises in France, absorbing the basics of wine by leading tours to French vineyards and wineries. In 2010 she was working at the desk of a luxury hotel in Sicily. There was a boyfriend—an aspiring chef—who had signed on to intern at Feudi. She visited him there and met Antonio, who offered her a job answering phones. Impressed by her smarts and initiative, he soon proposed that she oversee the newly assembled Basilisco.

"We thought she would coordinate the welcoming efforts and the office," Antonio said as our dishes were cleared, and we started on the apricots. "We didn't expect her to turn into a winemaker and agronomist." He also had not expected to find in Viviana an intellectual equal with a more precise idea of Vulture wine. And now that he had, it seemed, he'd surrendered: "After two years, she didn't listen to us. She was making the wine."

We packed up the remains of lunch, took down the shading tarp, and put out the fire. Elena and Andrea went on their way. Antonio, Viviana, and I took a walk through the Storico vineyard, where the vines, with corkscrewed trunks and seemingly mellowed vigor, followed the contours of the hillside, punctuated every fifty paces with the tangled manes of southern Ogliarola olive trees.

"The vineyard is like an open-air museum of viticulture in the South of Italy," Viviana proclaimed, loosely corralling vine shoots that had strayed out of their tall a capanno nests. "Every plant is an individual, and there are no clones. It doesn't make the most pleasant drinking wine, but it is the most unique. It's like an eighty-year-old person—it can be rough and grumpy, but with time, it tells its story. In one plant you may have only two bunches of grapes, but the quality justifies it."

One or two bunches per vine meant yields were as low as a mere 10 percent of what was allowed in Aglianico del Vulture. From a business point of view, it was far from ideal.

"I suspected that," Antonio said, wincing.

Viviana lived alone in Basilisco's centuries-old palazzo at the edge of Barile, with its green-and-gold panorama that rolled on forever up the Italian boot. In late spring sunsets seen from this vantage turned a fiery red. Basilisco's founders in the 1990s used the palazzo as a boutique hotel and restaurant, but now, except for the occasional visiting colleague, Viviana had it all to herself.

She kept the keys to Basilisco—dozens of all shapes, sizes, and eras—on a long belt-like chain. She found the right key to open an iron gate that led onto a piazza with a line of eight archways rimmed with elaborately sculpted stone and set into the hillside. Each led to a section of ancient caves that had been converted for winemaking.

"I was left here with too much time alone," she said, walking toward one of the archways. "I was bored."

Viviana learned how to cultivate vines by watching and working alongside Sirch in the vineyards. In the winery she learned from a seventy-year-old cellar master along with Basilisco's Tuscan winemaker Lorenzo Landi, who was soon replaced by the Bordeaux professor and wine consultant Denis Dubourdieu, until his death in 2016.

"I didn't know anything, but I had one varietal and great teachers and not a lot to do here," she explained. "So if you're curious, you watch, you taste, and then you feel like changing things."

She turned the key to the heavy wood door that led us into a tall, cathedral-like cellar held up by brick arches set into the rock, and we walked down a set of stairs. I could feel the natural cool and damp of the cave, where more than a dozen large steel tanks were squeezed onto a floor of black lava-stone tiles. Viviana found some glasses and wanted to taste a sample from every tank in the place. They were incomplete wines, last season's white along with Aglianicos that had already made their one-year-plus tours in barrel and were waiting to be put in bottles, where they would soften for some more years. Through another doorway off the piazza was another, more intimate, rustic cellar of stacked Bordeaux barriques, gravel floors, and a series of low arches that led to a back chamber and the mother rock of the hillside.

"This was the cave that took me and made me want to stay," she said.

After Landi's departure, she began isolating vineyards, making wines from them separately, and aging them five years before release. "To me, it's a process that needed to be done—to understand what Vulture has, to listen more to the vineyard, the altitude, and the earth," she said. "I am a teacher, and to me the different soils are like a classroom of pupils. They are all different, and it would be stupid and blind to treat them all the same."

She found a wine thief and dipped it into the bunghole of a barrel, securing the wine in the tube by covering the air hole on the top with her thumb. Then, easing her thumb off the hole, she deposited the samples into our glasses. Again, she wanted to taste from every barrel, to show the nuances of fruit, flowers, herbs, and minerals from each plot of land to the next.

She had infused her winemaking with a colorful imagination that also assigned human personalities to her three crus: her Fontanelle was as simple and exuberant as a twenty-five-year-old guy, like her kid brother; Storico, the old a capanno vineyard we walked through earlier, was the musty grandfather; and Cruà, both strong and feminine, mixing floral aromas with tannic intensity, she asserted, "is me."

"Coming here as a foreigner, I was fed up to hear that Aglianico was wine you can chew and that you have to drink it while you eat a Brontosaurus," she said, walking to yet another barrel and removing its synthetic stopper with a rocking motion of her long fingers. "When I came here, the locals told me that Basilisco was an international wine, but that was because the winemaker, Landi, was not from here and was not oppressed by the local culture. For my first harvest, what I tasted in the vat was exciting: there was laurel, mint, and Mediterranean herbs." She filled our glasses again. "The more you work in a rough way, the more you lose that. By working gently, you preserve all the complexity and beauty."

When near every barrel had been tested, we walked out of the cave and into the summer-evening light. "What I love about Vulture," she said, "is that it is all to be done. It is yet to be figured out."

As I watched her, I wondered what could keep someone like Viviana—smart, attractive, and curious—living alone here at the edge of the world. But the more time I spent around Vulture, I realized that she and Elena and their group were on to something. Vulture wasn't chic like Etna. Gaja wasn't sniffing around here. In fact, Aglianico del Vulture was a Lilliputian appellation with thirty-odd producers in a seemingly insignificant region—Italy's second least-populated, ahead only of the alpine Val d'Aosta in the shadow of the northwest's Mont Blanc bordering Switzerland and France.

Yet with one grape and terroirs across more than a dozen towns to express it, Vulture felt like a frontier in more than one sense. Its poor, agrarian past had left what were its riches: a countryside that was varied, vast, and empty—an oversize canvas for those who wanted to project their dreams.

A great thing about Vulture's new-wave wine scene was that all of it could fit around one long table. When Generazione Vulture got together for a meal, it was often in an intimate medieval piazza in Lavello, which the young chef Savino di Noia had transformed into his own local-sourced gourmet world.

Savino, who was thirty-four and bubbling with creative ambition, had taken the family bar and pizzeria, with its long-abandoned wine cellar, and turned it into Antica Cantina Forentum. Here, on the Piazza Plebiscito, he cooked with his mom using ingredients grown in their garden or produced within a few miles. Other than his experiments with avant-garde presentations, including sushi-like rolls transformed with ingredients from the local larder, Savino stuck to a traditional playbook with time-intensive dishes: stuffed and fried zucchini flowers, braised rabbit, rolled veal braciole, and handmade pastas.

One evening I met Generazione Vulture here for dinner in a one-table room that had once been an underground cistern. Among the group was forty-year-old Luca Carbone, who, in 2005, with his sister, Sara, decided to sell the family's small chain of supermarkets to make wine in the family's vineyards. There was Michele Bisceglia, the thirty-one-year-old son of an affluent family, who had a Hollywood swagger and a pair of forearm tattoos—on his right inner arm was the logo of Bisceglia's top red wine, Gudarrà (which in local Lucano dialect means "to enjoy") and on his left 22/22. (In Southern Italian festival raffles, the number 22 is a symbol of "the crazy one"; a crazy-feeling Michel had gotten the tattoo on his first trip to Chicago when he was twenty-two.) And there was hyperactive Paolo La Torraca, thirty-four, the son of a contadino who ran his family's Madonna delle Grazie winery in Venosa and who was engaged to Elena Fucci's cousin, though he quickly turned evasive when his friends pressed him about an actual wedding date.

What struck me most about the group was the easy camaraderie among their disparate personalities. In a bigger, more connected place, there would be nothing to bind them, but out here, on the perimeter, they were practically family. And Savino was one of them. That evening everyone in the group brought a favorite wine from outside the area, and so we drank Pinot Nero from the Alto Adige, Fiano from Campania, and Merlot from the Maremma. There was a bottle of Giuseppe Rinaldi's Barolo, A Vita's Ciro, Tabarrini's Piantagrero, and Gaja's white Sauvignon Blanc Alteni di Brassica.

For some years I had journeyed through the cuisine of Italy's modern chefs, and I'd burned out on culinary tricks and sophistication. Who needed dishes that were served with preambles or deconstructed tomatoes or Italian foie gras when Nonna was in the kitchen? In fact, I ended up where I started—in love with the traditional combinations of common ingredients prepared without shortcuts. Maccarunar du Munacidd is a cornerstone of Basilicata's Lucano cuisine. Munacidd in Lucano dialect refers to a folkloric elfish figure animating the soul of a child who died before being baptized. Savino's version combined homemade thick spaghetti tossed in a sauce of pumpkin, tomatoes, and wild fennel sausage, sprinkled with sliced almonds and tangy aged sheep cacioricotta (a hybrid of classic cheese and whey-based ricotta) and topped with a pointy crusco resembling an elf's hat. With every bite you could feel the care put into the assembly of the dish. Over the course of a week, everywhere I went, I was fed the cuisine of someone's mamma or nonna, who generally remained out of sight, communicating to the world through works of southern soul food. And, in each winemaker and family, I found some deeper meaning in wine as a kind of hope. Aglianico had become a way to explore and be in the world.

Elisabetta Musto Carmelitano at thirty-seven looked like a rock 'n' roller from the last days of vinyl. She wore a black leather jacket and her phone's ringtone played the intro to Kim Carnes's hit "Bette Davis Eyes," recorded in Elisabetta's birth year. Elisabetta was a contadina from tiny Maschito, ten miles east of Barile, where she worked in her winery below the family house and where her neighbors were her parents, grandparents, aunts, and uncles.

She drove me from Barile through what on that morning were wet, muddy backroads, past the already harvested wheat and barley fields, carpets of wildflowers, stands of cane, and long-abandoned stone houses and churches. "I never wanted to work for someone else," Elisabetta said, flicking on her windshield wipers on to swat away the light rain.

After her schooling at *liceo*, she joined her father making wine they sold out of the winery by the liter to local families. They turned an old rabbit pen into a new winery, and Elisabetta took over in 2007, when her father got a job as a cook in a nearby hospital. Helped part-time by her younger brother, Luigi, who worked in the Melfi Fiat factory, she began putting her wine in bottles and looking out to the world as her market.

The sky turned black as we drove up to her vineyards outside Maschito, and she whispered instinctively, "Madonna, guarda questa roba! [Madonna, look at this stuff!]" As she drove she pointed out the color of the runoff of the different terroirs—white in chalky soils, red in iron-rich soils, and dark gray from volcanic ash. On the way to her family's oldest Aglianico vineyard—a tiny red-clay-and-sand plot called Pian Del Moro—she spoke about her heritage and how the vines had been planted by her grandfather. This quickly led to a topic that everyone here wanted to talk about yet had left them baffled: the sale of Paternoster just two years earlier to Tommasi, the Verona area Valpolicella and Amarone producer.

"Paternoster was a historic estate," she said, shaking her right hand, her small fingers gathered together like the petals of an artichoke. "How does someone arrive to sell it?" She took both hands off the wheel, pressed her flattened palms together as if in prayer, and shook them again. "I can never understand it."

As she pulled into Maschito's center, she stopped for a bent old man hobbling across the street with a walker. "You see, we are a town of young people!" she said and laughed. "Maschito in the 1950s had five thousand people. When I was little, there was two thousand five hundred. Now there is less than two thousand."

In a nook in the winery, a lunch table had been set by her grandmother, with grilled peppers, local pecorino cheese, and pasta tossed with a peasant sauce made from zucchini leaves and flowers sautéed with tomatoes. We were joined by three skinny, bearded young men: Elisabetta's brother, Luigi, and Andrea and Lorenzo Piccin, Tuscan natives who grew up on their family estate in Montefalco and now ran Grifalco nearby. We sampled all seven of her wines, which varied from a bottle-fermented white spumante to rosé to a series of Aglianicos—all of them had a wildness to them. Like Elisabetta herself they fell between youth and ageless rusticity.

"You know there are more Maschitani in Fresno, California, than there are here," she said of the local-born populace. "That is why Aglianico del Vulture is better known in America than Italy."

"In America," said Andrea, the younger of the Piccin brothers at twenty-seven, "people know where Basilicata is. In Italia—no!"

I empathized with the Piccin brothers and their wide-eyed sincerity and youthful convictions, which reminded me of my own son. Andrea, who lived half the year in Milan, focused on administration and sales; Lorenzo, who was married and lived part-time in Turin, made the wine. The pair grew up in Montepulciano, where their parents founded the Salcheto winery in the 1980s, which they sold before falling for Vulture and buying land here for their sons' futures. They were earnest young men—socially and ecologically aware, from a family steeped in organics. They fretted about their generation, Italy's faltering pension system, and its newly installed right-wing interior minister, who was turning away boats of desperate refugees. And, they proclaimed as a fact, "capitalism is dead."

When it came to wine, however, they brightened, enthralled with Aglianico and its near indestructibility in the cellar. "Aglianico is much easier than Sangiovese," Lorenzo said. "Sangiovese is a much more delicate grape—if you mess it up, forget it. With Aglianico, if you do something wrong, it's okay. It always has something more."

But the brothers' gloom again took over when they got to talking about the bulk of Vulture's thirty-odd producers in the appellation consortium, their overuse of barrel aging in carelessly chosen wood to make wines that were often as heavy and lifeless as lead.

"It's twenty years that Aglianico del Vulture has been about to become the Langhe of the South or the next Tuscany. And for twenty years, it's about to have a boom," Lorenzo said. "It's always about to be or about to become, but it never happens. The institutions in this area have been run by the same people for twenty, thirty years, by people sixty, seventy years old, with old ideas and old methods of communicating."

While Luigi ate with two-fisted gusto, shoveling with a fork and a piece of bread, the Piccins picked at their food with ascetic disinterest. "Mangia," Elisabetta instructed them, bringing around the bowl of pasta for a second tour, "Ragazzi mangiate!"

My last meal in Basilicata was at Elena Fucci's house, but, before I went, I stopped to meet her neighbor, Vito Paternoster at Paternoster. Vito's grandfather Anselmo Paternoster returned from his army service after World War I and began bottling Aglianico here in 1925. He was a négociant who selected grapes from local growers and made wine that—typical of the day, because of high sugar content and rustic methods—continued to fizz in the bottle and was labeled as spumante. Paternoster achieved mythic heights due largely to its success at something unheard of in the isolated and impoverished economy before World War II: exporting to the United States.

The Volcanoes of Vulture

Two generations later trouble arose between Anselmo's grand-sons. Vito was an autodidact who learned from his grandfather and father. His younger brother, Sergio, was a trained enologist, who came to join the family business in the 1980s but soon learned that there was not enough room for two Paternoster winemakers. Sergio struck out on his own, becoming a noted consultant in Basilicata and across Italy, eventually becoming winemaker for his daughter's small organic Barile wine label, Quarta Generazione.

There were years of strain in the family among the stakeholders of Paternoster, who included Vito, Sergio, and their three siblings. Finally, in 2016, at lunch outside of Verona, the Tommasis broached the idea to Vito of their buying a majority stake in Paternoster. After that papers and money moved quickly. For Tommasi it was a way to expand the footprint of their sprawling family farther south. For Vito it was a way out of a familial conflict.

Vito Paternoster is a gracious gentleman who had aged well to a fit sixty years. He had a tanned, serene face on that late spring day. We walked the vineyards outside Paternoster's sleek, modern winery, the twin arcs of a steel roof separated by a concave dip in the center designed to resemble Monte Vulture. He told me proudly that he still had a minority stake. In fact, he tried to convince me, nothing had changed. Nothing, he repeated. He was still here, after all, and his nephew Anselmo was the enologist. Paternoster's top wine, which we drank together, was still it's beautifully austere Don Anselmo.

"It's not a sale," he said. "It's a partnership. We needed to have a partner with a global communication presence. It is not a funeral," he added. He seemed tired of having to defend himself. "It is a rebirth."

In Elena and Andrea's small, modern white apartment in the familial house above the winery, Andrea poured glasses of a white sparkling Franciacorta for a midday aperitivo. Elena made her version of Munacidd macaroni. Joining us for lunch was Elena's dad, Salvatore, who wore a button-down shirt with rolled sleeves and came around and shaved cacioricotta on the top of each serving. But just as I was digging into Elena's delicious pasta—the last I would eat for some time after a week in Basilicata—I mentioned their neighbor.

"Paternoster was like a Ferrari in this region," said Andrea, hunched over his bowl as he stirred in the cheese with his fork. "And it has now become like a Fiat Cinquecento."

"It was a shame," Elena echoed. "It was something for the two brothers—Sergio and Vito—to work out between themselves, but that didn't happen."

Salvatore finished his first bite and put down his fork weightily. It was as if the mention of Paternoster had let loose demons in the room, and it was up to him to exorcise them.

"I was at Vinitaly in 2016 when I saw Tommasi in the Basilicata hall with Paternoster," Salvatore said softly. "And when I saw that, tears fell from my eyes." His face had turned red and his eyes were wet. Then his voice boomed. "To see two brothers fight like that and not find a solution, that hit me in the heart." Salvatore's voice cracked as he dramatically mimed a knife going into his chest. "They didn't fight over the money—you can always find money—but for odio [hate] between brothers."

In Basilicata Paternoster had become a cautionary tale of biblical proportion. The thought of the moral decline of his neighbor's house revved Salvatore's emotions and sent him off on a sweeping analysis of Basilicata, its agriculture and wines. "In fifteen years, the mentality in Basilicata has changed," he said. "In the 1960s, it was difficult for a contadino to find a wife. Who wanted to marry a contadino? Now it's a prized thing; a contadino is an entrepreneur, a contadino can talk to journalists and go to New York."

The images this conjured played in my mind. There had been change on both sides of the Atlantic. Indeed, now Southern Italian farmers could rub elbows over their wine with urban hipsters or billionaires. A man or woman who lived off the land in the twenty-first century was no longer a slave but something close to heroic.

"It's changed not from an economic standpoint but cultural," he went on. "If you think you will become rich from wine, that is always a mistake. This is the reason for the sacrifice." Salvatore drew a vertical line in the air. "That my daughter can go to Hong Kong or London. That Meryl Streep buys her wine in New York. This is the advantage of grapes." Salvatore's voice crescendoed as he spoke about Elena's education, enology in general, and the family terroir. "But what is the guarantee of her wine?" he asked, nearly shouting.

I was trying to formulate an answer when Salvatore responded for me.

"It is her face," he cried. "Her face is the wine. If she does something wrong, she destroys her reputation . . . but she wouldn't only hurt herself, but me, her grandparents and great-grandparents, and all our other ancestors who were not rich people but contadini who worked as slaves for no money."

"Slaves," he repeated.

I looked over at Elena, who was slowly nodding her agreement. Then I looked back at Salvatore, who took a breath and concluded, "She would destroy it all. And that is what quality means and what ethics means."

I had come to Basilicata to learn about a new generation of winemakers but came away with an understanding of something more—a sense of what family and place can mean in the South of Italy among the so-called peasant *terroni*. *La terra* is more than just something to be owned or cultivated. Here in the South, it is personal—a crucible of life and death, generations and patrimony, sweat and prayers. It is a complete sense of terroir that goes beyond soils, expositions, and climate.

"If Benetton or some big company comes here and buys a vineyard, they could make a technical wine that would please the sommeliers and the journalists," he said and pirouetted an imaginary glass above his head. "But it wouldn't have anything behind it. The earth," Salvatore concluded, "is a sacrifice."

There was an awkward silence as Salvatore seemed to deflate. Everyone had stopped eating for what was something akin to a moving invocation of grace.

"Papà," Elena said, interrupting the silence, "you're not eating— you're just talking. Mangia."

With that plea from his daughter, Salvatore picked up his fork and lustily stabbed his macaroni.

14. Elena Fucci.

15. Viviana Malafarina.

16. The Piccin brothers, Andrea (*left*) and Lorenzo.

7   *Gioia and Suffering*

The Puglian town of Gioia del Colle sits on the Murgia plateau in the center of the heel of the Italian boot, its narrow stone streets of whitewashed buildings radiating outward from an imposing medieval Norman castle.

In modern times Gioia is known for several things. Aside from being a central producer of cow's milk mozzarella, it was the birthplace of Sylvester Stallone's father, Frank, who immigrated to the United States as a youth and pursued the familial trade of barber and hairstylist. It is also considered the cradle of Puglia's Primitivo, Southern Italy's equivalent of Zinfandel.

"There is a legend in Gioia that Primitivo was brought to California by Sylvester Stallone's family."

There was laughter around the table, which was covered with antipasti: salumi, balls of breaded and fried ricotta, and braids of that morning's fresh mozzarella. The idea of a Stallone connection is, of course, a joke, though some may believe it, proving that there are people who will take any two facts and connect them like two dots on an empty page.

The speaker was Marianna Annio, an unlikely winemaker of a new generation in Gioia, where she worked at her Pietraventosa winery. She was at lunch with her husband and winery partner, Raffaele Leo, in the antique pink-painted room of Locanda del Melograno, a farmhouse restaurant on the edge of town. The couple were both about fifty—Marianna the more extroverted of the two, with a broad, toothy smile and Raffaele the cooler, cerebral engineer.

Primitivo's origins are likely Croatian. For centuries it was known by names like Zagarese. But here in Gioia del Colle, in the eighteenth century, local monk Don Francesco Filippo Indellicati identified, selected, and propagated the grape, giving it the name *Primativo* for its early ripening characteristics. The grape is believed to have taken an entirely different route through Austria—with no relation to Gioia or the Stallones—to get to America in the nineteenth century. The link between Zinfandel and Primitivo was only established relatively recently thanks to a pair of University of California professors. In 1967 a UC Davis phytopathologist visited a colleague in Puglia and noticed the similarity, and, later in 1994, another Davis researcher proved the varieties were genetically identical.

Within Puglia, Primitivo spread—most notably around 1881, with the marriage of the young Countess Sabini di Altamura, who brought Primitivo cuttings as part of her dowry to her noble groom's family in the lowlands of southern Puglia, around Manduria. With the end of World War II, Primitivo's spread accelerated through the region; its inky, high-alcohol wines were shipped to Northern Italy, France, and Germany for boosting the local vino or making Vermouth. By the end of the twentieth century, the Baroque wines of Manduria had become the gold standard, eclipsing the lighter, more balanced wines traditionally produced at Gioia's higher elevations, which stretched up to twelve hundred feet above sea level.

"It was like they were making an orange to have the taste of a peach," Marianna explained. In her analogy the orange referred to the original Primitivo of Gioia, eclipsed by the "peach" of Manduria. "So when people tasted an orange with an orange taste, they didn't recognize it anymore."

I hadn't traveled to Puglia for thirteen years, and in that time I hadn't touched Primitivo. I'd long given up on Zinfandel. The wines were simply too flabby and sweet, tasting more like cola cocktails than wine. Plus, there was too much else out there to drink that resembled fine wine. Why bother? But the Primitivo of Gioia was different. Somewhere up north, someone had poured some. The wines were lively, fresh, a couple of shades lighter. If you were to compare them to an actor with an Apulian father, they were more nervously edgy John Turturro than pumped-up Sly Stallone.

On my first day in Puglia in September 2018, I'd met Marianna in Bari, Puglia's capital city that sprawled along the Adriatic, where it is fronted by miles of strollable Mussolini-era *lungomare* seawall.

"I love the smells of Bari," she said. "There is always the sea."

She led me on a tour. Old Bari with its narrow streets and alleys had long been known as a center for criminal gangs and disorder, but were now cleaned up at least enough that it was safe to walk by day—far more orderly than, say, Napoli, Bari's white stone piazzas were scrubbed and free of trash and tagging. The neighborhood shrines to local Madonnas embedded in the old walls were lovingly cared for and skirted with clean white linens.

We walked through the old market square, where the landmark sixteenth-century Colonna Infame (Infamous Column) stands on top of a circular pedestal of four steps and is flanked by a Roman lion. The pedestal, just below the Palace of Justice, was used to chain up insolvent debtors for public humiliation. We peeked into Bari's two great Romanesque churches. There was a large, splashy wedding in the San Nicola Basilica, built to house the remains of the original third-century Saint Nicholas, which were smuggled out of Turkey nearly a thousand years ago by Bari sailors. The church, with its exuberantly gilded wood ceiling topping seventeenth-century paintings, on this afternoon smelled of incense mingled with the wedding guests' perfumes. There was a more somber scene at the stoic San Sabino Cathedral, where white-gloved pallbearers shouldered a coffin arriving for a funeral.

We walked through a low archway and down the alley of the Strada Arco Basso, otherwise known as the Strade delle Orecchiette, where groups of women sat at folding tables in the street making fresh orecchiette, or ear-shaped pasta. As they chattered in dialect, their plump fingers rolled out snakes of pasta dough made with varied flours, including toasted dark *grano arso* (originating from a time when peasants harvested the burnt wheat that remained from the clearing of fields). With a single motion, they held their knives in one hand between forefinger and thumb, simultaneously cutting off a bit of dough and pressing it with their thumb to make a dome. The action was repeated all day from midmorning to evening, the orecchiette laid out on screens to dry and then bagged for sale on the street. The effortlessly fluid way these ladies handled their knives made me think this strada was more secure than most banks.

The following day Marianna picked me up in Gioia in her dusty, faded red Peugeot, which emitted a loud ticking from somewhere under the hood, and in which a wad of packing tape held the head of the stick shift in place. On the way northwest to the countryside, Marianna told me her story—sort of a riches-to-rags tale. She had grown up in a working-class family, her father a refrigerator technician. She studied in high school to become a bookkeeper and after that worked for an Italian furniture maker near Gioia. In 1998 she met Raffaele, a mechanical engineer for a company that produced steel wine vats, and he expanded her view of the world beyond Bari. Their courtship included a trip to Tunisia on his scooter, which they rode onto a ferry in Bari. Two years after they met, they were married and spent their honeymoon driving to Europe's most northern point, Norway's North Cape, where they watched the summer sun set and rise within minutes.

"I had my own work. I made money and my husband made money," Marianna said as she drove off the two-lane onto a dirt road that led through farms and small vineyard plots. "We had a good life without any problems. We went on holidays. We went to nice, expensive places. My husband changed cars every two years. When we decided to invest in this adventure, we changed our life. We invested everything."

"The adventure" began later in 2000, after Marianna discovered she was pregnant. Through his work Raffaele had learned more about winemaking and was hooked. He proposed it to Marianna. "He told me, 'We are going to have a baby. What will he have in the future?'" she recalled. "We wanted to leave our son something that was in contact with the territory and nature."

Now, eighteen years into the life change, Marianna opened her car door and stepped out into a corner of a rustic contrada where she and Raffaele rented about two acres of vineyards. Beyond a small patch of white wine grapes and cherry trees, there was a plot of old Primitivo—alberello-trained and resembling half-wild small trees in deep-red soil pocked by broken limestone and wild chicory. The recently completed 2018 harvest had been a disaster for Gioia del Colle; instead of their usually hot and cloudless summer, the year had been full of incessant rains that pumped the Primitivo grapes full of juice until their skins popped. Some of the juices began fermenting in the vineyards and continued on toward vinegar.

"This year is not normal," Marianna said. "It never rains in summer. This year it rained all the time. It's not a happy year for Primitivo."

As we walked back to the car, it was hard to imagine a less-than-perfect summer. The sky loomed over us big and clear, with a few high wisps of clouds and a constant northern breeze. The silence was total. A cloud of small white butterflies with black-spotted wings hovered at the end of a vine row. A caramel-colored cat lightly tiptoed by.

On the way to the cantina, we stopped at another old vineyard—this one rented from Marianna's uncle—which was dotted with apricot, prune, and hazelnut trees. We picked green figs hanging over the road from a neighbor's tree, eating them on the spot while Marianna gathered some for her husband.

Their adventure, she explained, did not play out exactly as planned. "In the beginning, it was all made on enthusiasm," Marianna said. "It was 'Wow—everything was beautiful. The wine will be great.'"

Those early days at the winery are preserved in an array of modern-day pastoral photos in Marianna's phone and on the walls of the winery. In those images Marianna is slender and young with a dark, flowing mane, and Raffaele is unshaven and wild-haired. The two of them, sunburned and grinning, seem electrified in every moment. They raised their son, Vincenzo, in the vineyards. As soon as he could walk, he was harvesting and stomping grapes with the tender soles of his feet.

"Then we made the wine and we realized, 'Who is going to buy a case of wine from people who have nothing to do with wine?'" Marianna said soberly. "In our first vintage, nobody wanted our wine. In the beginning, we gave away a lot of it."

Marianna pulled into the winery gate and drove along a dusty road that wound through about ten acres of vineyards she and Raffaele had planted with neat vine rows trained on wires and drip hoses for emergency irrigation. She parked at the back end of the winery, which looked onto a busy two-lane road and its neighbor, a shoe and clothing outlet.

Inside we found Raffaele, a naturally and nervously lean man with dark eyes, a prominent nose, and thinning hair pulled back in a small ponytail. As we said our introductions, I couldn't help but notice the large hunk of gleaming steel behind him in the fermentation area. There were several steel tanks of different sizes and cylindrical and conical proportions, but one in particular caught my attention: a horizontal cylinder on its side with torpedo-like conical ends, cradled by large support rings that rose to the ceiling. It looked more like a submarine or a weapon system than a piece of winery equipment.

Raffaele explained that this was his invention, produced in the interest of the gentlest fermentations for their wines. In Raffaele's system the wine must in the tank was automatically refrigerated, but unlike a conventional vertical tank that required pump-overs of liquids or punching down of the cap of solids, Raffaele's was an all-in-one solution. His fermenter was set to slowly rotate every twelve hours with a series of fins inside that submerged the skins. His invention could be set to turn once clockwise, another time counterclockwise. As Raffaele spoke about it, he became animated, describing all the nerdy features built into his tank, including a system for micro-oxidation. But the conversation naturally turned to what was inside his wonder tank and the other vertical ones alongside it. No amount of tech would save this vintage.

"Normally we produce about thirty thousand bottles," Raffaele said. "This year we will make fifteen thousand." He laughed at the thought, effortlessly blending drama with the comic self-mockery of his own misfortune. Implicit in his laugh was the irony that he had given up comfort and security to work with the whims of nature. And, this year, nature had screwed him.

Pietraventosa made a half dozen wines; the first one they produced was a Primitivo-Aglianico blend called Ossimoro (Oxymoron). But the one I found most compelling was made from the younger Primitivo planted by the two of them up front from 2002 and fermented and raised in steel tanks. It was called Allegoria.

We went to their small, light-filled tasting room and Raffaele began opening bottles. The 2015 version of the wine was young and undeveloped. The first vintage, 2006, was past its prime and tired. The 2008 was the sweet spot. It had a slightly cocoa flavor, the delicate, sensual feel of a new fine suede garment, and it flashed energetically from spice and tartness. As we contemplated the wine, Raffaele became more and more exuberant. "You see, with time," he said, "the acidity becomes less aggressive. Primitivo doesn't have great tannins; it's the acidity that supports it . . . You have the fruit and the acidity . . ." In a matter of seconds, Raffaele was off on a tangent talking about his love for Piedmont wines and aged wines in general.

Marianna interrupted him—or at least she tried. "Raffaele, you talk too much! Basta!"

"Look at the color," he said of the ruby liquid. (I don't think he'd heard her.) "This is wine."

It was. He set down his glass and mimed his words with his entire body. I lost track of what he was saying and watched his movements. He held his hands to his chest, fingers pressed together, then flung his arms out to his sides, palms open. Then he tented his fingers outward, the heels of his palms on his abdomen. Finally he held his hands in front of his chest holding up an imaginary globe.

"Wine needs time," he was saying. "With Primitivo, you need to work on the acidity. With time, there are other flavors that come out and integrate with the acidity."

As he spoke I could see that for Raffaele this wine was indeed an allegory of each vintage and their understanding of wine. We returned to the first vintage of Allegoria, the edges of the wine beginning to turn orange. "It's no longer living, but it's still wine," he said. Then we returned to the 2008 and he shook his head: "For me, this wine is perfect."

At lunch at Locanda del Melograno, we drank Pietraventosa's cheerful and easy Primitivo, called Volere Volare (literally "To Want to Fly") along with the opened bottle of 2008 Allegoria. Raffaele described how he'd entered the world of winemaking. He was the son of an engineer. His grandfather was a contadino who grew apricots near Brindisi, but his family had no connection to wine. "As a mechanical engineer, I worked in a world of metal, machines, and the noise of the factory," he said. "I wanted to leave the closed air of the factory." About the time he'd met Marianna, he'd asked his boss to learn more about winemaking so that he could better design and supervise the manufacturing of the winery equipment. His boss let him stage at the wineries of a few clients, and wine took hold of him. "It was a drug," he said.

During the second half of the meal, we ate Zampina (literally "small paw," a coiled veal and lamb sausage ground together with pecorino cheese, tomatoes, basil, and parsley and grilled over wood coals). After an interlude of nearly silent eating and drinking, Raffaele blurted out, "We have had highs and lows—it has not all been roses and flowers." He put down his knife and fork and shook his head. "There were times I thought it was all a big mistake."

Marianna held up the bottle of "perfect" 2008 Allegoria and added, "To sell this wine took three years!"

Today Pietraventosa sells mostly outside of Italy, in northern Europe, with a big allotment going to a Virginia importer who sells the wines in Washington, DC. The turning point for the couple came after 2011, Raffaele said.

"No," Marianna corrected, "it was 2013."

"2012, 2013," he said, holding up his hand and rocking it back and forth.

"No. 2013," she repeated.

I was witnessing a friction I've seen countless times among couples and families who work together—the bonds of affection rubbing against annoyance like worn bearings.

"End of 2012 to 2013," he offered in compromise.

"No," she said. In 2013, with the help of positive reviews, Pietraventosa wines distinguished themselves for a great quality-to-price ratio.

Raffaele threw up his hands and, without any edge in his voice, capitulated. "You are right, you are the accountant."

At the end of the meal, Raffaele and Marianna each stirred the crema on top of their espressos vigorously with a tiny spoon. It was an Italian ritual, but one that I have never seen performed so physically as I have in Puglia. It was as if the coffee were somehow not whole until it had been whipped. Raffaele got up first; he had to meet a trucker who was picking up a pallet of cases of wine at a local distributor some miles from the winery. Then he would lead the trucker to the winery. There was a discussion of exactly where the meeting place was.

Marianna drove me south of town, going around a steel roadblock that had closed a section of street on the outskirts of Gioia—for no apparent reason—and thereby was impeding her route. "Shhhh!" she said, holding a finger up to her lips as she veered around the offending barrier. As she finished the turn, her phone rang. She fumbled in her purse for it and brought it to her ear. It was Raffaele, telling her that the driver wasn't at the winery. In an explosion of curses that turned to prayers, Marianna asked every saint and Madonna that held sway over this part of Puglia to help her husband. Then she reminded him that the meeting place was not at the winery.

"Ahhhhhhhh!" From the passenger seat, I could hear Raffaele exhale as his realization sank in.

Marianna dropped the phone back into her bag, turned to me, and said, "Do you know the phrase 'idiot savant'? That is my husband. He is a genius, but in the little things, he is like an idiot."

Cristiano Guttarolo looks like a guy who never strays far from the beach. After our lunch, Marianna dropped me off at his farm—an old whitewashed house and adjacent barns he had inherited from his grandmother and converted to winemaking.

Cristiano, who was wearing baggy blue linen pants, a matching shirt open to his abdomen, and sunglasses, looked on as a pair of workers in rubber boots and gloves did the dirty work of the afternoon. They rolled a wood basket press out of his rustic winery and, under the cover of a makeshift portico, shoveled the black pomace from an afternoon pressing into a tiny flatbed truck.

Though Pietraventosa and Guttarolo's winery share some workers between them, the personalities of the proprietors are opposites. Marianna and Raffaele ran on dreams, Cristiano on an unruffled cool that bordered on indifference. At forty-four he was a middle-aged hipster with a goatee and a deadpan smoker's voice. He exuded the unhurried vibe of a southern *ragazzo* from his minimalistic movements to the way words rolled off his tongue and finished in a decrescendo, as did everyone's in his hometown of Salerno, on Italy's opposite coast. He'd studied mechanical engineering and at thirty, after deciding he didn't like the mathematical strictures of that life, came to Puglia while studying agronomy and took over the few acres of wine grapes on the family's farm. He started making

wine, planted new vineyards, farmed organically, and began experimenting with biodynamics.

"I make wines that are particolare," Cristiano said. He took a
pack of cigarettes out of his shirt pocket. "Molto particolare. Every
year I make the wines I want."

He is a free spirit with no recipe for his "very particular" wines,
other than that they were fermented with wild yeasts in steel tanks
or in clay amphorae. The latter were made by an artisan in Umbria
with the Guttarolo name and a series of personal hieroglyphs drawn
into the surface of the clay as if with a stick. Cristiano now lives
here alone with his mutt and is occasionally visited by his girlfriend
from the south end of Puglia.

In the last decade, he has had little trouble selling out the Masseria Guttarolo wines which fill about fifteen thousand bottles. In
the United States, he is represented by the hippest of hip importers.
"People are always looking for new things," he said. He jostled a
cigarette out of the pack, put it between his lips, and ignited it with
a disposable lighter. "If I wanted to follow a protocol I would have
stayed a mechanical engineer."

What surprised me the most about Cristiano is that, with all
his aloof-itude, and his little experience, he produced some delicious wines. He led me to an open-air former barn built from tufa
limestone blocks that had been refurbished and decorated like a
dream-sequence stage set with old props of antique barber chairs
and bicycles and the living wood sculpture of dead vines and olive
limbs. A dark plank table ran down the center of the room, a few
empty bottles scattered over it along with pieces of white chalk
that had been used to scribble on the wood. His classic Primitivo
Lamie delle Vigne was a cloudy, mouthwatering wine with the
saltiness of capers. That country elegance carried through to all his
wines—his more rustically barnyard amphora-fermented Primitivo
called Amphora; his dry, grassy Negroamaro; and his spicy, earthy
Susumaniello, made from an obscure Puglian blending grape in
comeback mode.

Cristiano's farm lay in a part of Gioia positioned at a slightly lower trough in the Murgia plateau where fog collected. Cristiano saw the microclime as a plus—it produced fresher wines—but the humidity had its inconveniences in higher levels of vineyard fungal diseases and molds. When I asked him what he did about the maladies, he shrugged nonchalantly and said, "I produce fewer grapes."

He sat at the table, pulled out his pack of cigarettes, but this time just left them there. Reflecting on his life, he said, "This place—Gioia—is very small for me. I always lived in the city. To come here was difficult. It is not a place that is open. The Gioiesi are *particolare*. I have friends from here. But I am used to the city by the sea, where there is always activity, always people. Here, it is dead."

I asked how he had adapted to country life in Gioia.

"I don't really *live* in Gioia," he said. "When I am here, I don't go anywhere. I am here. I am here."

Just as the existential meaning of that thought "I am here" sunk in, the afternoon calm was shattered by the sound of an inhuman mechanical scream from above. We wandered outside and looked at a series of fighter aircraft from the nearby Italian military airbase just south of Gioia, diving and climbing in formation, cutting through air and covering distances that made everything else seem small. Cristiano, with a tone somewhere between irked and bored, explained this was the afternoon routine here. "It's the same every day. Every day," he repeated. He looked up at the sky and pointed to his wrist, but there was no watch on it. "The same moment."

While Cristiano matches the image of certain type of Italian winemaker, Mariangela Plantamura, less two miles to the northwest at the edge of Gioia, is unlike any other *viagnola* I've ever met. She is a tiny, bespectacled woman of fifty with chestnut hair styled in an accountant's bob, and with small hands that are well muscled from doing most of the work in the family winery next to her mother's house. Ask her for the details of any of her wines, and instead of rattling figures off the top of her head or consulting technical vintage printouts, she pulls out her master notebook—the cloyingly cute kind you see in stationery stores, with a laminated cover illustration of a kitten nuzzling a sleeping puppy, all surrounded by pink hearts. She gives you the first impression of a quiet, cheerful functionary who helps you out at the bank or government office. But her Primitivos—she makes only Primitivo—are bold and fantastic, probably the best, most-focused versions of the wine I've tasted. The prices are more than fair. But, at the time I met her, to buy a bottle of Plantamura wine in the United States you'd have to travel to North Carolina, where her sole U.S. importer happens to reside.

When Mariangela picked me up at my bed-and-breakfast in Gioia, she brought her husband and vineyard manager, Vincenzo Maggialetti, and elder daughter, Alessia, twenty-one. They were a shiny, smiling family, perfumed and dressed in what looked like their Saturday clothes for a stroll on the town. We piled into the family's small, dusty Nissan. Vincenzo drove us west of town, out to the vineyards. Mariangela warned me repeatedly that she was not a communicator.

"I am not great with words," she said from the back seat. "I am a woman of action." The way she said the last part was convincing.

Vincenzo, who is two years older, is the talker. With a broad, open face, rectangular-framed glasses, and lightly fuzzy scalp, he is a personable dad who looks like he could be a family doctor or volleyball coach. Or both. Actually he is a cop—a career officer in Italy's Carabinieri force, with a desk job answering emergency calls in Gioia from an office in a medieval palazzo.

"I will tell you the most important thing about this *azienda*," Vincenzo said. He looked at me meaningfully and then back at the two-lane provincial road. "The most important thing is that this azienda was born in poverty."

At that moment I noticed something about Vincenzo the *carabiniere*: he didn't wear a seat belt.

"This azienda was born without even one lira," he added.

Vincenzo pulled off the road directly into a vineyard of tall, sentry-like, cordon-trained vines in the deep red soils of Contrada Parco Largo. The vineyard is responsible for about half of Plantamura's production, its "red-label" wine. Plantamura wines are color-coded in a way to save expenses. Mariangela had drawn her own logo: a sun with a bunch of grapes that was printed in gold on three colors of paper that differentiated the wines—red for the wines from Parco Largo, black for the wines of Contrada San Pietro, and a white label was for the Plantamura's old vines Riserva. To avoid waste the labels were used from year to year with vintages and vintage-specific information, like the percentage of alcohol, stamped on the back label.

It was a morning of clear light and sharp shadows. We walked through the vineyard, tasting the ripening small, delicate secondary Primitivo bunches, or *racemi*, that had yet to be harvested. Mariangela had worked with her father in his vineyards from the time she was a little girl. The family's Primitivo, like most of the area's crop, was sold to cooperatives or large producers. Typically, vineyards in Puglia passed to an eldest son or sons. But Mariangela's brother was occupied by a "posto fisso" (literally, "fixed post"), a bureaucratic government job for life and had no interest in wine. Her older sister worked in a bank. Mariangela studied business and economics in high school and worked as a part-time bookkeeper. She married Vincenzo when she was twenty-five, and the couple moved to a Carabinieri post up the coast in the Marche. A few years into their life in Central Italy, the September 1997 earthquakes—which famously collapsed the roof of Umbria's Basilica of Saint Francis of Assisi—badly damaged their rental house in Macerata, forcing the couple to move while Mariangela was in the late stages of her first pregnancy. Five months and one daughter later, Vincenzo had just arrived home from work one evening when a quake aftershock shook their new home.

"He picked up the baby, and we went out to the car," Mariangela said.

"I went back into the house, took the most important things, and we left like that," Vincenzo remembered. "I said, 'We're not going to die here. We're going back to Puglia.'" He arranged a transfer back to Gioia, and Mariangela began working for her father, organically farming about six acres of vineyards with the help of Vincenzo during his off hours.

"It was the only opportunity I had in Puglia," she explained with clear-eyed frankness.

To modern American ears, the thought of going to work on the family farm because of a lack of opportunity might seem depressing. But there is nothing at all depressing about Mariangela Plantamura. "I am a donkey," Mariangela said with a smile, chopping the air directly in front of her. "Head down, move forward."

She and Vincenzo were inspired by the entrepreneurial spirit they had witnessed while living up north. Mariangela took over the estate and became a supplier of grapes to a Tuscan wine group that bought their Primitivo crop, fermented it in Campania, and sold it in Switzerland. In 2001 their clients brought them a bottle of wine made from their grapes and sold in Switzerland. It had a retail price tag on it of 11.50 Swiss francs (today worth about the same in U.S. dollars). Mariangela and Vincenzo recalled their astonishment. Nearly twelve dollars for a bottle of wine seemed a colossal amount of money. "We said, 'How is it possible?'" said Mariangela.

"We knew then: we must make wine!" Vincenzo chimed.

In 2002 the couple began to experiment, producing about twenty-five hundred bottles. With the blessing of their Tuscan clients, they also sold them in Switzerland.

"With my salary, we could eat," Vincenzo said. "After that we saved and we invested in the azienda."

Little by little Plantamura grew to forty thousand bottles and twenty-two acres of vineyards. They said they would stop there; the scale is the maximum for their family economy, which includes Mariangela in the winery and Vincenzo part-time in the vineyards with four workers ("three Italians and one Albanian—all our friends").

Both their daughters—Alessia, who studied languages at university, and her younger sister, Chiara, who was off studying viticulture in Tuscany and whose role model is Elena Fucci of Vulture—planned to work for the company. "They have been breathing wine since they were babies," Mariangela said.

Thanks to their Swiss connections, the winery's renown spread through northern Europe. Plantamura has never had a problem selling its wines and, in fact, turns down requests for more bottles. Strangely, only fourteen hundred of them make it to the shores of the United States, all in the area around Durham, North Carolina—the result of a young Durham importer, Jay Murrie of Piedmont Wine Imports, intrepidly stumbling through here on a trip across Puglia.

Vincenzo drove to the nearby San Pietro vineyard that Mariangela had bought from her brother six years earlier. Mariangela pointed out its clear division between red and white bands of soil. The crop from both sectors were vinified separately, then blended into Plantamura's "black-label" San Pietro wine. "The perfumes are different from the different soils," she said. "Also, the white soils make for more elegance; the red soils are richer, stronger."

The family winery sits at the suburbanized edge of Gioia. Behind an electric gate is the family house, flanked by Mariangela's mother's house and an old whitewashed barn that had been converted into a winery: one white room with steel tanks and a red-painted floor. We sat around a mosaic tile table on Mariangela's mother's terrazzo terrace overlooking the neatly trimmed Mediterranean garden and a kitsch plaster garden statue of what I figured to be the biblical Rebecca at the well, her robe showing off ample leg and one bared breast as her white arms cradled a pair of water jugs. We tasted the wines. Mariangela consulted her kitten-and-puppy notebook, and I made hyperbolic notes about the wines like "wow—pinot noir-like," "dark cherries, tobacco," "fresh. Wild. Sunshine."

At lunch we drank their wines in Gioia's modern Osteria Borgo Antico, run out of old stone arched stables in town by twentysome-thing chef Ottavio Surico, whose cooking combined his creativity with the channeled spirits of countless Pugliese grandmothers. We ate his version of the classic *Spagettoni alla Poveraccia* (poor man's pasta) a seemingly simple mix of thick spaghetti sauced with olives, capers, tomatoes, anchovies, and fried bread crumbs.

"This is the territory," Vincenzo groaned with pleasure as we ate.

The dish was indeed terroir—another treasure born in poverty. I thought about something he'd said that morning at the wheel of his car: "In life, when there is suffering, beautiful things result." He'd been talking about Plantamura wines. But he could have been speaking about this pasta born from a scarcity of more noble ingredients. Or any of a number of recipes from this corner of Italy. Or countless other stories used to weave the fabric of the South.

17. Marianna Annio.

18. Mariangela Plantamura with daughter Alessia and husband, Vincenzo Maggialetti.

8 *In Rome's Shadow*

Like so many corners of Italy, Anagni once really *really* mattered. Forty miles southeast of Rome, its soaring Romanesque cathedral, Santa Maria Annunziata, dominates the old center of town. Consecrated nine hundred years ago, it boasts swirling-patterned Cosmatesque mosaic floors and vivid frescoes in its crypt nicknamed the "Medieval Sistine Chapel." Anagni produced its greatest hits in the thirteenth century—a time when the town gave rise to four popes, three of them from the powerful Conti family, which helped fund the great cathedral. On the winding, now-sleepy cobblestone streets, the peeling, richly decorated medieval palazzi are a reminder of another time, when local sons were doing ambitious things like organizing crusades and excommunicating kings.

I had come to Anagni in October 2018 for its wine heir Anton Maria (Antonello) Coletti Conti, a descendent of the union of the powerful papal Contis with the son of Anagni's famous nineteenth-century international opera baritone Filippo Coletti. Antonello is a purveyor and believer in Cesanese—the red Italian grape synonymous with Rome's region, Lazio. Perhaps because of their proximity, both rural Lazio and Cesanese can elicit scorn or indifference from Romans.

Cesanese—I have noticed the word is accompanied by a world-weary sigh when many Romans say it, as if to say the wine is probably a lost cause, not worthy of much interest. But

Cesanese—late ripening, difficult, rustic, and lending its wines a bitter finish—does have its fans. One of them is Andrea Franchetti, a Roman who planted Cesanese's best subvariety, Cesanese di Affile (as opposed to the larger berried Cesanese Comune) on his Tuscan Tenuta di Trinoro and later on Sicily's Mount Etna.

Perhaps Cesanese is an underachiever because few winemakers other than Franchetti expect much from it. When it comes to wine, culture always matters. Great wines come from cultures of excellence, mediocre ones from cultures of indifference. Cesanese, I figured, had been saddled with a culture that treated it as a commodity, whereas it takes time, study, experimentation, and selection to transform a grape into something finer. The efforts on behalf of Cesanese were scattered at best.

On my first evening in Anagni, I stopped at a small greengrocer and noticed local wine on display in plastic one-liter bottles selling for less than two euros—cheaper than the colorful, artificial-flavored teas and soft drinks on the shelf below. For centuries Lazio's rolling hills encircling Rome with volcanic-origin soils produced plenty of the staples of Mediterranean life: olive oil, wine, and wheat for the capital. Lazio's modern wine story has been one of *in vino quantitas*—its abundant wines quenching the thirsts of the Eternal City without much consideration.

I met Antonello in Anagni. He was a silver-haired fifty-nine, clad in jeans, an autumnal brown sweater, and wire-rimmed glasses. He was immediately affable and unassuming and as unremarkable as an insurance agent. Yet in the eccentricity department he did not disappoint. One of his quirks is a particular revolutionary reading of history that annuls the validity of the Italian State. He is also an expert on and devotee of the rock band Pink Floyd, a vegetarian in meat-heavy Roman countryside, and an advocate for a particular style of oft-misunderstood Cesanese.

"I like wines that are chewable," he said with an easy grin, as he wheeled out of town in his suv, heading a couple of miles to the family farm in the Sacco River Valley. "There is a trend to harvest earlier to have grapes that are less ripe—it's a different style. There are two different styles of Cesanese."

In other words, I figured, he made the style of Cesanese I wouldn't like. But I liked Antonello. His wines sold at fair, modest prices, and he seemed a sincere custodian of his familial lands, which were vast. His Caetanella farm, at about 250 acres, was only half the family land in Anagni. Caetanella had less than 40 acres of vineyards, with the rest given over to grain fields or left as forest.

Antonello pulled up to the center of the farm's activity, where a few nondescript buildings stood. A near-century-old granary had been converted into a small two-story winery, and out front, a pair of cellar hands were pressing red wine and bees were swarming around piles of discarded, dry-skin-and-seed pomace. A hundred yards or so down the hill was the stone carcass of an open-sided barn that once stored hay bales, the tarpaper roof set on a steel frame peeling off in sheets. Antonello told me that his brother, an architect, had drawn up plans to turn the structure into a restaurant—plans that I guessed would remain in the dream stage for some time.

"Cesanese isn't an easy grape," he proclaimed. "When I harvest I don't measure sugars or how much alcohol there will be. I taste the grapes, and when the tannins are no longer green and bitter, I harvest." Antonello was a more or less self-taught winemaker. He didn't use an enologist and spouted aphorisms that oversimplified his craft, such as "You make wine with the skins. That is the key."

He drove us next to a nearby eighteen-acre expanse of vineyard on a hilltop plateau that he had converted from grain fields to vineyards about fifteen years earlier. "It's a hill that gets sunshine all day," he said. "It is inundated with light from morning to evening, and when I came here to harvest cereals, I found it was a place I liked to be."

Growing up in Anagni, Antonello never dreamed of being a gentleman farmer like his father, who sold grapes to the local cooperative in Piglio for its Cesanese del Piglio appellation wines. He had studied law in Rome and was working in a law office in the 1980s, on the path to becoming a notary—an important, near-baronial profession in Italy entrusted to certify all manner of contracts, deeds, and estates. But when his father fell ill with cancer and could no longer work, he abandoned his career path and stepped in. It was a time of qualitative tumult in the Italian wine industry, and Antonello pondered bottling wine under Coletti Conti's own label.

"I had a dream to make wine," he said, "but I was fearful—I had no idea what the grapes would make here. Other than a noble dream, it was a dream without much substance."

The "without substance" part was amplified by a couple of factors. First, he knew little about growing grapes and nothing about making wine. The other impediment was that when it came to *drinking*, he didn't actually like the taste of wine. "I drank the local wines here," he explained. "So I didn't have much knowledge to know that wine could be very good."

Let us stop here and reflect for a moment on these words. Here was the descendant of one of Old Italy's most important families, with ancestors who ruled the world and others who traveled in international artistic circles. He owned vineyards. He came of age in Rome. And he didn't know that wine drinking could be a pleasurable experience? I was stunned with wonder: How far exactly had the Italian aristocracy fallen?

Antonello went on to explain that he finally lost his wine virginity, so to speak, in 1995, at the age of thirty-six. A friend brought a bottle of wine to dinner: Allegrini 1990 Amarone. From the first sip, the wine—powerful, complex, and velvety—was like a revelation. "I never realized wine could taste so good," he said.

This statement required more mental gymnastics on my part. Amarone—a wine made with attic-dried grapes in Northern Italy, outside Verona, for a dense and often sweet effect—is relatively modern style that came of age from the 1950s, achieving appellation status only in the year of that bottle, 1990. That this was the first wine that touched him also seemed incredible.

For years Antonello still wasn't convinced that he could make wine. His farming duties were based on selling cash crops like wheat, along with grapes. Then, in the late 1990s, a group of towns in the local Cesanese del Piglio appellation hired Roberto Cipresso, a Montalcino winemaker, to study the potential of Cesanese. "We had a meeting in which he brought three unlabeled bottles of a wine made from Cesanese," Antonello recalled. "We tasted the wine. It was a marvel. We were shocked. We had no idea that Cesanese could make a wine like this." The wine was revealed to be a Cesanese called Cincinnato produced by Franchetti at his Tenuta di Trinoro in Tuscany's Val d'Orcia. A week later a group of the Lazio producers visited Franchetti. Antonello quickly befriended the fellow eccentric aristocrat, an autodidact who, in turn, encouraged Antonello.

Beginning in 2000 Antonello selected cuttings of Cesanese di Affile vines from Franchetti's vineyards as well as his own, choosing lower-yielding plants that produced the ripest fruit. He had them propagated at a nursery in Burgundy and soon began planting them on the hilltop where we now stood, where he also planted small amounts of French international varieties Cabernet Franc and Merlot. In these volcanic soils, Cesanese thrives with vigor, often too much. So, as a result, Antonello never used fertilizer and let wild grasses grow between the vines to serve as competition.

"We try to keep Cesanese calm," he said.

In his first vintage, 2003, Antonello produced about thirteen thousand bottles total of three red wines: his flagship ripe Cesanese called Hernicus, raised in a mix of oak barrels and cement; an even riper (and woodier) Cesanese called Romanico; and a French barrique-aged blend of French varieties and Cesanese called Cosmato. Over time production tripled, and he added a white wine made from local varieties, but just as full-throttle-ripe as his reds. Response among the Italian press was quick and enthusiastic at a time when ripe wines with scents of French oak were in fashion.

In the mid-2000s he had another epiphanic experience. While attending a course with the Italian Sommelier Association in Rome, he tasted the 2002 vintage of Saint-Emilion's legendary Chateau

Cheval Blanc. "It made me cry," Antonello confessed. "It was a masterpiece."

As we walked through his vineyard, he explained his somewhat conflicted view of agriculture. He never used herbicides or pesticides in his vineyards. And, from 2015, he worked organically—meaning that, to combat vine fungal diseases, he treated the vines with copper-based Bordeaux mix and sulfur. "In 2015, it worked great. In 2016, it was great. And in 2017, it was great." Antonio looked forlornly at his vines. This season, many leaves had turned a mottled yellow in summer. The vineyard was full of unpicked bunches that had molded on the vine. "This year I lost most of my production to Peronospera."

Peronospera, or downy mildew, is a pathogen that spreads quickly in wet years if vineyards aren't treated at the right moment. It is controlled organically with copper-based mixes. Antonello treated in spring but did not follow up enough as the southern half of Italy was drenched by storms that continued into summer.

"Organic is a scam!" he spat. He cursed his decision to shun lab-developed, systemic fungicide that would have prevented such an outbreak. "Why renounce scientific research? The question is not what you use but how you use it!"

"Why, then?" I asked.

"Because I was a cretin!" he said, shaking his head, his voice rising to its most emphatic range, which compared to most Italians south of Rome was only about a three and half on a scale of ten. We climbed back into Antonello's SUV, and he drove to another hilltop within sight. It was less than three acres at the edge of his property abutting a warehouse for a German supermarket chain, emitting the clanking and grinding din of machinery. Here, in 2015, he'd planted another propagated selection of his Cesanese vines that produced the smallest of berries—about half the size of most of his vines. Because smaller berries mean more skin and thicker juice with concentrated sugars, the plot seemed destined to make high-octane wines.

"I think this will be a revolution for Cesanese," Antonello said. "It is like a Ferrari."

That year he was producing a sample vinification, the grapes so ripe they could naturally approach alcohol levels of a fortified wine like port. This "Ferrari" wine was, he explained, slowly fermenting, still sweet and fizzy, in his cellar. He would ultimately choose when he would bottle a vintage of this "Super Cesanese." As of this writing, it hasn't been unleashed.

"We have to wait," he said. "The important thing is to do everything with delicatezza." Then he added, as though passing on a great secret, "Delicatezza is the key to winemaking."

He drove to a small house near the winery, where, at a kitchen table laid with bread and local cheeses, we tasted some recent vintages. "I make wines that please me," he explained. Indeed, Antonello is a solitary winemaker who leads a team of seven full-time workers. He is married without kids but has several nephews who help him. "If I made two million bottles, I would have a problem. I make few bottles, so I don't have concerns about the market. I sell everything."

His Hernicus red was, year after year, his best: rich licorice and spice with the alluringly raw smell of a winery on pressing day. At the end of each sip was the bitter-fruit Cesanese kick. His Romanico bottlings, which sold for nearly twice the price—in the mid-twenty euros—obviously strove for a kind of "importance" that I found excessive. They seemed too rich and sweet feeling for my taste. Were they any thicker, you could spread them on toast.

"I can't tell you how many people say Romanico is the Amarone of Lazio," he said proudly.

Yet for all Lazio's seeming potential—its history with wine, its soils, and its grapes—how had it remained so obscure?

Antonello took a deep breath and began what became that afternoon's history lesson. "One hundred fifty years ago," he began, "this wasn't Italy—it was part of the Papal States. It was owned by a few families who had tens of thousands of hectares." Of course, one of those families were the Contis. "We had the mezzadria [sharecropping] system, and we didn't develop an entrepreneurial mentality. For centuries we treated the land like a pump for profits. Rome is a market that bought everything we produced without regard to quality. There was no push to do better. Now all of that is changing. But in twenty years, you can't make up for centuries."

It was lunchtime, and he drove to Anagni, where the streets are named after the typical Italian historical mix of religious, cultural, and political figures, including Dante, Saint Pancras, the Madonna, and the first Italian king, Vittorio Emanuele II. Yet there was one Italian hero commemorated by a small section of street that galled Antonello.

"Garibaldi was a horse thief—a bandit," he hissed. "He conducted massacres."

Giuseppe Garibaldi is Italy's most world-renowned founding father. He was a global freedom fighter (in South America before Europe), a Republican, and an Italian patriot whose military victories led to Italian unification under the Piedmontese House of Savoy. It is a testament to the flexibility of the Italian spirt that the intently anti-Catholic Garibaldi is so honored in overwhelmingly Catholic Italy, including a nineteenth-century monumental equestrian statue near the seat of the global church in Rome. But, in the South of Italy, there remain rebellious revisionist schools of which Antonello was a proponent.

"The Piedmontese took everything from the South and left us poor," he said.

It was not the first time I'd heard *that*. "But without Garibaldi," I countered, "there might not be an Italy."

"That for me"—he snickered as he parked the car near the center of town—"would be a beautiful thing." He elaborated with a cool, bemused smile. "Italy is chaos. It was born badly. Italy is too many cultures, too many languages, cultures, and people. And we have a political class that is stupid, corrupt, and incompetent."

I was sure that any gathering in any bar across Italy would agree with that last lament, but Antonello seemed deluded in his faith about how Lazio would run under papal rule.

"Without united Italy, we would be a series of small states," he said. "Here would be the Papal States. So what if it would be small? San Marino is a nice country. Luxembourg is a nice country. They are small. It would be much better."

We walked to the main square named for Innocent III, the first Conti pope, who flexed his power over European kings and organized the Fourth Crusade. It was Monday afternoon, and the only beings that seemed to be out that afternoon were a couple of coy cats making the rounds of restaurant kitchens.

"I would join the army to fight for the restitution of the Papal States," Antonello said, his voice seasoned with only a hint of emotion. "I would risk my life."

Those were strong words for a mild-mannered winemaker. I imagined aloud that Antonello was a partisan of the old system because of his legacy. Did the Contis sit around after Sunday dinner and reflect on the "good old days" of sacking cities and torturing enemies?

"Oh, no!" He stopped in his tracks before the great cathedral and smiled gently. "It's personal. For my father, the House of Savoy was the ultimate, the paragon. For me, I would have strangled them with my own hands."

The rising tintinnabulation of David Gilmour's repetitive guitar riff—the one about four minutes into Pink Floyd's epic "Shine on You Crazy Diamond"—sounded from his pocket. He pulled out his telephone and pressed it to his ear. "Si, Mamma," he said.

For lunch we ate Lazio's famous spaghetti *cacio e pepe*—a deceptively simple dish that is artfully prepared with only with pecorino cheese, black pepper, and pasta water. Antonello's Hernicus proved what a great wine Cesanese can be at the Roman table. Like the spaghetti it had its own spice and power. But neither one dominated.

The food and wine wrapped around each other like the "Shine on" synthesizer and guitar parts.

Later I walked through Anagni, the autumn sunlight hitting the layers of peeling stucco on the buildings in bright tangerine and ochre and forgotten, dirty grays. The black lava-stone streets and its small bars were deserted. I watched as a woman in a housedress poured a bucket of soapy water on her stoop, a ten-inch strip of red granite. She went at the stone with a bristled mophead attached to a long handle. She scrubbed back and forth intently as if in a futile struggle to return the stone to its former, unworn past—not unlike Antonello's and Anagni's unwinnable war with time.

The next morning I drove north about a half hour across the Sacco Valley, littered with twentieth-century ruins of abandoned factories, before climbing into a higher and verdant country of steep olive groves and vineyards around Olevano Romano.

Olevano Romano lies within the limits of what is now the Metropolitan City of Rome. Yet it is much smaller, more agricultural, and more intimate than Anagni. It also sits higher, topped by the ruins of a castle lookout at about nineteen hundred feet. The shark-fin-shaped pitch of the old walled town and its cultivated slopes below were immortalized by nineteenth-century European landscape painters, among them Jean-Baptiste-Camille Corot, whose luminous Olevano landscapes hang in museums from Fort Worth, Texas, to the Louvre.

Olevano Romano also has its own Cesanese appellation, and I had come to meet the leading edge of its new wave. At forty-one Damiano Ciolli was in many ways the opposite of Antonello Coletti Conti. The son of a contadino family, his wines were in the fresher, easier drinking camp, with sparing use of wood casks. He farmed organically without regret. And, perhaps because of his upbringing in wine, he'd never been afflicted with Antonello's doubts.

His family winery lay on the ground floor of the family's 1960s block of a house built into the hillside below town, with a panorama facing west, toward the long limestone chain of Pre-nestini Mountains. Here he lived with his girlfriend and wine partner, the enologist Letizia Rocchi, who was now off consulting with a client in Walla Walla, Washington. His mother lived in a separate apartment.

Damiano looked casually thrown together—shorts, an olive-colored Lacoste jersey, his thick dark hair hastily combed, his beard flecked with gray. We drove in his Fiat to his vineyards, and, passing one vineyard that had been abandoned, Damiano lamented the decline of local viticulture. "In the 1960s there were six hundred hectares (nearly fifteen hundred acres) of vineyards in the Olevano Romano DOC," he said. "Now there are eighty hectares."

He spoke in a deep, throaty, rustic country Italian that swallowed the ending of words and sounded like it came from a man twice his age. The problem, he went on, as with everything in Lazio, was Rome. "Most of the people here work in offices in downtown. There was a time when people worked in the office during the week and, on the weekends, worked in the countryside. But working in the countryside is difficult, and eventually they stopped. That, and politics." He cursed the European subsidies that paid landowners to uproot old vineyards.

Damiano had worked with his father in the vineyards as a small boy; he learned to drive a tractor when he was six years old, he boasted. He'd grown up helping his father peddle wine door to door in Rome, filling plastic bottles from containers they carried on their backs. In his boyhood Cesanese Olevano was a sweet wine, as it had been since antiquity. Like many old Italian wines, it often did not finish fermentation. When drunk it was still fizzy and kept enough fruit sugar to cover any rough edges or bitterness.

What was always certain for Damiano is that he would never sit in an office, which to him represented the kind of paper-shuffling purgatory he experienced after high school, when he completed his year of mandatory military service working a desk job at a military airport nearby.

"I did nothing all week, and on the weekend, I came home to work," he said.

About that same time, in the late 1990s, he discovered the world of wine with his friend from Olevano Mauro Mattei, who was as fanatical about Italian wines as most youths were about *calcio* (soccer). Coincidentally, I had once met the inspired and encyclopedic Mattei in Italy's far north, when he was sommelier of the Michelin three-star Piazza Duomo restaurant in Alba, not far from Barolo.

"We went to Montalcino and to the Piedmont and to Burgundy together, and I discovered another world of wine," Damiano said. In 2001 his father turned the vineyards over to him so he could pursue his dream of putting his wine in bottles. "People said I was crazy," he recalled. "They said, 'Cesanese is not a wine like *that*.'"

He drove along a dirt road and parked near a crumbling stone cabin with peeling green shutters and wood doors that barely hung on their hinges—his grandfather's and father's vineyard cabin and winery. Under a sagging roof overhang were a rusted old basket press and a manual destemming machine. Hitches for farm animals were built into the flaking walls. Out front was a family garden, the last small, sweet, oblong tomatoes of the season clinging to desiccated vines. An old vineyard stretched for about ten acres, most of it south-facing and planted with Cesanese di Affile in bushy alberello format that had been somewhat adapted to cordon vine rows.

Damiano's entry into the wine world had not come without difficulty. In the early 2000s, he flogged his wines in the one market he knew—Rome's streets. "I sold it in the markets where they sold prosciutto, vegetables, and fruits," he said. "I offered samples in the little plastic cups they use for espresso. At the end of the day, I did well to sell thirty bottles for five or six euros each. People would tell me, 'It's not Cesanese.' Because they were used to wines from here that were mixed with Montepulciano. I had two and a half years of wine in the cellar—nobody wanted it."

When he started, his competition in Olevano was one large commercial producer and one now-defunct local cooperative. Today there are more than a dozen producers, some of which followed his example. Damiano succeeded by abandoning Rome for a time. He hit the road, registering for wine fairs in Northern Italy and northern Europe, where "people didn't know Cesanese and didn't have this prejudice." By 2008 he was selling most of his wine abroad. With that recognition he gained acceptance in his backyard—the Roman restaurant trade became his biggest business.

"Roman food is heavy," he said and recounted a number of dishes, including oxtail stews, slow-roasted and seasoned *porchetta*, and Amatriciana pasta seasoned with pork jowl. "Heavy cuisine demands wines that are lighter and fresher, lively wines. Cesanese is the opposite of Amarone. Cesanese is not a *vino nobile* like Nebbiolo. You can't age it for thirty years. But it's a wine that's versatile at table. It's spicy, it's floral, and in a cold year, it can be like Pinot Nero."

Damiano drove to a second vineyard, a north-facing hillside that belonged to Letizia's family and that the couple planted with Cesanese in 2007. "We planted it for climate change—it's a cooler vineyard," he explained. "The thing with Cesanese is if you harvest it a few days too late, it makes too much alcohol. If you harvest it a few days early, the tannins are too green."

In Olevano, before lunch, we walked toward the high part of the old town. Damiano seemed to know just about every local in the town and greeted them with an accent as thick as Roman tripe. What sounded like "Aò [Roman dialect for the greeting *ciao*], Mo," he sung out to the service station mechanic. A few blocks on, a man came from around the corner. "Aò, Bo!" he said. "Ciao, Be," he called to another guy.

"The crazy thing is that most Romans don't know Lazio," he said. "Especially in the north of Rome and in the richer areas, where they go to Tuscany. We have more Danish and Germans who buy houses here than Romans."

The way grew steeper, and we ascended steps cut into the side of the street. The higher we climbed, the more desolate the town became. Near the top we passed a Nordic-looking blond woman—a sole Viking up here—raking leaves. We took another route down, Damiano returning the greetings of a pair of sturdy-looking nonnas who stuck their heads out of windows at the sound of our shoes.

At the foot of old Olevano, I followed him into the 1950s-era Trattoria Sora Maria & Arcangelo, now run in the third generation by Damiano's friend Giovanni Milana and his mother. Milana, with his wine cask of a torso, wild black curls and beard, and proud Roman nose, looked like a figure you'd see in the backgrounds of Renaissance paintings for local color. But he cooks like a nonna. His restaurant has a pan-European wine list that you would normally expect to find at big-city culinary palaces. And he was one of Damiano's early patrons and boosters.

We ate *animelle* (sweetbreads) with onions, fried *baccalà* in tomato sauce, and broad, flat pappardelle pasta in a sauce of ground rabbit seasoned with juniper berries and orange peel, and we drank Damiano's wines from his 2015 vintage. Both his wines were Cesaneses labeled with the Latin names of wild flowering plants in his vineyards. Silene (named for *Silene Vulgaris*, a.k.a. the bulb-flowered bladder campion) was his joyful, fruit-driven wine raised in cement tanks. Circium (common thistle) aged partly in wood casks was more ephemerally complex. Both of them cut through the rich dishes more nimbly and sharply than Coletti Conti's riper versions.

"It's not an international wine," Damiano said. "If you find it on a list in New York or London, you'd never buy it unless a sommelier or restaurant owner told you to try it. It's Cesanese," he said with a slow, accepting tilt of his shoulders. "It's not perfect."

Well before Rome's age of empire, Cori had its moment. Perched on the first line of hills of the Lepini mountains twenty miles inland from the Tyrrhenian Sea and about thirty-five miles south of Rome, Cori—originally known as Cora—was at the center of ancient Latium, whose Latini tribe spawned the original Latin language around 1000 BCE, long before Napoleon III coined the term "Latin America" and twentieth-century marketers applied "Latin" to just about every corner of modern life, starting with Puglia-born Rudolph Valentino, the first "Latin lover."

For a time, when the Roman Republic's emblem boasted SPQR (the Senate and People of Rome), Cori proudly had its SPQC. In the fourth century BC, Cori and the loose-knit Latin League of city-states went to war with the Roman army, resulting in their conquest. Today the old town—topped by the pillared remains of the Temple of Hercules—is surveyed by a league of skinny roaming cats, who can look out over the Pontina plane and its former marshlands, which were drained less than a century ago by Mussolini.

On my first morning in Cori, I went for espresso on the main square. On the terrace of one café, about seven women of retirement age sat together in a loose group, drinking, smoking, laughing, and talking over one another. Across the plaza about the same number of men were lined up at individual tables facing the sun. Except for one man, who held a newspaper in one hand while angrily gesticulating with the other, they were as silent and stolid as the travertine that lined Cori's streets.

Lazio, I was coming to learn, is a paradox—a backwater in the shadow of the eternal capital. Cori's local traditions live on through its Corese dialect, its elaborate, acrobatic flag-waving competitions, and its once-endangered grapes, championed by Marco Carpineti above all. At fifty-nine Marco had built his success over twenty years, exalting the area's two near-forgotten local grapes: white Bellone and red Nero Buono. He was born into a family of contadini with about ten acres of gently undulating vineyards. As a young man, he helped his father on the farm while working as an electrician for the town. At twenty-four he married the daughter of a local marquis. Soon after his father died, Marco quit his job to work the family vineyards and olive groves.

Marco began his new career in viticulture growing grapes to sell to the local Cincinnato wine cooperative and, in the early 1990s, became co-op president, championing local over international varieties. Then, in 1996, he struck out on his own, producing about 5,000 bottles of wine in his father's rustic wine shed in the vineyards. Over more than two decades, his growth has been spectacular. Vineyards now cover 160 acres—all farmed organically or biodynamically and some plowed by horse—that produce up to 350,000 bottles per vintage: white, red, sweet, and sparkling, and experimental.

I met with Marco on a pair of days in his large, modern winery overlooking his vineyards in Contrada Capolemole. The winery—an oversized modernistic rendering of the family's old house in town—hovers over a small valley. It's a place where he spends little time, preferring to act as the estate's vineyard foreman and agronomist and leave the winemaking to those he calls the "technicians." The first morning I spent a few hours with Marco's son, Paolo, the winery sales manager, who was dressed in a white shirt and suit pants for a meeting later in the day. Thirty-four, boyishly charming, and as fine-featured and handsome as a fashion model, Paolo struck me as too refined to follow in the footsteps of the heroic agriculturalist who was his father.

"Me and my father don't have a passion for the winery—we have a passion for the countryside," Paolo said as we climbed into his suv. He may have had a passion for the land, but he exuded the relaxed and gentile manner of a manor-born young prince. Perhaps unfairly, I couldn't imagine him getting his hands dirty.

"My father's family and my mother's family were very different, but very similar," he explained with no prompting. "They were different in that my father's family was all contadino. With them at dinner it was always 'Mangia, mangia.'" Paolo laughed. "And my mother's family were marchesi who talked about culture, art, and philosophy. But the two families were similar in that they both lived from agriculture." Paolo, I assumed, fit in the aristocratic camp. That was confirmed when he later told me that, even though he was sales director, he didn't like selling. He particularly loathed peddling to the public at wine fairs, preferring to direct a staff that actually did the vending.

He led me on an impressive tour of the area, starting with Carpin-eti's volcanic tuff stone vineyards of Capolemole and the old familial hovel of a winery where Marco produced his first vintage and where old farm machines and oak casks decayed under the shade of thick, shaggy olive trees. Then he drove to Pantanello Natural Park; in 2005, Marco planted vineyards not far from the park's Giardino di Ninfa, one of Europe's most beautifully evocative gardens criss-crossed by babbling brooks and ponds on a site named in antiquity for the supposed presence of water nymphs. Then it was on to the Tenuta San Pietro farm Marco bought from an uncle in 2009, where he plowed vineyards with farm horses. Finally we ended up at Carpineti's latest project—at six hundred meters, his highest-altitude site, on a north-northeast limestone plateau in Bassiano, where Carpineti was planting vineyards in cordoned rows staked by fat chestnut posts. One parcel was planted with vines propagated from shoots of an old specimen he and Paolo had found growing in an adjacent woods and that, on testing, turned out to be the old and rare Lazio red variety, Abbuoto. It was an expansive project in a secluded setting surrounded by forest and sky. Paolo, with hands on his trim waist, heartily breathed it all in.

"My father would like to plant all the land up here, but I would like to do something different . . . incorporating animals, a garden." He looked off to a series of rounded, scrub-covered hills that rose up from the plateau. "It's something that needs a new philosophy, a new way."

On the way back to the car, he added, "We don't know the agricultural results here yet, but in my opinion"—he nodded and pushed out his lips in a sign of considered confidence—"tranquillo."

We returned to the winery midafternoon for lunch, where we were joined by Marco, in a simple plaid shirt and jeans that hung off his wiry frame. He was a quieter man than his son, with a shaved head and dark eyes that underlined his resolute look. When he learned that we had visited his family's old winery, he reverently spoke of his father and his struggles selling wine to unreliable businessmen whose price offers declined as the year wore on and harvest approached.

"I remember my father telling me that to give a product value, you have to follow it all the way," Marco said. "He told me what a humiliation it was after a year of work to sell your wine for nothing—it was almost throwing it away. But he had no other possibility. People didn't think you could have a life of dignity in agriculture." He picked slices of prosciutto off a platter to fold into a thick slice of bread. "My father died of heart attack. The soils here wore him out. No one encouraged me." It was a refrain I heard from everyone who had any hope for achieving anything in wine in Southern Italy.

Marco recounted how, in the boom after the war, Lazio farmers, including his father, planted varieties from other regions as well as France. The root of the problem, in his eyes, was Rome as one of the world's first globalist powers with little interest in a local sensibility. "It's the story of Rome," he said. "Wine was the first drug, and the Roman army brought all the vines of the world back to Rome. Rome always thought of itself as having all the best from all the world." So, in modern times, he said, "Lazio producers brought in vines from all over the world. What the producers brought to Rome, Rome bought. People thought if you brought Chardonnay to Rome, it would make you more noble, and so we forgot thousands of years of our own history."

Marco spoke sotto voce. His eyes were deep set in weathered skin amid a web of laugh lines. His deliberate, muscled hands didn't venture out of a confined orbit. He ladled servings of a simple soup of pasta and chickpeas into wide, shallow bowls, and we ate with weighty oval spoons. Reflecting on his moves from electrician to wine producer, Marco said, "I was terrified. I had a wife and Paolo was born and we had a child to feed." As a grower, he toured other vineyards in Tuscany and Veneto, where he heard winemakers talk about centuries of history. "And I began to have faith in myself," he said, looking up from his bowl. "I said, with two thousand five hundred years of history, why are we planting Chardonnay in Lazio? People were taking the easy way out. Why didn't we make wines with our own grapes?"

Marco was outraged that Nero Buono—originally known as Nero Buono di Cori—was becoming extinct in his hometown. He led the first bottling of wines at the Cincinnato cooperative and paid a premium for Bellone and Nero Buono. When he struck out on his own, Carpineti went slowly. While he made Bellone as a monovarietal, at first he blended Nero Buono with better-known Montepulciano and Cesanese. "When I started out, I needed to expand to feed my family, and I borrowed money," he said almost apologetically. "To repay the bank, I wanted something that I knew would sell." As time went on, Marco kept pushing boundaries. In 2007 he worked with his enologist to produce *metodo classico* (Champagne-style) sparkling wines: white Kius Brut made from Bellone and rosé Kius Extra Brut from Nero Buono.

Carpineti's bubbles won't be seen anytime soon in the United States, where the market is dominated by a high-low combination of Champagne and Prosecco. At least now they can be enjoyed in Rome, which wasn't the case from the start. Marco remembered approaching the owner of well-known Roman trattoria in 2010 with his first Kuis Brut. "He told me, 'I don't want to taste it. It doesn't interest me. In Cori, they don't make sparkling wines. From Bellone? Organic? No way.'" As Marco spoke, he balled his right hand in a fist and held it lightly to his chest. In a near whisper, he added, "It was like a knife in my heart. Then a couple of years later"—his hand dropped to the table—"the same owner asked our agent in Rome, 'Why don't you sell me a few cases of that wine?'" Times had changed. Carpineti's sparkling wines were heralded as some of the best in Italy.

"Now," he said, "there are places that sell it as the Spumante of Rome."

As the afternoon wore on, Marco grew antsy. He had been away for two days at an industry ceremony, picking up an award in another part of Italy, and, he said, he was eager to get back into them.

"For what?" I asked. His harvest was finished. His crews were out plowing vineyards. What did he have to do?

"To think," he said. "To think."

I met Marco at the winery the next morning; he had already been out thinking in his young Bassiano vineyards and returned in his work boots, jeans, and field vest. We spoke of two of his most intriguing wines—both produced in small quantities and works in progress. One was his red, silky Nero Buono, made from the vineyards he planted near Ninfa, barrel-aged, and released after five years. It was called Apolide, meaning a stateless person—in protest of European labeling that reduced the name of Nero Buono di Cori to Nero Buono. The irony of this is that shortly after he began making Apolide in 2009, he himself became "stateless" by pulling his wines out of the Cori DOC appellation. The reason was an all-too-Italian dispute over having to filter wine samples to a tasting panel too soon. Of the wine Marco said, "The vines are still young." He was still experimenting to get the balance right. And that was the thing with Marco: he was still trying to understand the effects of expositions and soils—volcanic, limestone, and clay—on the local grapes.

"Each terroir gives something different to the wines," he said. "We don't know exactly what yet."

In recent years Marco had gone beyond organic and converted most of his estate to biodynamics and used other vineyard-balancing measures, mainly because he was searching for a deeper connection to his land. "If you care for the earth, the plants will do well," he said. He had begun working part of his San Pietro Bellone vineyards with a horse-drawn plow that he and Paolo trained to use in Northern France. He combined the grapes from the vineyard with some from his family's ancestral vines in 2015 and fermented a small amount in a few unlined clay amphorae where the juice of white wine was left to ferment—on wild yeasts, like all of his wines—and then rest for eight months.

"Why amphora? We feel Roman," Marco said. "The Romans put wine in amphorae." He'd even thought of it a decade earlier but hesitated because of Friuli winemaker Josko Gravner's fame in making wine in amphorae imported from Georgia in the Caucasus. "I was afraid of copying Gravner. It was a mistake, but I hesitated."

The resulting wine—called Nzù (meaning "together" in Cori dialect) and filling only two thousand bottles—was, for me, Marco's masterpiece. Vibrantly golden in color, it smelled and tasted like, I imagined, some kind of ancient flint fire starter or spent bullet casings wrapped in salted caramel. It danced lightly across the tongue and tasted like nothing else from Lazio—or Southern Italy.

"My idea is to make wine as they made wine two thousand years ago," Marco said.

There is a lot of romance that goes into such a statement—man, agriculture, clay vessels, and a grape with an ancient history. Never mind that Roman wines were produced on large estates off slave labor and contained all kinds of additives, from honey and seawater to spices and even sweet-tasting but toxic lead compounds. I doubted that the wines the Romans drank tasted anywhere near as complex.

When I think of Rome, I think of the first cosmopolitan city—a hard-edged hub of commerce and snake pit of politics—neither a sentimental nor nostalgic place. Yet if it makes sense anywhere to look back two thousand years, it is here in Rome's shadow, where the stones seem to scream out at you, *We were once the center of somewhere.*

19. Anton Maria (Antonello) Coletti Conti.

20. Marco Carpineti.

9 *Return to Vico Equense*

In the fall of 2018, fifty years after my childhood summer there, I returned to Vico Equense hoping to rediscover some of the magic. As I exited the tunnels that separate the smog-opolis of Naples from Vico and the Sorrento Peninsula, a big, bright October sky opened in front of me. I wound down the road that leads to Vico's Seiano waterfront and parked on the small lava-stone street.

The Vico waterfront had been developed but not overly so. A pair of white-stucco hotels and a row of restaurants stood along the marina, with its moorings of small fishing and pleasure boats. The midday sun warmed my skin. The light cast on the seafront was crisp, the air scented with hints of the last of morning coffee and the first frying fish.

At the end of the marina is a small bend in the road and a spillway from the low mountains above town. Just beyond that, O'Saracino and the pier that extended over its own blue bay were gone. The area had been scrubbed of any trace of beachfront, the gray lava sand and pumice sprouting patches of waist-high weeds. At the water's edge, a few sunbathers sprawled on black basalt boulders, basking in Indian summer sun.

I walked back toward the marina and approached a man setting tables on one dockside terrace. He looked about my age, and I wondered if he had been here in the summer of '68. I asked him what had happened to O'Saracino.

"Politics," he nearly shouted, shaking his head in a dramatic display of disgust. "It was the first restaurant here. Now look at all of them. It was best restaurant in all of Vico, and it was destroyed by politics. This is what happens when fights start. They end like this."

I later researched what "politics" exactly had befallen the familial restaurant—named for the squat, squared-off, fortified medieval Norman tower across the street that had once served as a lookout and defense against Saracen (Muslim) coastal invaders. O'Saracino, alone on the Seiano waterfront, was built after the war, before zoning laws or construction enforcement. A 1980s law providing amnesty for such older, unsanctioned construction might have allowed it to stay in place. But after a fire destroyed it and Ciro Aiello rebuilt, his landlords—a power couple, both regional politicians— claimed the amnesty as theirs. They had hoped to extend their own small resort on the old farm behind the restaurant to O'Saracino's old space. After years of court proceedings, O'Saracino was ruled illegal by a judge and razed in 2014. On this trip to Vico, I noticed that the landlords' adjacent property was shuttered and appeared neglected behind a chain-link fence. From the looks of it, no one won that fight.

Yet, long before O'Saracino's finale, Ciro made a smart move by purchasing the old Saracen tower. In the 1990s his daughter, Vittoria, opened La Torre del Saracino, built in and around the tower, with her then–life partner, the rising star chef from Vico, Gennaro Esposito. By 2008 La Torre del Saracino had earned two Michelin stars, and Esposito was hailed as one of Italy's great young chefs. At some point his relationship with Vittoria, a pastry chef, fell apart, and he fathered a child with another woman. Still, they remained business partners. When I returned in 2018, La Torre del Saracino was still at the top of its game. The cherub-faced Esposito had opened restaurants in Capri and Ibiza and was a star chef on Italian television. I had contacted Vittoria earlier in the fall, and she insisted I come for lunch when on my way south. Minutes after I arrived in town, my phone chirped—Vittoria checking on my arrival.

Vittoria was a commanding presence. A fast talker with a pair of dark sunglasses propped atop her head of long black hair, she had an encyclopedic knowledge of wine, food, and people. On this day, in her midforties, full-figured, she sported a black dress with white polka dots and a pair of glittery, flat sandals.

The look of the place recalled nothing of O'Saracino's mid-twentieth-century beach-shack feel. Le Torre del Saracino is all modern architecture and minimalistic design, with mostly white interiors, lots of glass, and lights that glow from wall niches. In the tower itself was a cool lounge with an impressive retro-style stereo that showed off its mercury vapor tubes like jewelry. It lay on squat, white cubes next to a massive old stone mill that had been built for making olive oil but was used for milling grain during the food shortages of World War II.

Vittoria and I are related by a common Cioffi great-grandfather; her grandmother was my grandfather's sister. In the sunlight-filled steel kitchen, she introduced me as her *cugino* to her staff, from the cooks to the crisp-suited servers and the sommelier. The one person she notably did not introduce me to was her ex. Esposito, in his chef whites, was sitting at a table with two men on one of the restaurant's terraces. She breezed right by as if the space around Esposito were filled with dark matter. She led me past the kitchen and down into La Torre's wine cellar, which was loaded with treasures that defined how far modern Italy and its South had come in the last years.

I sat in a glassed-in, panoramic terrace behind the best table in the house—the one set in corner, walled with glass, that pointed directly over O'Saracino's old spot and was currently occupied by a Japanese couple dressed as if they had fallen out of the pages of an Italian fashion magazine. In the O'Saracino bay, a couple in a plastic kayak paddled through the calm waters. A few hundred yards down the shoreline the sheer cliffside rose up to Vico Equense's old town, with the landmark peach-and-white baroque-fronted church and bell tower of Santissima Annunziata, whose panorama put it at the top of magazine lists of Italy's most *bellissima* wedding locations. Across the Gulf of Naples, a pair of symmetrical white clouds framed the peak of Vesuvius in the brilliant blue sky.

I have eaten at many two- and three-star Michelin restaurants, and I find many sad. What ruins many for me is the overly formulaic vibe, which in Italy often means robotic waiters and a lack of spirited young children. I didn't see any high chairs, but it was a weekday lunch, and the waitstaff didn't seem stiff either.

Giusto Occhipinti, the Sicilian architect-turned-pioneering-winemaker at cos in southeastern Sicily's Vittoria, once opined to me about Michelin stars, "The first star is for the food, the second for the service, and the third for the parking lot." There may be some truth in this; Esposito had publicly complained that the reason his Vico restaurant had not obtained a third star was the lack of parking in Seiano.

My main beef with elite restaurants is the cuisine, where technique often reigns, and food loses all connection to anything real. A faux tomato that actually contains no tomato may one day be a marvel to space travelers on their way to Mars, but it means nothing to me. A great chef doesn't need to be an artist, but they need to be rooted to something and somewhere. Esposito, Vico's favorite culinary son, seemed to be deeply rooted in his hometown. His guiding maxim translates to "Forgetting one's origins is a mortal sin—remember."

The common image of the Sorrento Peninsula is its coastline, which wraps around its point and leads to the south-facing Amalfi Drive. But Vico climbs from the sea through groves of giant lemons and olives to the chestnut forests at the mountainous center of the peninsula. Esposito was known for combining surf with Vico's varied Mediterranean turf in new, meaningful, and beautiful ways.

I lost count of the dishes at that meal, mostly a collection of small bonsai-like creations featuring the local bounty in combinations such as anchovies stuffed with white figs and dressed with crushed nuts and fig vinegar. There was also the poetic revisiting of traditional foods like fried mullet—his not fried, but instead vapor-cooked, with its anatomy rearranged into a tiny sandwich topped by its fins and algae.

La Torre's sommelier poured me half a dozen glasses of white wines from Campania, including a Falanghina, with its tropical flavors, a more delicate and salty Greco di Tufo, and a floral and almond-tinged Biancolella from Ischia. There was a new glass for every course, each of which was worthy of a #foodporn shot on Instagram. Yet, despite the stylized presentation, to Esposito's credit, you could recognize the foods, flavors, and ingredients. Deep brown and intensely flavored, Esposito's famous *minestra di pasta* was a collection of grandmothers' soup recipes combined into one hand-painted ceramic bowl; it contained eleven types of pasta and, it seemed, just as many cephalopods, crustaceans, mollusks, and mugilidae. But as I pondered a dessert of salty-and-sweet crème brûlée and sipped sweet *passito* from Caserta, I missed what used to be—the simple world that lived across the street at O'Saracino, with the large, voluble families, the clanking dishes, the platters of food, and the house hound, Lupo, who roamed the place looking for table scraps.

After coffee with Vittoria in the tower, I began walking back to my hotel on the other side of the marina. I had taken only about fifty steps when I heard a whistle from behind. I turned to see a familiar face—the silver hair had thinned, but the unmistakable Cioffi smile underlined the family's substantial nose. His still-jaunty frame was clad in shorts and an untucked short-sleeved shirt that bulged at the paunch.

"Cugino," he called out.

His arms curled around me, and he kissed me on each cheek. I responded in kind before I remembered his name. Vittorio is a first cousin of my mother. A retired tailor who'd spent his life in Vico, he had accompanied us to O'Saracino a decade earlier. Vittoria, he explained, had alerted him to my presence. Within a minute, Vittorio arranged to pick me up at my hotel at seven for dinner.

When he picked me up that evening, I noticed how dramatically the cars seemed to have changed from my memories of the 1960s. Of course, the models were different, but the cars themselves had lost their sheen. In the postwar years, Fiats were a cherished object to pamper and polish. The small, plastic vehicles that now replaced them resembled most cars across Southern Italy: like old slippers that had been left out in the rain and pounding sun.

Vittorio parked behind his fifties-era apartment building, which stood five stories tall in Vico's bustling little downtown. It took us about a half hour to tour the whole of Vico. Vittorio, who had exchanged his shorts for long pants, walked with an uneven bounce in each step. When he wasn't talking, he hummed or whistled, greeting fellow *Vicani* about every thirty seconds in either heavily accented Italian or Neapolitan. Vittorio did not speak a word of English. In fact, on our last trip, he had counseled our son, Alexander Dante—then in high school—that if he wanted to make himself understood throughout the world, he did not need English, French, or Chinese; the only language he needed was Neapolitan. Fortunately, our son did not take the advice and went on to study in London, where Neapolitan doesn't yet make the cut outside of the Mamma Mia Pizzeria.

It was a warm evening, and, as night fell, we walked to the cliffside esplanades of Vico's thirteenth-century fortified castle and ducked into Santissima Annunziata. Originally constructed as a gothic cathedral, the church had been restored in a lighter and more inviting baroque style in the late eighteenth century. That evening what appeared to be a civic meeting was taking place in the church nave, and we stayed just long enough for Vittorio to give me a lesson on American history. Entombed in the church are the remains of the Neapolitan jurist, economist, and philosopher Gaetano Filangieri, who died of tuberculosis in Vico at a mere thirty-five years old, in 1788. Though his name is not taught in American history classes, his impact on the world is legendary in parts of Italy, particularly around Naples.

Filangieri had achieved international acclaim for volumes of his progressive opus *La Scienza della Legislazione* (*The Science of Legislation*). His work attracted the interest of Benjamin Franklin, with whom he corresponded. Some Italian scholars and Filangieri fans even suggest that Filangieri's concept of national well-being led the drafters of the Declaration of Independence to include "the pursuit of happiness" as an inalienable right. Never mind the more accepted view that the idea came from Englishman John Locke's influence on Thomas Jefferson. On the Gulf of Naples, the case is closed.

"Filangieri did all the writing for the American Constitution," Vittorio said, matter-of-fact.

I had to laugh.

"He was friends with Washington or Franklin—one of them," Vittorio said. "He had all the ideas. And they used them."

We walked back through the dark medieval quarter and the turn-of-the-last century downtown with its brightly lit shops and piazzas lined with outdoor cafés, to arrive at another important Vico institution: Da "Gigino," Vico's "University of Pizza," which coined the now oft-used term *Pizza a Metro* (pizza by the meter) in the 1950s, is now a light-splashed, multilevel modern restaurant that could seat the entire population of Vatican City and still have room to spare. We stood up front where the *pizzaioli* rolled out the dough made with *lievito madre* (sourdough starter) into oblong shapes, sprinkled on toppings, and fed three domed brick wood-burning ovens with their long wood paddles. Vittorio approached the cashier in her bulletproof glass booth (Da "Gigino" takes no chances with its pizza proceeds), pulled out a crisp fifty-euro bill, and slid it through the slot. He took his change and an order number for our half-meter pizza margherita. We stood with a group of locals waiting for our number to come up on an electronic counter while basking in the hunger-summoning redolence of baking dough, tomato sauce, and melting *fior di latte* (cow's milk mozzarella).

Minutes later, out on the street and carrying the steaming-hot pizza box, Vittorio reflected, "In Vico you can eat for less than five euros for a person, or for more than two hundred euros." The latter was a reference to La Torre del Saracino, where Vittorio had been invited a few times but concluded, "It's not for people like us. I prefer to eat family style, like this." As he asserted this, he lifted the pizza box under his nose.

The door of Vittorio's third-floor apartment still bore a plaque with his father's name: Giuseppe Cioffi. By Italian standards it was a large two-bedroom, decorated like an Italian time capsule, with floors an earthy-colored jigsaw of large-format terrazzo, with lots of antique dark-wood furniture and lace. It was arranged along a central hall—the first bedroom on the right before the living room, he explained, had been his parents'—and looked as though it been untouched for years: the bed neatly made, a modestly bloody crucifix on the wall above the headboard. Vittorio, who'd never married but entertained a series of girlfriends over the years, pointed out his room, on the other side of the living room, where he slept in a narrow cot. At the end of the hall, he'd converted a small room into a sewing studio that was littered with fabric scraps, and where, deep into his retirement, he still worked.

On the other side of the hall was the kitchen, lined with sixties-era lime-green tiles that seemed to have not aged. He set the pizza box down on the weathered marble-slab kitchen table and pulled plates, glasses, and paper napkins out from a cupboard. He took a whole salami off the kitchen counter and placed it with a knife on a cutting board. From the refrigerator he pulled out the evening's wine: a half-drunk bottle of prosecco. The handle of a spoon dangled inside the bottle neck with its face resting above—a trick he said he learned to preserve the bubbles.

"I prefer eating family style, like this," he repeated, "to going out to a restaurant. Don't you?"

In that moment I agreed.

The basil on top of the pizza had wilted in the box on the way back to Vittorio's home, but the crust and cheese were both browned to the color of caramel, and it had those magic qualities of Neapolitan pizza:

a fall-apart delicacy that translated to a lightness on the stomach. We folded the slices and ate with our hands as Vittorio told family stories, including his version of O'Saracino's history. The problems, he said, began long before the zoning fight. Back in the 1980s, a group of men from Vico's neighboring town Castellammare di Stabia, on the other side of the mountain tunnels toward Naples, began hanging out at the restaurant. Castellammare, Vittorio said, was the hometown of Ciro Aiello's in-laws, and, in Vittorio's opinion, it was a cesspool of crime and shady characters. Vittorio tugged the skin below his lower eyelid for emphasis. He recalled run-ins between Ciro and one particular young tough. He recounted—with a succession of more eyelid pulls—stories of men running contraband cigarettes through the O'Saracino dock, of arrests, and then suddenly, one night, of the kitchen fire (another eye pull) that destroyed O'Saracino.

Castellammare is one of those little-known Italian towns that periodically makes big news for nefarious reasons. In 2016, for example, Italian authorities found a pair of Van Gogh paintings, stolen in 2002 from Amsterdam, hidden in the wall of the farmhouse owned by drug boss Raffaele Imperiale's mother. Imperiale, who was hiding in plain sight in Dubai, where he was building luxury villas, confessed in a letter his part in a syndicate that supplied cocaine to Neapolitan Camorra dealers on the Bay of Naples. In 2017 he was convicted and sentenced in absentia to eighteen years in prison. Through his lawyers he said he bought the paintings knowing they were stolen because they were a good deal and he was fond of art.

So I asked Vittorio who would have burned O'Saracino. He flipped open the top of the box, and we both took more pizza. If you discounted the idea of an accident, it was impossible to know exactly who bore a grudge against whom, he said.

We drank the wine from small etched wineglasses, and Vittorio cut slices of the salami, which had been made by a friend. On the outside, it looked as dried and mottled as old stucco, but inside it was moist and peppery, with just enough fattiness to make you want to drink more of his day-old prosecco.

"I am poor, but I live like a rich man," Vittorio said proudly, his broad smile unfurling. "My pension is five hundred euros a month." His abrupt accounting of finances surprised me. "The apartment rent is four hundred, and the utilities and the cleaning lady are a hundred." By my instant calculation, that should have left exactly zero to live on. But Vittorio didn't act like a man who was short on cash.

"I have plenty of work." He nodded in the direction of his sewing studio. "I am the last artigiano, so people come to me."

Vittorio worked with his hands and had learned the art of tailoring at a young age. Neapolitan tailors—like Neapolitan espresso—have long been considered the best in Italy. On our family trip a decade earlier, I recalled him showing off the detail of the work he'd done dressing a foot-high statue of the Virgin Mary for a local church. He'd lifted up the Blessed Mother's dress to show us the all the detailing of her lace undergarments.

"I have four doctors as clients." Vittorio grinned. "An orthopedist," he said, tapping the back of his shoulder, "a cardiologist"—he put a hand over his heart—"everything."

Earlier that year Italian voters had somehow put a government in place that was simultaneously at the extremes of both the right and left wings. The left part, the Cinque Stelle (Five Star) Movement, had carried the Italian South, largely with promises of a minimum family income of eight hundred euros. And the baby-faced leader of Cinque Stelle, thirty-two-year-old Neapolitan and college dropout Luigi Di Maio, had become the new government's labor minister.

"We have a labor minister who's never worked." Vittorio snorted. "I should be happy that they want to give me three hundred euros a month more."

But he was indifferent. Money? What would he do with it? He had no children. He didn't own or want a computer or Facebook or Instagram, or an app-laden smartphone—his phone was the kind with a postage-stamp-size screen and actual buttons that served the sole purpose of placing and receiving phone calls. To remember his number, Vittorio had taped it to the back of the phone.

"I am poor, but . . ." He laughed.

Vittorio stood and went to the hall closet, returning with what appeared to be a half-filled bottle of used motor oil. He folded up the pizza box, set out a couple of tumblers, pulled the cork out of the bottle, and poured out some of the thick, brown-black liquid. He announced that it was some of his homemade *nocino*, walnut liqueur. Nocino is an ancient digestive found across Italy with historic roots from ancient Rome. The Christianized tradition goes like this: on the feast of Saint John the Baptist, when walnuts are still green, you pick twenty-four of them (or, if you are really being traditional, a barefoot woman climbs the tree to do the picking). You quarter and macerate them in alcohol with the spices of your familial recipe: typically cinnamon and clove as well as licorice and orange peel. After forty days you filter the liquid and add a sugar solution. The Cioffi touch, used by Vittorio, was a shot of espresso.

"My parents didn't leave me any money," Vittorio said brightly. "But they left me all this."

He meant it too. As a Cioffi he'd inherited not just family recipes, but a way of living that fear and calculation didn't factor into.

I lifted the thick glass and clinked it with Vittorio's. The Nocino tasted a lot better than it looked: bittersweet, herbal, and nutty all at once. I could sense the dark forests above Vico, where walnuts grew, and the coming of winter. We drank. He refilled our glasses, and we drained them again. I asked Vittorio to clarify a delicate point about the Cioffi name: the nickname by which the family was known in Vico. In this part of the world, last names tend to repeat often. There are so many Cioffis, the name is like Smith. So families take on nicknames—giving you, say, "Cioffi the cheesemaker" or "Cioffi with the olive mill."

The nickname of my familial Cioffi branch was first related to me by mother's late cousin, the legendary ABC news correspondent Lou Cioffi, who had carried himself with aplomb covering the Korean War—in which he was wounded and was awarded a Purple Heart—and Vietnam. He later served as United Nations correspondent and

Paris bureau chief and won an Emmy for his interview with Libyan leader Muammar Gaddafi. Lou was the first man of the world I'd ever met. When I was a young boy, he'd once signed a picture of himself in Vietnam with words that implored me to "stay small and never grow up." Yet what I most remember about him was his impeccable style—the cut of his suits, his fitted shirts, his manly cologne, and his cool, despite all the horrors he'd seen. As Lou had once related to me in the 1980s, our branch of Cioffi was named for his (and my mother's and Vittorio's) grandfather Francesco Cioffi, a contadino who worked in the hills above Vico and fathered eight children. He was the first to be called by the local nickname "Cioffi-Cazzinale."

So what exactly is a *Cazzinale*? Well, at first look, to most anyone outside of Vico, it sounds lewd. *Cazzo* is a vulgar term for "penis." *Che cazzo* can mean "bullshit" or "a dickhead." Not a very flattering handle to go by. But the Cioffi were proud of it. On my previous trip to Vico, I'd learned that, somehow, in this Neapolitan town at the end of the nineteenth century, it referred to a man of good, upright character.

"Negative is Cazzo!" Vittorio explained, the first of many times that evening. "But my grandfather was an esteemed man that people trusted. He was"—Vittorio straightened his back, circled his thumb and forefinger in front of his chest, and pulled his hand downward—"Cazzinale."

Vittorio stood and led me into the hallway, where he had a series of old photos stuck between a mirror and its wooden frame. He pulled down a yellowed black-and-white photo of my great-grandfather, whom he introduced in vowel-reducing Neapolitan, with what sounded like *Franjesch-Cioff-Cazz'nal*. The man in the portrait, stamped by a local photo studio, looked about Vittorio's age. He wore a light, crisp button-down shirt and over it a vest and a baggy wool coat. His hands looked as though they had turned to arthritic claws from the work he'd done, and he clasped a slightly crooked cane that he may have fashioned himself from a hazelnut branch. He had a thick silver moustache, neatly combed white hair, big ears, and a meaty nose. But the most striking thing about him was an intense light in his eyes that looked like it would never go out.

Before we parted ways, Vittorio insisted I return the following evening. "I will make linguine with clams . . . like you can't get in a restaurant," he promised.

How could I say no?

"Good, I will buy the clams in the morning."

The next day I drove over the hills of Vico, cutting across the Sorrento Peninsula to its south side and the Amalfi Coast. The route began with passing through the tunnels toward Naples and cutting through a section of tall apartment blocks in notorious Castellammare di Stabia before rising up to Gragnano. Gragnano is Italy's most famous pasta town, long known for its pure mountain waters for making pasta and its gentle winds for drying it. I'd imagined strands of spaghetti, spaghettoni, bucatini, and linguine hanging in the streets like so much laundry. But I was disappointed. Today it's all done behind factory walls.

After Gragnano the road switches back and forth, climbing through the chestnut and oak forests and wildlife refuge of the Monti Lattari, the mountainous spine of the peninsula. Just over the crest of the mountain, at two thousand feet, sits the small, tidy town of Agerola. Only about twenty miles as the crow flies from Naples, Agerola seems another world, with its oxymoronic nickname "the Neapolitan little Switzerland." From here the road descends south to what was about a thousand years ago the powerful seafaring Republic of Amalfi. I stopped at a point about fifteen hundred feet above the sea in a gathering of small farms, olive groves, and ruggedly steep vineyards with their rustic system of tall chestnut pergolas that held vines overhead. This was Furore, a quiet agricultural hamlet of seven hundred souls between the touristic playgrounds of Amalfi and Positano.

On this day the garage-like door of the Marisa Cuomo winery stood wide open, steel equipment spilling into the narrow, unstriped road. From this vantage I beheld one of the most spectacular views I'd ever seen in the wine world: the jagged vineyard terraces and citrus and olive groves that climbed up, from Furore, toward Agerola, and down to the bright blue infinity of the Tyrrhenian Sea. At the edge of a farm below the road, a single century-old vine, with a treelike trunk and enough leaf canopy to cover a small house, sprouted from a terrace dry stone wall. The morning sun bathed it all in ethereal light and shadow. A sailboat glided maybe a kilometer to the south in a dark sea. There was something so compelling—so damn poetic—about it all, it made me wonder: Who, given the chance, wouldn't want to make wine here?

The man who came out to greet me was Andrea Ferraioli, Marisa's husband. The two of them had been working on what seemed a tedious and laborious process at the opening to the winery: preparing a large steel drum filter caked with diatomaceous earth and volcanic glass. The drum turned slowly as Marisa—a tall, broad-shouldered woman in her midfifties, with gray eyes and handsome Eastern European features—leveled the surface with a long-handled scraper. In contrast to Marisa's focused aura, Andrea bristled with electric energy. He was a bit older, sixty-one, with combed-back gray hair, a slight frame, and a quick Vic Damone smile.

"It is a terrible day," he said dramatically.

His smile fell, and my daydreams of Amalfi Coast winemaking came crashing to earth. They were at the tail of the harvest, he lamented. There was a lot of work to do in the winery, and two cellar hands were sick. His uncle, who helped manage the painstaking vineyard work, had died just days earlier, and he hadn't even had time to mourn. His and Marisa's daughter was also pregnant and not feeling well. So much for Eden.

Andrea then called the winery agronomist, Gaetano Carrano, to come and take me through the vineyards. While we waited in front of the winery, Marisa continued working quietly while Andrea chatted with me, arms folded across his chest.

"Wine is subjective," he said. It seemed a practiced line. "I don't want to make a wine better than the next one. I want to make a wine that tells a story—the story of our territory."

There was nothing to argue with there. His words, I'd come to realize, could be a sine qua non for the Italian South, with its long local histories that sprung from its soils, people, and happenstance. But I was struck by his use of the first person. The winery was named Marisa Cuomo, after all. But it had come from Andrea's side of the family and was given by Andrea to Marisa as a wedding gift in 1983. I had to wonder what kind of gift it had been. Marisa—the more introverted of the couple—actually makes the wine with the help of her son, Raffaele, producing about two hundred thousand bottles a year. Andrea is general manager, directing work in the vineyards and the office and its beautiful marketing videos. He also does most of the talking.

The day, it seemed, was destined for confusion. Just as Gaetano came ambling up the road to greet us, a small busload of young Chinese tourists was let out in front of the winery office, where one secretary—who doubled as a guide—worked. The tourists quickly fanned out in the road, posing for 360 degrees of selfies.

Gaetano and I escaped. A calm and balding brick of a man with blue eyes and rounded shoulders, he led me around for the next few hours, in a small winery truck and on foot, through what were some of the most extreme vineyards I'd ever seen. As it often does, beauty here comes at a price. These vineyards were as steep, irregular, and remote as vineyards I'd seen in Northern Italy's Valtellina, along the mountainous Swiss border, or in the largely abandoned, hardscrabble hills above the Ligurian coast. Crossing them was a hike up along tall, narrow paths of loose stone and up and down sets of centuries-old steps held onto terrace walls without mortar.

The plots were tiny but required what seemed like an unimaginable amount of work. Marisa Cuomo employs about twenty workers to cultivate its ten acres of vineyards and another twenty-five acres under lease from nearly thirty owners. In addition, along the Amalfi Coast, the winery contracts to purchase grapes from sixty-seven growers. All of it is hand harvested and carried out of vineyards on workers' backs, donkeys, roadside cranes, or, in a few cases, small, private, mechanized rails. Gaetano, who lived on the other side of Amalfi in the fishing village of Cetera, was at forty also one of the youngest of the growers who sold grapes to Marisa Cuomo. And, in addition to grapes, he cultivated Sorrento lemons and olives on his familial land.

You could say these vineyards were older than dirt—or certainly older than their topsoil—considering that soils have been brought down from the Lattari forests for generations. The mountain slopes themselves were pure dolomitic rock pushed up from the seafloor by the collision of tectonic plates. For centuries farmers set up elaborate traps to catch soils that eroded with the rain from the forests above. Occasionally Vesuvius added a dusting of volcanic ash. Today those same soils are brought in by truck and wheelbarrow.

"In what little soil we have, we try to have viticulture," Gaetano said. Driving on a straightaway, he took his hands off the wheel and held them about a foot apart to illustrate the depth of some top soils.

The vines, which root into the rock, are old as well. Most are planted *piede franco*, without American rootstock. Phylloxera never made it here. Was it the volcanic sand? Were they too isolated? Or was the place just too grueling even for burrowing aphids?

Gaetano led me to a vineyard in Agerola at the side of a gorge, way above the coast, along a vertiginous trail that was fighting a battle against the creeping Mediterranean broom and wild fennel, ash saplings, figs, myrtle, mastic shrubs, and small oaks. "Zero machines," he said, explaining the handiwork that went into each vineyard, including shearing wild grasses with scythes, replacing old chestnut pergolas, and tying up vines to the pergolas using thin, pliable willow branches. "Only those who love it can do the work," he said. "To manage all of this takes lots of hands, a lot of time, and a lot of economic force."

Amalfi is one of the few vineyard areas where the term "terroir" seems small and insufficient. The earth doesn't come to mind at these heights. Once you step out of the intimate, shaded spaces directly under the vine trellises, the vista is dominated by the dark blue of a deep sea and the azure sky meeting on a brilliant horizon. The sea breezes mix the scents of wild vegetation and salt that seem more "air-oir" than "terroir." Or perhaps it's better said by the Sicilian Chef Pino Cuttaia of La Madia on Sicily's southern coast at Licata, who pays homage to the *mare* (sea) as "mar-oir."

As for the grapes, they are a local jumble that defy our tidy, modern visions of monoculture. The red ones—mostly tannic Aglianico and fruitier Piedirosso along with smaller amounts of full-bodied Sciascinoso and Tronto—are planted alongside the white grapes that make Marisa Cuomo's more distinctive wines: Falanghina and Biancolella and the local-to-Furore Fenile and Ripoli. Everything goes into the harvest basket—segregated by color only—after Gaetano and Andrea choose the ideal moment to pick. "The grapes that are ripe have to wait for the grapes that need more time to ripen," Gaetano said—a flagrant but necessary contradiction of modern precision harvesting, in which the winemaker exerts supreme control. Here, the vineyards, shaped by the decisions made by previous generations, hadn't ceded that power.

On the way back to Furore, we looked down to the natural landmark that gives the place its name: the steep, natural fjord cut into the cliffsides where the Schiato River cascades to the sea. Furore and its fjord were immortalized in Italian director Roberto Rossellini's grainy black-and-white 1948 short film *Il Miracolo*, shot onsite with his lover, Anna Magnani, and his friend Federico Fellini. Magnani plays a disturbed goatherd who sees Saint Joseph in a traveler (Fellini) who, in turn, plies her with wine and (it's implied) takes advantage of her, resulting in her "miracle" pregnancy. The film is a grand metaphor of the Italian South, with its relentless sun and endless sea, childlike faith in local miracles, and provincial cruelty. As with all postwar Italian movies, I can't make it through with dry eyes. But American censors weren't so moved at the time of its release in 1950. New York State banned it for "blasphemy." (The controversy resulted in the landmark Miracle Decision, with the U.S. Supreme Court recognizing film, for the first time, as artistic expression protected by the First Amendment.)

When we returned to the winery, Marisa and her son were filtering wine. The tourists had left, and Gaetano walked back down the road. Andrea had changed his work polo for a button-down white shirt patterned with blue diamonds. "Let's go to lunch," he said, enthusiastically rubbing his hands together. And so the two of us walked about fifty yards down the road, leaving his wife and son to work.

The Hostaria di Bacco is a near-century-old Ferraioli family restaurant and inn run by his cousin Raffaele, the longtime mayor of Furore. The Ferraioli and Cuomo families intersect here too. Running the kitchen is Raffaele's wife, Erminia Cuomo, the eldest of Marisa's twelve siblings all born from a Bosnian mother and Furoresi father.

We sat in the white dining room with its linen-covered tables and modern sliding doors that looked out to the big blue. The *hostaria* didn't have the sophistication of Le Torre del Saracino. But what the kitchen lacked in culinary invention, it more than made up for with dishes like its signature Ferrazzuoli alla Nannarella: double-barreled pasta twists dressed in a southern mix of savory, sweet, bitter, and spicy flavors from stewed tomatoes, swordfish, raisins, pine nuts, arugula, and hot peppers.

We leisurely sampled Marisa Cuomo wines, starting with the 2017 white Costa d'Amalfi wines—one from Furore and another from Ravello—both a blend of the Campania grapes Falanghina and Biancolella. When I taste Falanghina the first thing that usually comes to mind is pineapple, and that is a dangerous thing. In the wrong hands, Falanghina can be immediately cloying. Cuomo's wines were balanced by several things—a healthy mar-oir saltiness, good winemaking, and the component of more delicate, leaner, and slightly bitter Biancolella. "Our wine is not the best in the world, and it's not the worst—it is unique," Andrea said. I felt as if he was continuing to recite lines from a winery brochure. "We have a microclimate on the back of a mountain facing the sea. We don't find balance in one parcel but the whole area." He is certainly a salesman with a palpable drive. I sensed that striving had less to do with making good wine than in building *something* here as a legacy. His significant role in the preservation of Amalfi Coast vineyards and a renaissance of Amalfi wines was only a byproduct.

Andrea's family had been making wine since 1942—a year before Italy switched allegiance to the side of the U.S.-led Allies in World War II. Here in Furore, next to the family inn, Ferraioli cousin Vincenzo Cavaliere began his Gran Furor Divina Costiera label, which flourished in postwar peacetime. But, by the 1970s, business and interest fell when faced with the competition of cheap, mass-scale wines, modern cocktails, and the call of more prosperous lives elsewhere. Though the family still made wine for itself, the winery as a commercial venture was no more.

Andrea initially had no intention of becoming a wine producer. He entered what was then seen as a more lucrative and important trade: electrician. But, in 1977, after returning from his military service, where he encountered other Italians whose families made wine, he was determined that *someone* in the sprawling family should reactivate the winery. He called a meeting of dozens of uncles, cousins, and siblings who owned part of the family vineyards and old winemaking operation and asked, "Does anybody want to put the winery back in business? If they do, they can buy out the others." There were no takers. Three years later he bought out the rest of the family for the equivalent of about twenty-five thousand euros. Another three years later, he gifted it all to his new bride as a wedding present.

"I was born in wine," he said. "I remember from when I was little the smell of the cantina and the fermenting must. That was something I could not abandon and let die."

Marisa and Andrea made simple wine with the guidance of his family for about a decade, while he continued his work as an electrician. Then, in 1995, the year Amalfi appellation was established, he quit his day job and got serious. He recruited the Campania native, winemaker, professor, and enologist Luigi Moio, who had studied in Burgundy and later founded his own winery, Quintodecimo, in Irpinia. "Luigi taught us an idea of what a quality wine was," Andrea said. "Luigi taught us that to make a balanced wine is something that starts at the beginning of the growing season and goes through to the harvest."

Using two hands and with his brow furrowed and gray eyes expressing the seriousness of the moments to come, Andrea carefully poured the most recent vintage of Marisa Cuomo's flagship white wine, Fiorduva, made from a trio of grapes found only within a few miles of where we sat. As we began the usual swirling and wine sniffing ritual, Andrea's phone went off. He looked at the screen, answered, and asked the voice on the other end what was going on. He impatiently repeated something about a button that needed to be pressed on the machine. Then he told the caller he would be right there.

"Excuse me," he said. He stood and threw up his hands. "My wife is making a casino [mess]."

It was an embarrassing moment. As it turned out, I had a come at a bad time and was witness to a collision of winery and marital stress. Andrea's man-in-charge attitude would surely confirm my wife's prejudices about the Italian South. I didn't expect Furore to be a bastion of feminism, but here was a case of a husband lunching while his wife worked—and then getting peevish when she summoned him to help. Then again, these petty human details seemed small in that moment compared to the view from where I sat, with the light dancing over the sea, on the white tablecloth, and into my wineglass.

During Andrea's absence, I reflected on the wine made from Ripoli, Fenile, and Ginestra grapes. I'd had no idea what to expect.

I knew the wine was aged and partially fermented in French oak barrels, that Italian wine critics swooned over the stuff, and that the celebrity sommelier Luca Gardini called the three-years-earlier 2013 vintage "a miracle of native grapes." I drank in the golden color, smelled the wine, and opened my lips to taste the "miracle." It was indeed the big and complete wine that the critics loved, and I thought: *That is its problem.* The wine seemed to be trying so hard to be important, and that was all I tasted. Maybe my cousin Vittorio's Nocino had ruined my taste buds, but Marisa Cuomo's great wine tasted too refined, too tame, too French. I could have mistaken it for Burgundy Chardonnay, which I understand many great wine palates would be happy with. But sitting here in Furore—just the name conjures passion—I wanted something wilder, something that smelled like the stands of fennel we'd walked through that morning, that conjured the sea, wind, and sun on the rocks, and the impossible, sweaty labor of harvest here. I wanted (why not?) some vile-meets-sublime mar-oir flavor like that of fermented *colatura di alici*—the sauce made from drippings of fermented anchovies down the coast in Cetera.

After lunch Andrea and I sped around Furore in his small electric car past some of the vineyards I had visited that morning, and he explained the complex way he tried to balance their wines. "In the east-facing vineyards, we have low alcohol and high acidity and aromas," he said. "In the vineyards that face west, we have more alcohol and less acidity. The southern exposures are in between. It's a mix of altitudes and exposures that brings the equilibrium. It's enough to make you crazy." Then he shouted convincingly into the wind: "I am crazy!" He flashed the Vic Damone smile and put his foot to the accelerator.

Back at the winery, Marisa was cleaning out the equipment from the day's work. Her clothes, hair, and face were spotted with white wine sludge, and she looked beyond tired. She smiled with the weary satisfaction of an endurance athlete, handed Andrea the gun of the power washer she'd been using to clean, and took a break. We sat in the small office of the winery, which was plastered with a mix of professional vineyard photos and shots of celebrities who'd dropped in from chicer spots along the coast. She explained that for the nearly two months of harvest she had been working up to nineteen-hour days, from seven in the morning until past midnight.

"I don't know how to talk about wine," she said apologetically and adjusted the bridge of her fashionable, multicolored sunglasses. "I only know how to make it. It's heavy work for a woman, but I find it satisfying." She used the back of her hand to brush away strands of hair that had fallen into her face. "I don't think there are many women who do the work in the cantina. But when someone tastes my wine, I know I can say, 'I made it.'"

It was true. I knew hundreds of winemakers and wine families. Most embrace the noble-seeming part of wine—owning the land, making decisions for others to carry out. Marisa doubted the glamorous Wonder Woman ideal of the Italian female winemaker who does it all, then finds time to go on globe-trotting marketing tours. "How can you be traveling the world talking about your wine if you are the winemaker?" she asked with an exhausted smile. "The wines are like children—they need attention all the time."

Marisa said she preferred to make red wines, but she didn't drink wine at all because of a metabolic intolerance to alcohol. I was taken aback at the thought of a southern winemaker who didn't talk much and didn't drink at all. Yet there was one thing I needed to know from her about Andrea's wedding present and the founding of Cantina Marisa Cuomo. Was it a gift for her? Or was it really a gift for himself?

"He gave it to me," she said with a serious glance that softened as the words sunk in. "But it was like if you give someone a bicycle so they will learn how to pedal."

It was a prophetic statement—not just because the bicycle was such an important symbol of progress in Italy's not-too-distant past, but also because the act of pedaling is one of the best ways to describe Italians, at least in the twentieth century: crossing oceans, obsessed with work, the "sticking together" of the family, the thorough integration in new countries, the untiring pursuit of something like happiness. My own family's generations that I had known weren't reflecting much or looking where they were going. They pedaled all their lives. In my travels across Southern Italy, I'd seen it everywhere—people seemed to have little choice but to improve what their piece of earth had given them. Marisa Cuomo, like generations before her and probably many to follow, wasn't obsessed with the finer points of the wine world. She was simply moving forward—for thirty-five years now—so as not to fall.

That evening I found my way to Vittorio's apartment building. He was waiting on the corner and whistling when I arrived. After the usual embrace, we turned and walked down the street, past the door of his building.

"Aren't we going upstairs?" I pointed.

I learned that there had been a slight change to the program. When Vittorio had said, "I will make linguine with clams," I had taken it at face value. And I'd brought a bottle of Marisa Cuomo wine to accompany his meal. But, as it turned out, "I will make linguine" didn't mean that Vittorio would actually do the cooking. He explained that he had recruited his sister, Teresa, for that. And, of course, he said, it was best that we not disturb the cook while she was working. "Let's go for a caffè," he suggested, and we walked into the balmy Vico night.

It was Friday, and the town seemed to have an added bustle. Vittorio doled out good-evening expressions in Neapolitan to select passersby. He stopped to talk to a couple near his age, outfitted in their finest. As it turned out, they were going to a reception for the new Mister Italia, Nicola Savarese—a thirty-one-year-old civil engineer from Vico with black hair and beard and a build like a statue of a Roman hero. His title was apparently a matter of local pride, meriting civic celebration. We continued to Vico's busy central square,

Piazza Umberto, built around the Fontana dei Delfini: a spring-fed lava stone fountain with dolphins carved out of marble, built in the mid-nineteenth century to solve Vico residents' chronic lack of water.

The tables in front of the Gran Caffè Zerilli on the piazza's southeast corner were filling up with people, a mix of ages and nationalities, sipping colorful cocktails and eating baroque-looking pastries. I followed Vittorio through the big open doors into the bright white interior and to the bar in front of the gleaming espresso machine. At the bar were gathered a number of local male pensioners who all knew Vittorio. The café is now famous beyond Vico because it was founded by Bruce Springsteen's maternal great-grandfather and run by the family until his grandfather, Antonio Zerilli, left his hometown to emigrate to the United States. In 2015, after decades of being called Bar del Sole, and three years after Vico Equense made Springsteen an honorary citizen, the new owners reopened the café with the Zerilli name.

Vittorio explained that we were waiting for a friend, the son of a shop owner for whom he had worked. The son, now working as a jack-of-all-trades in Britain, called Vittorio to meet for espresso whenever he returned to Vico. I asked Vittorio if he wanted to sit at a table outside in the warm evening air to wait for his friend. He looked at me as if I were spouting heresy—like pineapple on pizza. Had I said something wrong?

"Never!" he said. "Caffè must be drunk almost boiling!" He stretched the three syllables of the Italian *boll-en-te* over his tongue. "If we sat at a table, by the time it got to us, it could be frozen!"

I looked at the distance between the bar and the outside terrace. It was maybe twenty-five feet—about a fifteen-second journey for a waiter in shirtsleeves weather. But I didn't argue. Vittorio obviously felt at ease by the bar. Besides, I was sure that there might be some nominal charge for table service that repelled him and his fellow pensioners.

One corner of the place was dedicated to Springsteen: three thick shelves headlined with the painted words BRUCE'S TIME. A poster-size photo of the Boss onstage in Naples, unfurling a large print of an antique image of the café, balanced on the top shelf, beneath it a copy of the Springsteen biography *Bruce* and a CD box for the album *Lucky Town* on one shelf, and on the bottom miniature guitars and American flag–themed drums.

Vittorio's friend, a man in his forties, arrived with his British wife, and some news was exchanged. The prodigal *Vicano* bought a round of espresso at the bar. The coffee came in small ceramic cups with lips as thick as beer goblets. The espresso required stirring for half a minute to cool down—no possibility of freezing there. After it reached a drinkable temperature, I closed my eyes to savor the sweet and bitter, almost chocolate flavors and the rich texture that combined to reach their apogee only around Naples. Vittorio belted his cup down in two sips, spooned out the *crema* left at the bottom, and said ciao to his friends.

Back at Vittorio's apartment, Teresa, who stood less than five feet tall, was hunched over the stove. She was thin and wore short-cropped hair, glasses, and her family's infectious smile. Her pink athletic polo was emblazoned with the word SLAM. The way she moved authoritatively in Vittorio's kitchen said "nonna" in the best sense of the word. She was the person you would call, before a doctor, when you had a fever. She was of a class of people most Italians entrusted with their greatest treasures—their regional cuisines. In other words, she was qualified to turn ordinary supermarket pasta and olive oil with the day's fresh clams into an exquisite *linguine alle vongole.*

The smell of garlic frying in oil rose from an iron skillet on the gas burner. Teresa added a large bowlful of thumbnail-sized lupini clams, which slowly opened, spilling their juice into the oil. She removed the open clams with a wooden spoon and placed them back in their bowl, adding chopped parsley to the pan juices. When Teresa could tell, through some sixth sense, that the linguine was near al dente, she strained the noodles in the sink, then poured them into the skillet for a second cooking in the sauce. She spooned the linguine into two dishes, putting a few clams on top of each and leaving the rest in their bowl, then lifted the pan at a right angle to pour the last of sauce on top of the pasta, guiding it with a crust of bread. She set the skillet down, wiped the bottom clean with the bread, and popped the crust into her mouth.

There is something that happens in the creation of this simple dish that is far greater than the sum of its parts. The day's fresh clams, with their sweet-salty flavors, are obviously the key ingredient. But, as with Teresa's pan-finished version, the linguine absorbs the clam juices, oil, and garlic, leaving a slick coating on its outer surface that exalts and amplifies everything. In Naples spaghetti or linguine with clams is an important part of the late Christmas Eve dinner. It would no doubt be my proverbial last meal, but I am much happier to have it as my next meal.

After tidying up a bit, Teresa and her husband, a retired cruise ship captain who had been watching television in the other room, went off into the night. We ate in reverent silence. Vittorio pushed the bowl of clams my way.

"Ecco, mangia," he said. I took some, and he begged me to take more, insisting in Neapolitan, "*Magnia.*"

We drank from the bottle of Marisa Cuomo wine I'd brought—the simplest white blend of Falanghina and Biancolella that Vittorio pronounced "buono."

After we'd finished our pasta, he did a strange thing with the wine. He went to his refrigerator and pulled out a peach, then a fruit knife from a drawer. He sat down and sliced the peach in his hand, placing the slices in a jar. He poured the wine over the peaches.

"What are you doing?" I asked reflexively.

"What?" He shrugged and laughed and placed the marinating fruit mixture in the fridge to chill. "It's good. You'll see. For dessert."

Vittorio's homemade concoction—sipped and forked out of our glasses—wasn't half bad. I thought about how, at that moment, many of my colleagues were gathering in New York at a large wine fair to taste some of the world's great wine with food served by top chefs.

And here I was in Vico, drinking Vittorio's tableside peach sangria. But I had no desire to trade places. As I have traveled across Italy, and particularly the South, I have learned that when we drink wine, about half of what we taste is the wine, and the rest of what we sense is what we *feel* while we are drinking it. I do believe it is possible to taste wine very objectively, though I am not good at it. My feelings and memories of wine are far messier—more southern—than that kind of objectivity. And I'm happy about that. I remember very few of the wines that I have drunk at tastings, and when I do remember one, it's usually not for a positive reason. Whereas the memory of the wine I drank that evening with Vittorio—that I'll keep with me for a long time.

Before I left Vittorio bid me to return. I should bring my wife. He had plenty of room, he said. I promised I would, not knowing when that might be. In the hallway he took down a picture of his grandfather again. This time he offered it to me as a gift.

"Cazzinale," Vittorio said, giving a noble weight to the word.

Before I left Vico to head north, I dove into the same small bay I swam in as a boy. It still felt like late summer, and I stood on the beach where O'Saracino had been, surveying the volcanic stones for a souvenir. I sat on a black volcanic boulder in the morning sun and thought that, for me, Italy still begins at Vico Equense. Though O'Saracino was gone, Vico hadn't been swallowed by Naples's sprawl or Castellammare gangs, or trash, or the indifferent march of plastic that turned so many places into copies of somewhere else. Perhaps because of some morbid reflex, I have sometimes imagined my last moments on earth. Invariably—likely the influence of too many early Fellini movies—it ends at the sea. I imagine I am watching some kids play on the stones here, the hulking silhouette of Vesuvius in the distance. One of the boys finds the carcass of a spider crab that has washed onto the shore. There are no signs of life, and, as the boy picks it up, I realize the crustacean is me. The boy throws it into the water, but another boy dives in to retrieve it. He looks like I did at ten years old.

When he emerges from the surf, crab in hand, I am seeing through his eyes. I look to a wooden terrace and the restaurant on its pier. My family—healthy and bronzed in their sunglasses and simple, sixties-era cottons—is there at a long table, with plates of food and golden wine that reflects the bright light.

They are calling me back to the table.

21. Marissa Cuomo and husband, Andrea Ferraioli.

22. The coastal site where once stood O'Saracino in Vico Equense.

The Food and Cooking
of Eastern Europe
Lesley Chamberlain
With a new introduction by the author

The Food and Cooking of Russia
Lesley Chamberlain
With a new introduction by the author

The World on a Plate: A
Tour through the History of
America's Ethnic Cuisine
Joel Denker

Jewish American Food Culture
Jonathan Deutsch and Rachel D. Saks

The Recipe Reader: Narratives,
Contexts, Traditions
Edited by Janet Floyd
and Laurel Forster

A Chef's Tale: A Memoir of
Food, France, and America
Pierre Franey
With Richard Flaste and Bryan Miller
With a new introduction
by Eugenia Bone

Masters of American Cookery:
M. F. K. Fisher, James Beard,
Craig Claiborne, Julia Child
Betty Fussell
With a preface by the author

My Kitchen Wars: A Memoir
Betty Fussell
With a new introduction
by Laura Shapiro

Good Things
Jane Grigson

Jane Grigson's Fruit Book
Jane Grigson
With a new introduction
by Sara Dickerman

Jane Grigson's Vegetable Book
Jane Grigson
With a new introduction
by Amy Sherman

Dining with Marcel Proust:
A Practical Guide to French
Cuisine of the Belle Epoque
Shirley King
Foreword by James Beard

Pampille's Table: Recipes and
Writings from the French
Countryside from Marthe Daudet's
Les Bons Plats de France
Translated and adapted
by Shirley King

Moveable Feasts: The History,
Science, and Lore of Food
Gregory McNamee

To order or obtain more information on these or other University
of Nebraska Press titles, visit nebraskapress.unl.edu.